LANDMARK VISITORS ...

# Iceland

## Cathy Harlow

Cathy Harlow first visited Iceland as a child, thanks to an academic father with a passion for the land and its literature. After a degree in Spanish she was drawn back by its rugged landscapes and came to live on the island. Learning Icelandic, she trained as a local guide and since 1987 has shared her enthusiasm for the country with many hundreds of visitors. She now guides natural history and walking holidays in many parts of the world which fuels a successful career in photography and travel writing.

### Acknowledgements

Many people helped with updating this 3rd edition special thanks to:

Sari Kaufmann, Pálina Hjaltadóttir, Magnús Einarsson, & Bára Jóhannsdóttir

### Dedication

To the 'Icelanders' in my life – my father Geoffrey and son Ari

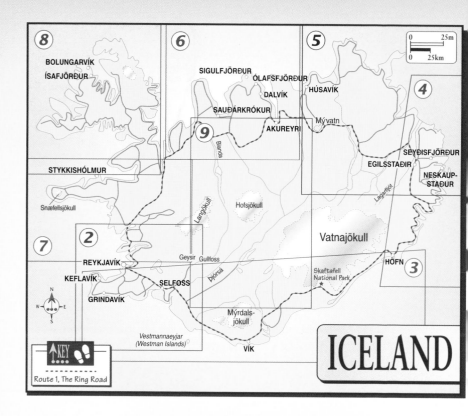

# ICELAND

Route 1, The Ring Road

Below: Hornvík Bay on Hornstrandir
Opposite: Laki craters

LANDMARK VISITORS GUIDE

# Iceland

Cathy Harlow

# • CONTENTS •

• FEATURE BOXES •

Getting by in Icelandic 39-41
Nightlife in Reykjavík 44
Icelandic food – palatable
or poisonous? 49
Iceland's Silent Enemy –
Soil Erosion 208
Festivals 248

# • TOP TIPS •

## REYKJAVÍK

There are great hotels, some of the freshest seafood on earth and as unusual an array of things to see and do in and around the capital as you could wish for.

## LANDMANNALAUGAR

Its vivid mountains are an unforgettable sight and its walks and views among the most inspiring in Iceland.

## SKAFTAFELL

Its glaciers are awesome and the views from the national park's scenic walking trails, breathtaking.

## JÖKULSÁRLÓN

The boat trip among the icebergs of this glacial lagoon is simply a must.

Above: Höfði at Lake Mývatn

Opposite: Landmannalaugar

## LAKE MÝVATN

Possibly the greatest concentration of unusual volcanic features on earth, and huge numbers of wildfowl.

## ÞINGVELLIR

Historical site of major importance and the cradle of the nation. A place to quietly contemplate the island's great natural beauty and the extraordinary forces that have created it.

## SNÆFELLSJÖKULL

Viewed from across the bay in Reykjavík, or ascended on a midnight sun snowmobile expedition, the shimmering snowcapped cone of this volcano has a unique lure.

# • TOP TIPS •

## THE WESTMAN ISLANDS

Offshore islands whose fishing town was engulfed by lava in 1973. Keiko, the orca of *Free Willy* fame was relocated here in 1998.

## THE WATERFALLS

Iceland has waterfalls of every imaginable shape and size. Delicate plumes like Seljalandsfoss, shapely Goðafoss and thundering Dettifoss are just three out of... well, hundreds, even thousands.

## THE GEYSERS & HOT POOLS

Geysers, mud pools and gushing hot springs plus places like Hveravellir, Landmannalaugar, Askja and Laugafell where you can bathe in natural hot pools. Pure magic! The Blue Lagoon – surreal and atmospheric.

## SNOWMOBILING

These exhilarating snow machines may be expensive, noisy and polluting but they are enormously good fun. A ride across one of Iceland's huge icecaps is a once in a lifetime experience.

## WHALE AND DOLPHIN WATCHING

With more than six species regularly seen, Iceland is fast becoming acknowledged as a world-class whale and dolphin watching destination.

## WHERE THE SUN SHINES

If you have a flexible itinerary, watch the forecasts and head for the sunniest weather regardless of your original plan.

# GOING OFF THE BEATEN TRACK...

## THE WEST FJORDS

Dramatic fjords, golden sand beaches, friendly fishing villages and some of the greatest concentrations of nesting cliff birds in the world.

## HORNSTRANDIR NATURE RESERVE

Adventurous hiking, wonderful flowers, birds, arctic foxes and a journey back in time to the Iceland of days gone by.

## ASKJA & KVERKFJÖLL

A journey through Iceland's uninhabited highlands is incredibly bleak, yet hauntingly beautiful. The sky is as vast as in Africa and the views can stretch forever.

## LAUGAVEGUR

Long distance hiking trail from the brilliant landscapes, steam vents and lava flows of Landmannalaugar, to the glaciers of Þórsmörk and the waterfalls of the Skógá River.

## THE SOUTHERN FJALLABAK ROUTE

Adventurous four-wheel-drive track with awesome scenery and a chance to put your jeep through its paces.

## THE FAR NORTH-EAST

A forgotten corner. Borgarfjörður Eystri with its fantastic mountains and superb hiking trails; Melrakkaslétta – isolated but one of the best spots to enjoy the midnight sun.

Until recently, little was known about Iceland other than its chilly sounding name. Anyone intent on visiting was likely to be asked 'Why?'. For the discerning few who had been there, the answer was obvious and best kept a secret. But now, with easier flight connections and better facilities for visitors, more and more people are discovering the sub-arctic destination.

Drawn by its legendary natural beauty, visitors are refreshed by Iceland's breathtaking views and clear, clean air, that lends the landscape the vivid hues of an artist's palette, and its clichéd title of 'island of contrasts'. Its unpolluted rivers and lakes are teeming with salmon and trout, while the bird life and abundant whales and dolphins attract naturalists. Nature has always been a dominant force, but in among Iceland's volcanoes, waterfalls and glaciers, deserts and tortured lava flows, there are fertile farmed valleys and fishing villages snugly located on the shores of its scenic fjords. The capital of this nation of barely a quarter

## Climate

Lying just south of the Arctic Circle, Iceland seldom experiences the climatic extremes of other arctic and sub-arctic regions. This is because of its oceanic location and the influence of the Gulf Stream. Icelanders love to talk about their weather. Reports and forecasts are broadcast four times a day on the state radio, with over an hour devoted to the subject. 'If you don't like the weather, wait a minute', visitors are often told and 'changeable' is the word that most aptly describes the weather of the island. High precipitation, strong winds and comparatively low mean temperature variation are typical features of the island's weather throughout the year. Reykjavík's mean temperature in January is 30°F (-1°C), the same as that of Milan, while the July mean is 52°F (11°C) but winter lows of 5°F (-15°C) and summer highs of 77°F (25°C) are not uncommon.

The north and east of the island lie in the rain shadow of the ice caps and have drier weather and greater extremes of temperature, whereas the south and west get the bulk of the rainfall. The good news is that bad weather in the south of the island usually means good weather in the north and vice versa.

of a million people is Reykjavík, a vibrant and youthful city with a fascinating fusion of old and new.

Many visitors are struck by the tenacity and entrepreneurial spirit of the nation and people. Its early history is woven into the acclaimed sagas, fabrics of spell-binding intrigue and mastery that rank as world class literature. Shaking off centuries of colonial hardship, the island became an independent republic in 1944, developing a prosperous economy based on fishing. Situated midway between Europe and North America, Iceland's highly educated and forward-looking people have sought inspiration from both sides of the Atlantic to produce a modern culture that is uniquely Icelandic.

Iceland attracts all sorts of visitors: outdoor enthusiasts, naturalists, geologists and photographers; some go for a short break in Europe's most northerly capital, while others plan a lengthy back country expedition. Few, if any, come back indifferent to Iceland. For some, the island quickly becomes an addiction. Read on with care!

# When to visit

Most people choose to visit Iceland in summer, with mid-June to mid-August being the most popular period. This is the busiest season and the most expensive. However, July and August offer the warmest, though not always the sunniest weather and the scenery is at its most spectacular. From mid-May to late July there are 24 hours of daylight. Late May to mid-July is the best time for bird watching while the latter half of June and early July are good for wildflowers. From late August onwards airfares are lower, there are fewer visitors around and the northern lights can be seen, though October, November and February are generally the best months for observing this phenomenon.

From early September to late May, many visitor facilities in Iceland close down outside of the Reykjavík area. This makes travelling at this time of year more challenging but if you want the country to yourself then this is the time to do it. It is usually possible to drive the main coastal

|  | Jan | Feb | Mar | Apr | May | Jun | Jul | Aug | Sep | Oct | Nov | Dec |
|---|---|---|---|---|---|---|---|---|---|---|---|---|
| Warmest months |  |  |  |  |  |  |  |  |  |  |  |  |
| Longest hours of daylight |  |  |  |  |  |  |  |  |  |  |  |  |
| Darkest months |  |  |  |  |  |  |  |  |  |  |  |  |
| Cheapest airfares |  |  |  |  |  |  |  |  |  |  |  |  |
| Most expensive airfares |  |  |  |  |  |  |  |  |  |  |  |  |
| Highland tracks open |  |  |  |  |  |  |  |  |  |  |  |  |
| Bird watching |  |  |  |  |  |  |  |  |  |  |  |  |
| Whale watching |  |  |  |  |  |  |  |  |  |  |  |  |
| Flora |  |  |  |  |  |  |  |  |  |  |  |  |
| Visitor facilities open |  |  |  |  |  |  |  |  |  |  |  |  |
| Northern lights |  |  |  |  |  |  |  |  |  |  |  |  |

routes even in winter. A stay in Reykjavík can be rewarding at any time of year and day excursions from the capital are offered all year round.

## A winter wonderland

Iceland is best known as a summer destination but a visit out of season can be as rewarding and it doesn't have to be that cold. Temperatures can plunge to –20°C but mostly they are between –5°C and 5°C. Flights, car hire and hotel prices are cheaper and many of the coastal roads are kept open for traffic. March and April, with plenty of snow and more daylight, are wonderful months for experiencing some unusual winter sporting activities.

There is usually enough snow around between January and April to enjoy both downhill and cross-country skiing, as well as snowmobiling and popular off-road jeep safaris, using huge balloon tyres and custom-built vehicles. Because Iceland is sub-Arctic, there is no polar night and even in December there are four to five hours of daylight, with some superb opportunities for photography.

## The travel options

### Reykjavík as a base

For a weekend break or a longer stay, Reykjavík is an obvious choice and a stay in Iceland's capital can be enjoyable at any time of year. There are often good package deals out of season. For a stay of up to a week, the city itself and day trips in its surrounds have plenty to hold the visitor.

### Two or three bases

With a week or more of holiday you can look at combining Reykjavík with a stay in one or more places around the country. Akureyri, in the north, Ísafjörður in the north-west, the fishing village of Höfn and Lake Mývatn are popular choices. Travel between the bases can be by scheduled bus, car or air.

### The Ring Road Circle

It is feasible to complete the Ring Road in a week. However, ten days or two weeks will allow much more time to enjoy the scenery and take side trips to explore as you travel around. The route can be taken in a normal two-wheel-drive vehicle or by scheduled bus.

### The East plus the Highlands

In two weeks you can travel the Ring Road east from Reykjavík, through the east fjords and north as far as Akureyri and then cut through the highlands on one of the mountain tracks to return to the capital. Four-wheel-drive vehicles with good ground clearance are essential for the Sprengisandur track and advisable for the Kjölur Track. A side trip to Askja or Kverkfjöll could be incorporated – the track is open to jeeps and coaches only. Allow two weeks if you have your own vehicle, but ideally three if you are using public transport.

13

## The West

The west of Iceland may be covered in two weeks, including visits to the Snæfellsnes Peninsula and West Fjords region. The route can be done with public transport but your own vehicle allows greater flexibility, particularly in the West Fjords, where public transport is limited. The Kjölur Track across central Iceland (four-wheel-drive and high ground clearance advisable) can be incorporated into the circular route.

## Package deal or independent travel?

The cost of hiring a vehicle, the complications of taking your own and the restrictions of public transport make many visitors think seriously about visiting Iceland on a guided tour. Though the concept of a package can be off-putting to independent-minded visitors, many people do opt for such an arrangement in Iceland. The advantages are many: it may often work out cheaper if you are travelling on your own or as a couple; you get to see the places that are off the beaten track, difficult to reach and hard to find; with a guide on board you get to know much more about the country and with accommodation and often meals included you don't have to worry about being left without a bed for the night. Package arrangements range from city breaks to fly drives and inclusive hotel based and camping tours that take in most of the island.

If you plan to bring your own vehicle, cycle or backpack then an independent arrangement will give you far greater flexibility. For those who plan to use public transport, it makes sense to book at least some of your travel and accommodation

arrangements in advance. The same uncluttered roads that make driving a pleasure, make hitchhiking a nightmare. Even on the Ring Road you may wait hours, even days, for a ride, and though Iceland may be one of the safer places in the world to hitchhike, it is certainly not the easiest.

## Eating and drinking

For hundreds of years Icelanders lived from the livestock they raised and what they could harvest from the sea. Sheep, horses and cattle provided meat and dairy produce, while fish was caught in season. Seals, beached whales and nesting seabirds and their eggs were a valuable supplement to the diet. Nothing was wasted and they developed ingenious methods of preserving food: smoking, drying and salting and pickling in barrels of sour whey. Wild berries and lichen were gathered on the fells and angelica roots dug up along the banks of rivers but growing of crops, other than grass for hay, ceased after the fourteenth century, when the climate got colder. Since then, all grain has had to be imported. Potatoes, turnips, red currants and rhubarb grow readily, but little else is worth cultivating, unless under glass.

It was a precarious existence but it was not until World War II that far reaching changes were made to the diet of Icelanders. Many thousands of British, and later, American soldiers were stationed in the country with a variety of foods imported for their consumption.

After the war, the emergent Republic of Iceland found ready markets for its quick frozen fish

Opposite: Núpsstaðaskógur, South Iceland

and salted herring, importing in exchange a wide range of fresh and packaged foods. Icelanders now travel widely, bringing back from abroad a taste for the exotic. Reykjavík has a huge choice of ethnic, as well as traditional restaurants, and imaginative use of the freshest of fish, shellfish and lamb ensure that every meal is a feast. Around the island, farm guesthouses, hotels and local restaurants serve simple but unpretentious food. Those with less adventurous palates will be comforted by the usual range of fast food outlets. Hot dogs 'heitar pylsur' are popular with locals.

Breakfasts are usually buffet style consisting of 'súrmjólk', a type of yogurt, cereals, bread and cheese, cold meat and herring. Lunches may be an expanded version of breakfast, or soup followed by a simple fish or meat course. For dinner, soup is often served as a starter, while fish or lamb is the staple main course. Icelanders tend to eat meat rare, including lamb and pork. If this is not to your taste, it is important to say so when ordering in a restaurant. Desserts are typically gateaux and as one might expect from a former colony of Denmark, delicious pastries line the shelves of cafés and bakeries.

The Icelandic national drink is coffee and, on any social visit, you are likely to be offered cup after cup. Coffee drinking is an expected accompaniment to a social gathering and a prerequisite to stimulating conversation, replacing the evening pub or bar ritual of other countries. If you order a coffee in a café, it is expected that a top up will be included free of charge.

## Wine, beer and spirits

For many years there was total prohibition in Iceland and even today, there is a strong anti-alcohol lobby. During the nineteen twenties, with some reluctance, Iceland agreed to import wine from Spain, in return for its exports of salted cod. Later, spirits were again allowed and vodka, in particular, is preferred among Icelanders. The locally brewed **Brennivín**, a schnapps spiked with caraway seed, is often marketed under the 'Black Death' label. But, until 1989, beer over 2.25 per cent alcohol could not be bought in Iceland. Nowadays alcoholic drinks are more widely available but outside of hotels, restaurants and bars can still only be purchased at the ATVR, official government run stores which are found in the Kringlan Shopping Mall in the capital, and in most larger towns around the country. Prices are high and in restaurants a bottle of wine may cost as much as your meal.

## Geography

Iceland is located in the North Atlantic mid-way between New York and Moscow. It sits just south of the Arctic Circle, and lies 606 miles (970km) from Norway, 499 miles (798km) from Scotland and 179 miles (287km) from Greenland. Slightly larger than Ireland in size, the island measures 190 miles (305km) from north to south and 312 miles (500km) from east to west.

Around half of Iceland's landmass lies over 1,300ft (400m) above sea level. While the coastal lowlands and valleys are fertile and allow cultivation of grass for hay, the interior plateau is largely devoid of continuous vegetation cover, though in part suitable for sheep grazing. Icecaps cover 12 per cent of the island and are located mostly in the southern half, which receives the bulk of the precipitation brought in over the Atlantic. Lava erupted in the last 10,000 years forms one tenth of the surface area and a staggering 50 per cent of the country is desert.

Stretching almost the entire breadth of the south coast is a black sand plain formed of debris brought down by flooding from the glaciers. There are no suitable anchorages for fishing vessels along this coast though the flat land is good farming country. The east, north and north-west of the island are more mountainous, carved and scoured by Ice Age glaciers into sheltered fjords that make ideal sites for fishing ports.

Sediment laden glacial rivers drain to the north and south of the ice caps, their flow dependent on temperature as well as rainfall. Spring fed rivers and numerous lakes dot the landscape and even the deserts have their oases.

# Geology

Iceland's position, astride the plate boundary known as the Mid-Atlantic Ridge, accounts for the almost entirely volcanic origin of its rocks. The island's landscapes, its mountains, river valleys and coastline are youthful because, on the geological time scale, Iceland is a mere infant. If the earth were 24 hours old, Iceland's existence would be measured

in seconds. Its oldest surface rocks, which are found in the east and north-west of the island, date back just 14 million years.

Around 65 million years ago, cataclysmic forces set in motion the process of continental drift in the region. The Atlantic Ocean began to form where the ancient continent of Laurasia broke up. What geologists term ocean floor spreading created a tectonic rift running north to south. Volcanic activity on the sea floor along the rift built up the submarine Mid-Atlantic Ridge. Where the activity was particularly intense, flooding basalt lavas built up sufficiently to form islands, of which Iceland is the largest. Known as the Tertiary basalts, these rocks are also found in Northern Ireland, the Hebrides and Scotland, the Faroe Islands, Greenland, Baffin Island and Spitsbergen, and are all associated with the same volcanic activity that followed the continental break up.

Sea floor spreading continues to this day, which is why Iceland, astride the Mid-Atlantic Ridge, is still volcanically active, while the other regions where Tertiary basalts are found, are not. With the rate of spread at around half an inch (1cm) per year, Iceland is still growing in size.

Around thirty volcanic systems have erupted since the settlement of the island in the ninth century. Most are sited along a roughly diagonal line, which follows the Mid-Atlantic Ridge though the island from the south-west corner to the north-east. Lying outside the main zone are several side belts of volcanic activity, which over hundreds of thousands of years have built up significant mountains.

Volcanic eruptions occur in Iceland

*Continued on page 20...*

17

Opposite: Svartifoss Falls; basalt columns,
Skaftafell National Park

Above: Laki craters, erupted 1783, South Iceland

Below: Lake Mývatn, Hverfjall explosion crater

## Shield volcano

Flat dome-shaped lava shield with an angle of slope less than 8°. Formed of thin ropy lava sheets of low viscosity from eruptions lasting months, even years. Examples: Skjaldbreiður near Þingvellir, Kollóttadyngja and Trölladyngja north of Vatnajökull.

## Subglacial volcano

Eruptions during the Ice Age formed many of the mountains to either side of the present volcanic zone. They produced tuff (also known as palagonite) instead of lava, which piled up under the ice in the hole melted by the eruption. When the Ice Age finished the material was left behind as ridges (from fissure eruptions) or free standing mountains (from a single vent). Where the eruption penetrated through the ice, a hard cap of lava was formed and such mountains have a flat 'Table Top' appearance. An example is Herðubreið.

## Spatter ring crater

Low viscosity lava erupts from a single vent producing a lava lake. Splashes from the lake build up a steep-sided, thin, circular crater wall. A rare type with examples Eldborg on Snæfellsnes and Eldborg near Krísuvík on Reykjanes.

## Scoria and cinder cones

Lava fountains throw out lumps which form hard scoria walls, building up a crater. Lava may break through the crater wall and flow in channels to form extensive lava flows around it. Examples are Rauðkúla on Snæfellsnes and Eldfell on Heimaey.

on average every three to five years but, because many happen in winter or under the icecaps, a visitor's chances of witnessing such events are slim. Even if they do not see an eruption, visitors cannot fail to notice the abundant volcanic material, in the form of lava, ash and its coarser form tephra, which litters the landscape.

Lava in Iceland is of two types – block or scoria lava, known also as *aa* (the Hawaiian name) and ropy lava or *pahoehoe*. Scoria lava is gassy, viscous and slow flowing, rough and clinker-like on the surface when it hardens, but giving way to columnar formations at a depth. Ropy lava is thinner, faster flowing and, as it hardens on top but continues to flow underneath, forms ropes or wrinkles on its surface.

## Ice caps and glaciers

Roughly twelve per cent of Iceland's landmass is covered with ice, in the form of smooth dome-shaped ice caps fringed by deeply crevassed valley glaciers, many of which almost

## Crater row

A row of scoria and cinder cones erupted along a fissure, often in groups indicating that different sections erupted at different times. Very common in Iceland, the best example being the Laki craters, along a 15-mile (25km) fissure. Þrengslaborgir and Lúdentsborgir at Mývatn are further examples.

## Strato volcano

The commonest volcano type outside of Iceland, Vesuvius, Etna, Mount St Helens and Fujiyama being examples. Formed of layer upon layer of lava and tephra and built up in repeated eruptions over thousands, even millions of years. Examples in Iceland are Snæfellsjökull, Öræfajökull, Eyjafjallajökull and Tindafjallajökull. Hekla, which erupts along a fissure, is a linear strato volcano.

## Ash and explosion crater

Very explosive eruptions produce only tephra, consisting of ash, pumice and rock fragments blasted from the vent. If the eruption is weak, the material will accumulate around the vent forming a crater, as in moon-like Hverfjall at Mývatn. In more violent eruptions the material is blown away, as in Víti at Askja.

## Maar

A deep crater-like depression from eruptions that produce mostly steam and gas. The hole is deeper than the water table and a lake forms. Examples are Kerið on the road from Selfoss to Gullfoss and Ljótipollur, near Lanndmannalaugar.

## Pseudocrater

As the name suggests, not really a crater at all. Formed when lava flows on marshy ground or into a lake. The lava absorbs water as steam, causing expansion and exploding it as tephra. In places, clusters of craters are formed, distinguished from true craters which normally occur in rows. Examples of pseudocraters are at Skútustaðir at Mývatn and Landbrotshólar near Kirkjubæjarklaustur in the south.

reach sea level. Pockets of ice also remain year round on many of the higher free-standing mountains. Contrary to popular belief, the island's ice caps and glaciers are not remnants of the Ice Age but have been formed in the last 3,000 years. Present day global warming is having a marked effect on Iceland's ice caps and most glaciers are retreating significantly. Visitors need not fear that they will all be gone before they arrive, however, as in places the ice is half a mile (1km) thick.

Many of Iceland's older landscapes, particularly in the northwest, the east and the north of the country, have been scoured and shaped by glaciers during the Ice Age, forming the fjords and dramatic steep-sided mountains that are characteristic of the regions. When it comes to eroding power, ice is a formidable force. Under pressure, it begins to flow, scraping and scouring the surface rock it comes into contact with. Eroded material is dumped as moraine to the sides and

# • VOLCANIC ACTIVITY •

Nowhere else on earth is such a showcase of volcanic features found. This accounts for Iceland's popularity as a destination for geology field trips. The sparse vegetation cover makes features easy to study and the island has many geological oddities. Some, for example shield volcanoes and spatter ring craters, are rare elsewhere in the world. The commonest eruptions in Iceland are of the fissure type, where lava and ash are ejected along a rift. As the eruptions progress, they often become concentrated at points along the fissure, forming small craters around the eruption site.

The large and often cone shaped mountains, which are what may spring to mind when we think of a volcano, are also found in Iceland. Known as strato volcanoes, they are built up of layer upon layer of ash and lava and can be active for many millions of years. The beautiful cone-shaped Snæfellsjökull and Iceland's highest peak, Öræfajökull, are examples.

Major volcanic areas, with a long active life, are known as central volcanoes. Under the surface lies a magma chamber, fed with molten material from the earth's mantle. When pressure builds up inside the chamber, the magma is forced upwards and sideways through fissures, often reaching the surface and causing an eruption. If the magma chamber empties very suddenly, its roof may collapse, leaving behind a steep-sided, roughly circular shaped depression, known as a caldera. Askja (meaning caldera in Icelandic) is one of the best examples in Iceland.

The type of eruption, the kind of material erupted and the crater formed depend on many complex factors, among them the origin of the magma and its mineral and gas content. The initial stages of an eruption can often be very violent and gassy, producing large amounts of ash that are widely dispersed but, as the eruption tails off, may build up around the vent to produce a cone-shaped crater. Later stages, or indeed whole eruptions, may produce just lava, which flows out from a small crater, forming extensive flows. Depending on its composition and origin, magma can be basic, resulting in dark basalts, or acidic, forming the lighter rhyolite in various shades of beige or brown.

in front of the moving ice mass. If the glacier later retreats, the moraines are left behind as ridges and hillocks. Fine examples are found all along the south coast.

Iceland's largest ice cap, Vatna-jökull, measures 3,200sq miles (8,300sq km) and is much larger than all the others combined, in fact larger than all of Europe's glaciers put together. Next in size are Langjökull 368sq miles (953sq km), Hofsjökull 357sq miles (925sq km) and Mýrdal-

sjökull 230 sq miles (595 sq km). The location of all four in the south of the island is explained by the pre-vailing southerly winds which dump their moist cargo as they encounter land. The only significant ice cap in the north of the island is 77sq mile-(199sq km) Drangajökull, in the North-West fjords.

Until the end of the nineteenth cen-tury, rather little was known about Iceland's ice caps. Almost certainly a route across Vatnajökull from north

Morsárdalur, Skaftafell National Park

to south existed up until the sixteenth century, used by seasonal fishermen to reach the rich fishing grounds off the south coast. It was an Englishman, W L Watts, who mounted the first official expedition in 1875. Accompanied by five Icelanders, he took twelve days over the south to north traverse. The first scientific expedition followed in 1919, when the Grímsvötn caldera and volcano were discovered by a Swedish team. In the last ten years, the ice caps have opened up to recreational use and many thousands of visitors enjoy snowmobile and jeep safaris.

## A land in the making

Iceland's landscapes are changing at a phenomenal pace. Volcanoes spew out lava and build up craters; retreating glaciers expose new valleys and form lakes; powerful glacial rivers and cataclysmic flooding from eruptions under the icecaps transport ton upon ton of sediment, dumping it along the coast; waterfalls cut through rock to form deep gorges. And it doesn't end there – frost, wind and sea also play a part in shaping Iceland's youthful landscapes. Visitors often bemoan the fact that Iceland's maps are less than accurate – hardly surprising really, a land in the making is a cartographer's nightmare.

# People and language

Though the least Nordic of the Scandinavians, Icelanders are principally descended from the Norse settlers, who migrated to the island in the ninth century from Norway. Quite a number of them had previously settled in Northern Britain, the Shetland and Orkney Islands and brought with them spouses and slaves of Celtic origin. There are

predictably many tall and blond-haired Icelanders, but a surprising number have dark or red hair and freckles, and research into the blood line shows that the Celtic element may be greater than once believed. Fishing brought French sailors to the east coast during the eighteen hundreds and it is joked that many villagers in the region have darker than usual hair and skin. Today, the nation's population of around 290,000 is fast becoming a fusion of cultures and ethnic groups as Iceland allows increasing numbers of immigrants from far and wide.

Sacred to the nation and dearer to the hearts of its people than any other issue, is the Icelandic language. Much as Latin is the source of modern Romance languages, so Icelandic is to the Scandinavian group the base language from which they have evolved. While Swedish, Norwegian and Danish have been influenced by other European languages, Icelandic has remained virtually unchanged since the thirteenth century. Gramatically complex, it is a minefield of tortuous declensions and conjugations that will baffle and frustrate anyone brave enough to take it on.

Even the alphabet is difficult for there are 33 letters, including two which exist in no other language today. The 'ð', pronounced 'th' as in 'the' and 'þ', pronounced 'th' as in 'thing' were once commonly used in Britain but by the sixteenth century had dropped from the English language. For the visitor it is well worth learning a phrase or two, even though most Icelanders speak remarkably fluent English. French, German, Spanish, Italian and the other Scandinavian languages are also taught and spoken, though less widely than English.

## Icelandic etiquette

A shyness towards foreigners may be mistaken for coldness, though Icelanders are by nature welcoming and hospitable to visitors, if a little curious as to what brings them to Iceland. Family ties are strong and especially on festive occasions, they travel great distances to be together. Everyone is on first name terms as surnames and titles such as 'Mr' and 'Mrs' are not used. It is customary to shake hands when greeting and leaving and Icelanders always remove shoes when entering their home.

To offer a toast raise your glass and say 'Skál' – pronounced 'scowl'. At the end of a meal in a family home it is usual to thank the host by saying 'Takk fyrir mig', before leaving the table. Even children are expected to do this at every meal!

## Economy

Though the founders of the nation were farmers, by the thirteenth century Icelanders had turned to the sea to supplement their livelihood. For centuries, dried fish and homespun wool cloth were the mainstay of the economy and its chief exports. Until the beginning of the twentieth century, most fishing was done using rowing boats with temporary camps set up for the season. When in the early twentieth century engines allowed much larger vessels to be built, which could travel further out to sea and fish for longer, they needed sheltered, deep-water ports, provided for by the fjords of Iceland's indented coastline. The larger catches demanded a resident workforce to process them and many of Iceland's fishing villages were born at this time.

Today's modern and sophisticated fleet is equipped with the latest technology but ironically, there are now strict quotas on practically every species of fish, which makes much of the technology redundant. Their fish factories at a standstill, many fishing villages face an uncertain future, while the villagers pack up and leave for Reykjavík.

Still, fish and fish products account for about three-quarters of export earnings and the industry employs ten percent of the workforce. Iceland's main markets are the USA, European nations and the Far East, especially Japan. The bulk of the fish exports are in the form of quick-frozen prawns, cod, haddock and red fish. Herring and capelin, once fished in hundreds of thousands of tons account for a small share of export revenue, along with salted fish.

Farming engages fewer people and contributes little to exports, but the island is self-sufficient in meat and dairy produce. Sheep rearing, traditionally the backbone of the rural economy, is on the downturn and the introduction of a quota system has left many farmers in deep trouble. Though subsidies encourage diversification into rural tourism and fish and fur farming, such avenues are not available to everyone. Hill farmers and others whose lands are steadily being lost to soil erosion may simply give up.

With no oil, coal or viably exploitable minerals, Iceland has had to

Saguaritun i Klaustrum

for the fishing industry. Tourism provides seasonal jobs, many of which are filled by teachers and students, as the school holidays coincide with the main visitor season. Dogged by double-figure inflation for decades, the country now enjoys one of the lowest rates in Europe and growth and stability that allow its people to be praising instead of cynical of their politicians.

Left: Akureyri Church window "Saga writing in the monasteries"

Below: Ingólfshöfði, landing place of first settler Ingólfur Arnason

Opposite: Statue of Viking boat 'Solfari' at Reykjavík

look at other ways of steering away from an unhealthy dependence on fish exports. Plentiful rivers have long supplied the country with most of its power but recent decades have seen development of massive hydroelectric schemes with a capacity well beyond domestic needs. Tax incentives to foreign investors are designed to attract power intensive industries to Iceland. However many Icelanders are deeply concerned about the impacts on the landscape brought about by hydroelectric schemes and would prefer to see investment in other fields they have gained recognition in, such as computer software, biotechnology and financial services.

The greatest employers are the service and construction industries, supported by light manufacturing outlets, which produce foodstuffs, clothing, furniture and equipment

# History

## Who discovered Iceland?

It is not known who first discovered it but one of the earliest sources is Pytheas, a third century Greek scholar and explorer, who wrote of a land he called Thule, though this was more likely to have been Norway, but the name stuck. From the seventh to the ninth centuries, Irish hermits in search of solitude were busily exploring further and further afield ultimately reaching Iceland. Some returned with tales of this vast empty island with useful advice such that it was light enough at night to pick lice from your shirt and that the land lay a day's sailing south of the frozen sea.

## The settlement of Iceland

Icelanders remark that they can trace their ancestry to the royal courts of Norway. Talk to any two people in the country and they may claim descent from the same saga age chieftain or Viking poet, not all that far-fetched, given that the original settlers may have numbered as few as 20,000 and that many of their names were actually recorded. The 400 or so entries written down in the twelfth century Landnámabók, 'Book of Settlements', list the settlers, their places of origin, where they made their new homes and the names of their descendants. Historians still argue over the accuracy of the manuscript but few nations in the world can boast as authentic a record of their origins as Iceland.

Iceland has been an independent republic since 1944 but its history as a nation goes back to the ninth century, when scores of families, complete with their livestock, left Norway for Iceland. Their journey across the North Atlantic, in open boats, ranks as one of the greatest sea migrations in the history of mankind. What prompted the exodus is still a matter of dispute. It may have been shortage of suitable farming land in Norway but Norway at the time consisted of many small kingdoms embroiled in turmoil and political unrest. The aggressive land-grabbing tactics of one of the kings, Harald Finehair, left those who opposed him with no choice but to emigrate.

It is also known from the Book of Settlements that a number of the emigrants came from the British Isles and were Viking colonists driven from their conquered lands. Whatever the truth, the romantic notion that some Icelanders hold dear is that their ancestors were chieftains driven by the dream of freedom and equality to escape King Harald's tyranny.

The title of first official settler is credited to one Ingólfur Arnason, who landed in the year 874 on Iceland's south shore. As was customary at the time when striking new land, he cast overboard the wooden pillars of his high seat and vowed to settle where they washed up. They drifted west and came ashore where the city of Reykjavík now stands. The early settlers were quick to grab the best tracts of land, which they found uninhabited, except for a handful of Irish monks. Unwilling to live among heathens, the monks departed, leaving behind bells, books and croziers.

By 930, the island was considered fully settled and its inhabitants had set up a legislative and judicial body of their own at a place they named Þingvellir. One hundred years later Christianity had all but replaced the worship of the Norse deities and skills at navigation led the Icelanders further afield to Greenland. Eirik the Red, outlawed from Iceland, founded a colony on Greenland's west coast, which grew to number possibly as many as 3,000. Worsening climate, epidemics and repeated attacks by the Inuit wiped the settlements out by the fifteenth century.

## Where was Vinland?

Eirik the Red's son Leifur, known as Leif the Lucky, continued the Norse exploration further west, reaching a land he named Vínland, 'Wineland', for the profusion of wild grapes he found growing there. His brother-in-law Þórfinnur Karlsefni later established the first European settlement in the New World, 500 years before Columbus. Excavations at L'Anse aux Meadows, a bay on the north-east of Newfoundland, reveal traces of a Viking settlement but as wild grapes have never grown north of Passamaquoddy Bay, between Maine and New Brunswick, it cannot be proved that this was indeed the Norse Vínland. In the event, the colony was short-lived, its settlers driven off by the native North Americans.

During her stay, Þórfinnur's wife gave birth to a son, Snorri, the first white man to be born in the New World. Their story and that of the other Norse settlers is told in the Vinland Sagas, written in the twelfth century during Iceland's 'Golden Age' of literature. Though their historical accuracy may be argued, the value of these epics as a record of life in ninth and tenth century Iceland is undisputed.

## Iceland under Norway and Denmark

From the outset, strong trade and cultural links remained with Norway and with no suitable timber of its own for shipbuilding, Iceland was dependent on Norway for its supplies. Though subject to the laws of its legislative assembly, the Althing, the people of Iceland were effectively ruled by their thirty-nine chieftains. A farmer was free to shift his allegiance from one chieftain to another and naturally, those with the greatest number of supporters became the most powerful. Keen to increase his influence in Iceland, King Hákon of Norway encouraged rivalry among Iceland's chieftains, upsetting the power balance with the result that in 1262 Iceland handed over legislative power and agreed to pay taxes to Norway.

With unification of the Scandinavian kingdoms under Denmark in the fourteenth century, Iceland came under Danish administration. At that time it was foreign merchants, among them British, who had Iceland in their grip but once the Danes got wind of this they quickly displaced the foreigners and took over all commerce. They eventually introduced a trade monopoly that stifled the struggling economy of the tiny nation for over 150 years. Successive epidemics and natural disasters began to take their toll on a country that was already feeling the effects of centuries of isolation from the rest of Europe.

## Recovery and independence

Iceland at the end of the eighteenth century was an entirely rural society and towns and villages did not exist. In an attempt to stimulate the economy, a few small-scale workshops were set up around the farm of Reykjavík and it was decided to move the bishopric and school to the same site from Skálholt, where they had stood for centuries. As Reykjavík was born, the first murmurs of independence were heard, stirred by stories of revolution brought home by those few Icelanders who had managed to travel abroad for an education. In 1844 the very symbol of national pride, the Althing, was re-established in Reykjavík and the island got its own constitution thirty years later. Home rule followed in 1904 and independence under Crown Union with Denmark in 1918. Finally, on June 17 1944, at an emotional gathering attended by almost every Icelander who could make the journey to Þingvellir, the Republic of Iceland was established.

## The post-war years and a new national identity

Iceland today has a sophisticated and highly educated population, enjoying one of the best standards of living in the world and a comprehensive welfare system. To support this, the tax burden is high and, for many, long hours of overtime and two jobs leave little space for leisure activities and family life. Over half of Icelanders live in the capital and surrounding areas. They own more cars, televisions and mobile phones, consume more soft drinks and sweets, yet live longer than most other nations in the world. It is hard to imagine that before World War II, life for most of the nation had changed little in hundreds of years.

Though committed to neutrality, Iceland was occupied during the war, first by British and later by American armed forces. The occupiers carried off their share of war brides but greater still was the impact on the island's infrastructure and economy. Roads were built and industries and jobs created to service the forces. This is turn provided the much needed cash to update the fishing industry in the post war years.

The fishing industry once provided a ready supply of holiday jobs for youngsters but nowadays few of Reykjavík's youth have set foot in a fish factory, nor would dream of doing so. The shift from an entirely rural to an essentially urban populace has had a far-reaching impact on society. Where it was once

## Is Iceland really so expensive?

Iceland has a reputation for being an expensive country to visit which to an extent is justified. There is a sales tax on practically all goods, including food. Alcohol is taxed even more and as almost all goods and raw materials have to be imported, there are freight costs and import duties. While prices overall are higher than in most of Europe and North America, most visitors remark that Iceland represents good value for money and goods and services are generally good quality. Hotels and restaurants are of a high standard and it is difficult to have a bad meal out. Fuel prices are similar to those of Europe, though a lot higher than in the USA. For budget visitors Iceland can be challenging, though by camping, self-catering, travelling by bus and exploring on foot it is possible to do things more cheaply.

customary when meeting a stranger to ask where he or she hailed from, with the idea of establishing links and even kinship, this is now pointless, as two whole generations have grown up in the capital.

It was once an accepted norm that city children spent at least some of the summer working on farms but as the supply of children far exceeds the number of farms and most of the hay is now cut, turned and baled by machine, the practice is dying out. The state television, which used to stop broadcasting in July, as well as having Thursdays off, now competes with private channels, satellite and digital TV for the attention of Iceland's screen addicted youth. Sports, among them soccer, basketball and handball are popular distractions, along with horse riding and the national pastime, swimming. A compulsory subject on the school curriculum, all Icelanders must swim by the age of ten. With unlimited supplies of hot water, most towns and villages, and many rural areas, have their own pools, complete with saunas and jacuzzis.

Icelanders are enormously fond of travel. For their annual leave, many head for the sun, sea and sand of Florida or the Mediterranean. Cultural trips to Europe and further afield are also popular, but for many the lure of the homeland is irresistible. When the weather looks promising, especially if it is a holiday weekend, the city of Reykjavík empties into its rural hinterland, taking up residence in the many 'Summer Houses' that dot the countryside.

Icelanders can indulge their other national obsession all year round. Super jeeps are specially modified four-wheel-drive vehicles, fitted with huge balloon tyres to travel on snow

Seljalandsfoss

and equipped with 'state of the art' navigation gadgetry. Decked out like this, they can travel in safety and comfort through even the most inhospitable and rugged of Iceland's backcountry. They are, of course, as likely to be seen cruising the streets of the capital on a Friday or Saturday night.

Though welcoming to visitors, Icelanders nevertheless have a touch of xenophobia when it comes to foreign interference in their affairs. This is altogether understandable in a nation that endured almost 700 years of colonial domination and exploitation. An interesting issue to ponder, but only for the brave to raise in the company of Icelanders, is that of local attitudes to whaling, a subject which is likely to remain polemic for some time to come.

## Natural history

What Iceland lacks in variety of flora and fauna, it certainly makes up for in terms of sheer numbers of individual species. Mountains and meadows are thick with wildflowers; lava is clothed in luxuriant moss and every boulder sports different splashes of bright lichen. On the coastal cliffs, no ledge is ignored and the air throngs with sea birds, while inland each and every pond and marsh is home to abundant wildfowl and waders. As if this were not sufficient, off shore, Iceland has some of the best and most varied whale watching opportunities in the world, making the island a choice for the discerning naturalist.

Because of their isolation, the flora and fauna of islands tend to develop rather differently from those of larger continental landmasses. Furthermore, islands of volcanic origin

have mostly never been attached to a major landmass. This explains why Iceland has only one native land mammal, the arctic fox, in contrast to Scandinavia, Siberia and Northern Canada, which have many. The arctic fox is assumed to have arrived on ice, probably during the later part of the Ice Age.

Rather few of Iceland's plants and animals survived the Ice Age and most have arrived in the last 10,000 years, again accounting for the rather poor numbers of species. In evolutionary terms this is also very recent, which explains why there are no endemic species in Iceland. Some plants and animals, the hawkweeds and the wren for example, show different characteristics from those found elsewhere in Europe, but are subspecies, rather than a separate species. Another peculiarity of the fauna is the complete absence of reptiles and amphibians and rather poor insect life.

### Land mammals

Iceland's ninth century settlers brought with them sheep, cattle, goats, pigs and horses, as well as cats and dogs. Over the next centuries brown rats, black rats, house mice and long-tailed field mice were all introduced by accident. Reindeer, snowshoe hare and musk ox were introduced experimentally but of these, only the reindeer has survived. The most recent arrival, and at that not a welcome one, is mink, which have escaped from fur farms.

Arctic foxes are found all over the island, but usually in uninhabited areas. For centuries, Icelanders have poisoned, trapped and shot them, in the belief that they are responsible for killing sheep. There is no conclusive evidence that this is true and it is more likely that they eat animals that have died of natural causes. The population today is unknown, but the greatest number are found in the uninhabited Hornstrandir Peninsula in the north-west.

Reindeer are more likely to be seen, particularly in spring, when they are still down in the lowlands before migrating to their summer mountain pastures. They were introduced into Iceland in the eighteenth century from northern Norway, with the idea that they would be farmed, as in Lapland. However, they very quickly became feral but now only remain in the wild area north-east of Vatnajökull. A limited number of reindeer are hunted during the summer, but this does not appear to affect the population, which remains stable at around 3,000.

## Marine mammals

Two types of seal breed around Iceland, the common or harbour seal, and the grey seal. Harbour seals are commonest and are found all around the island, except in the far north. In late summer, when they moult, they often haul out on rocks en-masse. Early summer, when they are pupping, is also a good time to see them. Iceland is thought to have around half the world's population of harbour seals, estimated at around 80,000.

Grey seals are less abundant, numbering around 10,000 in Iceland. They are mostly found along the south and west coasts and important breeding sites are the islands and skerries of Breiðafjörður Bay off Snæfellsnes. Five other seal species occur occasionally in Iceland's waters. The ringed seal and harp seal are most commonly sighted, while bearded and hooded seals are rare.

## The Icelandic horse

The Icelandic horse (note horse, not pony) is a unique breed descended from those brought over from Norway by the first settlers. No horses have been imported into Iceland since the settlement, so the breed has remained pure and has a unique gait, the tölt, a smooth fast trot, to which the rider sits, rather than rises in the saddle. Incredibly hardy, for centuries they were the only means of transport in a country where the wheel had almost no part to play until the nineteen hundreds.

Walruses have been spotted about forty in the last 100 years.

## Whales, whale watching and whaling in Iceland

The mixing of ocean layers off Iceland's west coast creates a nutrient rich soup that attracts life forms spanning the breadth of the food chain, among them whales and dolphins. Fifteen different species of cetacean are found here. Of these, the minke whale, harbour porpoise and several species of dolphin are resident, while others migrate south during winter, returning to their summer feeding grounds in June, July and August.

The first commercial whale watching trips in Iceland were pioneered some years back by UK tour operator Discover the World. A decade later, whale watching is being offered from locations all around Iceland,

*(continued on page 36)*

Above left: Dried fish, Húsavik
Above right: Iceland whaling station in the 1960s
Below left: Horse in winter, near Geysir, South Iceland
Below right: A humpback whale fluking

Above: Highlands; Mt
Herðubreið Arctic Riverbeauty
(Epilobium latifolium) in bloom

Right: Arctic poppy

Below: Puffins with Sand eels

## Whales and Dolphins

The following cetacean species are found in the seas around Iceland:

| | |
|---|---|
| Blue Whale | White-beaked dolphin |
| Finback Whale | |
| Sei Whale | Long finned pilot whale |
| Humpback Whale | Atlantic white-sided dolphin |
| Minke Whale | |
| Sperm Whale | Striped dolphin |
| Northern Bottlenose Whale | Common dolphin |
| | Bottlenose dolphin |
| Killer Whale | Harbour porpoise |

Five of the above species are regularly seen on whale watching trips in Iceland. They are minke whale, blue whale, humpback whale, harbour porpoise and white-beaked dolphin. Several others, the orca or killer whale, sei whale, finback whale and long finned pilot whale, are occasionally seen, while some, like the sperm whale, stay further out to sea.

becoming one of the fastest growing sectors of the tourism industry For minke whales and white-beaked dolphins, boat trips from the Reykjanes Peninsula, Húsavík and Eyjafjörður's offer good opportunities between May and September. Blue whales and humpbacks are most reliably seen 20-60 miles (30-100km) off Snæfellsnes from mid-June through August. Humpbacks occasionally also put in an appearance in the northern fjords. For land based whale watching, killer whales may be spotted, on occasions, from the Snæfellsnes Peninsula's south-west shore in the surrounds of Hellnar. On Iceland's south coast, the cliffs of Ingólfshöfði may yield minke whale sightings, as may the cliffs of the Tjörnes peninsula in the north of the island.

It is always a good idea to pre-book a whale watching trip and worth inquiring at the same time what species are currently being observed. Even so, sightings can never be guaranteed. There are several factors at play here. A clear sky and calm sea make spotting whales and dolphins very much easier, and more enjoyable. When feeding they may understandably show more interest in food than in us and when they are on the move, they are difficult to follow. It is often when they are interacting with one another that the most rewarding encounters are experienced as they may also come in close to investigate a boat, swimming around and under it. If you are serious about watching whales, allow time for more than one trip.

As a former whaling nation, there is still a strong pro-whaling lobby in Iceland and despite the IWC moratorium on whaling hunting whales for scientific purposes started again in August 2003. Several leading whale and conservation experts consider the potential for whale watching in Iceland to be outstanding. Already, the income generated from whale watching trips exceeds that derived from a good whaling year. It is hoped that by supporting local whale watching initiatives and raising local awareness of the value of cetaceans alive rather than dead, attitudes towards whaling in Iceland will eventually change.

## Birds in Iceland

Roughly 300 bird species have been observed in Iceland, though only 70 breed regularly. Of these, a handful are resident but many are migratory and only visit their breeding grounds for three to five months in the year, escaping the harsh winter by flying south. The remainder are either vagrants, which may be winter guests that arrive in autumn and depart in spring, or passage migrants which call in during spring or autumn on their way to or from more northerly breeding grounds. Knots and turnstones are passage migrants that stop off in Iceland in early spring en-route to Greenland and can be seen in mid to late May in huge flocks along the south coast.

Compared to elsewhere, there are rather few breeding species of bird in Iceland. To blame are its northerly location, oceanic weather conditions, isolation and lack of woodland and insect life. The species that are now considered Icelandic are almost exclusively species also found in the rest of northern Europe – with three exceptions, the harlequin duck, Barrow's goldeneye and great northern diver (loon). Though the harlequin also nests in Siberia, these three species are North American.

With the warmer climate over the last 80 years, 17 new species have been added to the list of birds that breed in Iceland regularly. The lesser black backed gull and starling are two of the recent additions. One species, the great auk, has died out completely, while several others are now considered doubtful breeders. Habitat destruction has had some impact on bird populations as extensive draining of marshland in the lowlands makes way for hayfields and grazing lands.

The species that dominate the bird scene in Iceland are seabirds, waterfowl and waders and there are very few passerines. Passerines actually make up sixty percent of the world's birds but are only seventeen percent of Iceland's. One third of Iceland's bird species are seabirds, but when it comes to numbers they are by far the majority, with possibly as many as 13 million breeding pairs.

## When to go bird watching

Early summer is the most rewarding time for bird watching in Iceland. During the last two weeks of May many passage migrants stop off on the south coast, particularly around Eyrarbakki and Stokkseyri, before continuing their journey further north to breed. By the first week in June, many birds are pairing up to breed in Iceland and courtship rituals can be entertaining. Once the females are on the nesting site, they become easy to observe but it is important to be careful not to disturb the birds at this critical point in the breeding cycle. By mid to late June, the young of many species are hatched. On the seabird cliffs, the greatest activity is from late May to late July. By mid-August most of the young are fledged and have left their cliff ledge perches.

## Vegetation and flora

When it comes to vegetation Iceland is a land of puzzling contrasts. At times the greens couldn't be greener, yet just around the corner there is barren desert, apparently devoid of vegetation. How can it be that lava in the south of Iceland that is covered with a thick layer of moss is only 200 years old, yet 6,000 year old lava in the interior has no vegetation? The secret is water, or lack of it. Much of Iceland's interior desert lies in a rain shadow north of the icecap Vatnajökull. Where there is surface water, around streams and ponds for example, vegetation is prolific, even at 2,000ft (600m) above sea level.

Soil type and geology also influence what will grow and where. The older pre-Ice Age basalts hold water and their soil cover better and vegetation grows continuously on even quite steep slopes. The younger palagonite or tuff rocks, formed during the Ice Age in sub-glacial eruptions, are very friable and easily eroded and the vegetation has a hard time keeping hold. Glacial sand and volcanic ash are easily windblown, so unless sown with soil-binding lyme grass, they are often bare of vegetation.

In Arctic areas most plants are perennial and there tend to be very few annuals. This is because conditions are harsh and the growing season short. Most plants cannot germinate, grow, flower and produce seed in such a short time. Plants have needed to evolve ways of coping with their hostile environment. Take seed dispersal for example – the viviparous fescue allows seeds to germinate on the plant. Others like the beautiful pyramidal saxifrage cope with lack of water and suitable anchorage by siting themselves in rock crevices, which drain run-off rainwater and provide a hold for the root systems. The moss campion has such a deep taproot that it is anchored even when all the surrounding soil has been eroded away. Birches and willows hug the ground in exposed areas, growing horizontally rather than upright. Their roots are shallow but extensive, allowing them to profit from the warmer soil at the surface.

For the visitor to Iceland, the most striking feature of the vegetation is the lack of woodland. Only one percent of Iceland has continuous forest cover, though this has not always been the case. At the time of settlement, it is thought that as much as one quarter of the country was wooded with birch, several species of willow and rowan. The only evergreen native to Iceland is juniper though many others have been introduced in gardens and forestry plantations.

# Visitor Attractions

These include museums, historical sites, excursions and special activities. Many attractions are not open in winter, or have restricted opening hours. Opening hours and departure times may change from year to year and Icelanders have always had a fairly flexible approach. People are often willing to bend the rules and open up on demand so it never hurts to ask, and it is always worth telephoning if the scheduled hours do not fit your travel plans. Many museums, particularly in the capital, are closed on Mondays in summer.

# · GETTING BY IN ICELANDIC ·

**A** complex language, Icelandic is a daunting prospect for visitors, but thankfully most Icelanders speak some English. However, a few phrases of the language are fun to try out and will be much appreciated when you make contact with the locals. Stress naturally falls on the first syllable of a word.

## Pronunciation

**a** as in *hard*
**á** as in *how*
**e** as in *get*
**é** as in *yet*
**i** or **y** as in *thin*
**í** or **ý** as in *seen*
**o** as in *fought*
**ó** as in *sold*
**ö** as in *first*
**u** as in *book*
**ú** as in *pool*
**æ** as in *eye*
**au** a sound between *date* and *oil*, as in the French *'feuille'*
**ey** and **ei** as in *day*
**ð** is th as in *the*
**þ** is th as in *thing*
**fn** is pn as in *open*
**g** followed by **i** (except at the start of a word) is y as in *yet*
**hv** is kf as in *thankful*
**j** is y as in *yet*
**ll** is tl as in *little*
**r** is always lightly rolled
**rn** is tn as in *mutton*
**rl** is rtl as in *heartless*
**tn** and **fn** at the end of a word are almost silent

## Useful signs

| | |
|---|---|
| Toilet | Snyrting |
| Gents | Karlar |
| Ladies | Konur |
| Open | Opið |
| Closed | Lokað |
| Airport | Flugvöllur |
| Campsite | Tjaldstæði |
| Parking | Bílastæði |
| Police | Lögreglan |
| Shop | Verslun |
| Garage Mechanic | Verkstæði |
| Hospital | Sjúkrahús |
| Health Centre | Heilsugæslastöð |
| Post Office & Telephone | Póstur og Sími |
| Swimming Pool | Sundlaug |
| Entry | Inngangur |

# · GETTING BY IN ICELANDIC ·

| | |
|---|---|
| Exit | Útgangur |
| Jeep Track | Jeppavegur |
| Prohibited | Bannað |
| Danger | Hætta |

## Some useful phrases

| | |
|---|---|
| Good morning | Góðan dag |
| Good evening | Gott kvöld |
| Good night | Góða nótt |
| All right | Allt í lagi |
| Goodbye | Bless |
| Yes | Já |
| No | Nei |
| Thanks | Takk |
| Thank you very much | Takk fyrir |
| Thank you (at the end of a meal) | Takk fyrir mig |
| Would you like? | Viltu? |
| Yes please | Já takk |
| No thank you | Nei takk |
| May I have? | Má ég fá? |
| When? | Hvenær? |
| Today | Í dag |
| Tomorrow | Á morgun |
| Yesterday | Í gær |
| Come! | Komdu |
| Cheers! | Skál |

## Numbers

| | |
|---|---|
| One | einn |
| Two | tveir |
| Three | þrír |
| Four | fjórir |
| Five | fimm |
| Six | sex |
| Seven | sjö |
| Eight | átta |
| Nine | níu |
| Ten | tíu |

But... beware because numbers one to four decline and have masculine, feminine and neuter forms. It is safest to use five and above!

## Days of the week

| | |
|---|---|
| Monday | Mánudagur |
| Tuesday | Þriðjudagur |
| Wednesday | Miðvikurdagur |
| Thursday | Fimmtudagur |
| Friday | Föstudagur |
| Saturday | Laugadagur |
| Sunday | Sunnudagur |

## Map reading made easy

A glance at a map of Iceland leaves many a visitor in despair. Icelandic place names are as long as they are unpronounceable. But, with a little knowledge of Icelandic geological and topographical terms, things can become a lot easier. Many place names are composite, that is to say made up of several elements. Take, for example the icecap Eyjafjallajökull, which is made up of Eyja (island), Fjall (mountain) and Jökull (glacier). Here are some other examples of common components of Icelandic place names:

| | | |
|---|---|---|
| Fell | hill, mountain | Búrfell (chest mountain) |
| Hlíð | slope | Reykjahlíð (steam slope) |
| Hraun | lava | Eldhraun (fire lava) |
| Gígur | crater | Lakagígar (Laki craters) |
| Gjá | fissure, rift, gorge | Eldgjá (fire fissure) |
| Laug | hot spring | Landmannalaugar (hot springs of the people from Land) |
| Hver | geothermal spring | Hveravellir (hot spring plains) |
| Dyngja | shield volcano | Trölladyngja (trolls' shield volcano) |
| Fjöll | mountains | Kerlingarfjöll (troll wife's mountains) |
| Dalur | valley | Vatnsdalur (Lake valley) |
| Hóll | hillock | Vatnsdalshólar (lake valley hillocks) |
| Vatn | lake | Álftavatn (swan lake) |
| Á | river | Jökulsá (glacier river) |
| Fljót | large river | Skjálfandafljót (trembling river) |
| Lækur | stream | Brjánslækur (Brján's stream) |
| Lindir | cold spring | Hvannalindir (angelica springs) |
| Höfði | headland, cape | Ingólfshöfði (Ingolf's cape) |
| Eyri | sand spit | Suðureyri (south sand spit) |
| Vík | bay | Reykjavík (smoke bay) |
| Nes | peninsula | Tjörnes (pond peninsula) |
| Sandur | sandy plain | Mýrdalssandur (marsh valley sand) |
| Fjörður | fjord | Breiðafjörður (broad fjord) |

## Whose son or daughter are you?

Icelanders do not have surnames, using instead the ancient tradition of patronyms. When christened, a child is given his or her first name, and takes the father's (or occasionally the mother's or grandfather's) first name to which is suffixed either 'son' or 'dóttir'. So, Kristín Magnúsdóttir is Kristín, daughter of Magnús. Women do not change their name on marriage as they cannot become someone else's son or daughter, which means that both parents, sons and daughters will all have different last names in Iceland. This raises a few eyebrows when Icelanders travel abroad.

The formal titles 'Herra' and 'Frú' are used in official correspondence but never in personally addressing someone. 'Mr' and 'Mrs' are simply unnecessary in a country where everyone is comfortable on first name terms. Even the telephone directory is listed under first names. When introduced to an Icelander you are likely only to be given their first name. To find out more you must of course ask: "Whose son or daughter are you?"

# REYKJAVÍK

*I*n recent years, Iceland's capital has developed a reputation as an exciting and rewarding destination and not without good reason. The city's stylish shops, bars and restaurants and vibrant nightlife combine to give it an invigorating and youthful appeal that matches the zest for life of its inhabitants. For quieter pursuits, the museums, galleries, tree-lined back streets and well-tended parks are the draw, while beyond the city limits, a rugged coast and splendid backdrop of mountains invite further exploration

Today, **Reykjavík** is a modern sprawling city of over 100,000 inhabitants, that still retains a lot of its small town charm. Its setting is beautiful, and the views in clear weather over **Faxaflói Bay** to the ice-capped volcano Snæfellsjökull, are little short of stunning. Struck by the columns of geothermal steam that rose from its surrounds, Ingólfur Arnason, the first official settler, named the place Reykjavík, meaning 'Bay of Smoke'. This is slightly ironic, as Iceland's capital is one of few in the world so unpolluted it can claim to be smoke-free. The hot water is still pumping out, and since 1930 has been used to heat the city's homes. A statue of Ingólfur, by sculptor Einar Jónsson, stands on **Arnarhóll** beside the National Theatre, by way of homage to his role as founder of a nation and its capital.

The old town is clustered round a pretty lake down by the port. Here are found most of the traditional wooden homes, clad with brightly painted corrugated iron sheets for protection against the elements. Narrow streets lined with delightful gardens give the quarter a tranquil ambience. The lake hosts around forty breeding bird species and the surrounding parkland is popular with families. Jutting out into the lake is Reykjavík's new and controversial **Town Hall**, which houses a huge relief map of Iceland. Open daily to visitors, it also has a delightful café with views over the lake, and a tourist information bureau.

Also flanking the lake is the **National Gallery**, housed in an old ice factory. From the lake, **Lækjargata**, meaning 'Brook Street' runs towards the port. The stream was covered over in 1840 but the name remains. Overlooking Lækjargata is the elegant **Menntaskólinn**, Reykjavík's oldest school, dating from 1844.

# • Nightlife in Reykjavík •

**S**uch is the transient nature of many establishments and fickle the loyalty of their clients that it is almost pointless to compile a list of night spots. Not surprising when you consider that until the nineteen eighties, the only bars in Iceland were in the hotels and that beer was illegal.

Today, the city's nightlife is focused on the heart of the old town, where the longest established pubs like **Gaukur à Stöng** compete with a new generation of chic cafés and bars such as **Nelly's, Vegamot, Víðalín** and **Hverfis bar**. The Irish themed **Dubliner** has a hard core of followers and often puts on live music. For dancing **Kaffi Reykjavík** and **Kaffi Victor** pull a mixed crowd, while Friday and Saturday nights at **Broadway**, Iceland's largest nightclub, can be lively, as can the enduring **Þjóðleikhúskjallarinn** – a night club in the cellar of the National Theatre. **Nasa** and **Pravda** attracts a younger clientele.

Things are pretty quiet during the early evening, with many pubs and cafés only open to diners but after 11pm it starts to warm up, with most establishments staying open until 3 or 4am at weekends, but closing earlier during the week.

Icelanders are not known for doing things half-heartedly, and Friday night on the town is no exception. The theme of alcohol consumption, mingled with youthful exuberance and joie de vivre is one and the same, but while the over-twenties fill the bars and clubs, the under-aged throng the streets, with their plastic bottles of spiked cola. On even quite an average night, it seems that the city's youth in its entirety empties on to the streets to celebrate another Friday. Dressed for the cat walk, the crowds display a total disregard for the weather and an extraordinary ability to look 'cool' in spite of the cold.

By one o'clock there are lines outside the bars and traffic queues start to form. Those not drinking are at the wheel, having borrowed their parents' car for the ritual street cruise. The Friday night frenzy reaches its crescendo at around 3am, leaving the streets littered with broken glass after a generally good-natured round of bottle-slinging. Drunken couples hover in the doorways, bands of teenage girls huddle together for shared tears and comfort and taxis cannot be had for love or money.

Several other restored timber houses flank the street, as do restaurants serving traditional Icelandic menus. The main tourist information bureau is situated in Aðalstræti, the capital's oldest street.

West of the lake is Suðurgata a street of elegant homes with leafy gardens leading to Iceland's **National Museum.** The museum contains the most valuable archeological finds in the country as well as priceless national treasures such as furnishings, costumes, embroidery and the few religious artifacts to survive the Reformation. Iceland's great literary heritage is housed in the adjoining **Árni Magnússon Institute,** where visitors can see many of the treasured Saga manuscripts on display.

Suðurgata continues past the domestic airport to **Skerjafjörður,** where remains of old fishing huts sit side by side with sought after luxury homes. A walking and cycling trail, with the distraction of some unusual sculptures, runs along the coast in either direction from here.

The city's main square, **Austurvöllur,** is a pleasant spot to watch life go by. The **old cathedral,** originally erected in 1796, was so badly designed that it had to be rebuilt, taking on its present form in 1879. Also facing the square is the austere stone **Parliament House,** built during 1880-1881. A statue of independence hero **Jón Sigurðsson** sits in the middle of the square, among pleasant gardens. Park benches and open-air cafés are testimony to the hardy nature of the Icelanders, who will never let a ray of sun slip by unappreciated.

Reykjavík's port originally lay alongside **Hafnarstræti,** then named Strandgata, but when the port was extended in 1913, land to the north of it was reclaimed to make way for further building. The port is now the largest in Iceland and fishing still an important activity in the capital. Alongside the large stern trawlers that fish the bulk of the catch are many smaller vessels. **Kaffivagninn,** a café on the wharf side, is one of

## Getting around Reykjavík

The city's public buses are easy to use once you get hold of a route map, available from the Tourist Information Centre. Most drivers speak English. A flat fare is charged and exact change must be given. If you plan to change buses, ask for a transfer ticket, which is presented to the driver of the second bus. Otherwise, no ticket is given. Most services run at 15 or 20 minute intervals during the day and at 30 minute intervals at evenings and weekends. **The Reykjavík City Card** is a special pass, which includes bus travel, museum, attraction and swimming pool entrances. The Tourist Information Centre in the city has full details and sells the pass.

Taxis can be found at taxi ranks around the city or called by telephone. Most accept payment by credit card, as well as cash. Tipping is not usual.

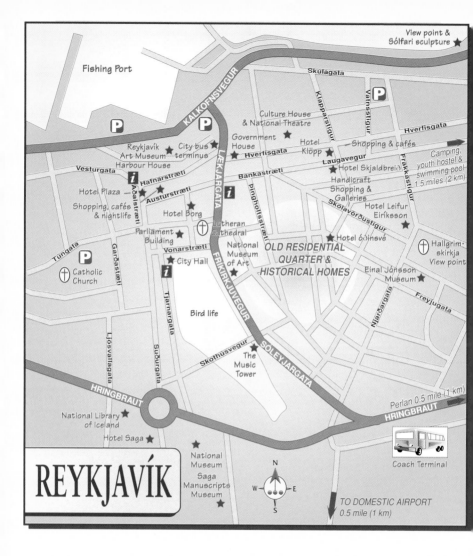

REYKJAVÍK

the longest established in the city and serves genuine and unpretentious Icelandic food, to a clientele of factory workers and trawlermen.

The main shopping street, **Laugavegur**, leads out of town. The name means 'hot spring road' and in the old days it led to a cluster of hot springs where laundry was taken. Though the hot springs have long gone, harnessed for hot water, the city's excellent **Botanical Garden** is on the same site in **Laugadalur** 'hot spring valley' and is well worth a

visit. Close by is the city's main swimming pool, which is heated by geothermal water.

An unmistakable sight are the glistening tanks of **Perlan**. Storing the city's hot water, they house an impressive history exhibition and a revolving restaurant and viewing platform, offering an excellent view of the city and surrounds. Pleasant walking trails criss-cross the hillside, where there are also remains of a British army camp from World War II and a simulated geyser.

# Places to Visit
# REYKJAVÍK

**Árbæjarsafn Reykjavík Museum**
☎ 577 1111
A collection of historical buildings moved to the site from all over the city. Special cultural events in summer. Located in the outskirts of the city. Open: 10am-5pm Tuesday-Friday and 10am-6pm Saturday and Sunday 1 June-31 August; Mondays partly open 11am-4pm.

**National Museum of Iceland**
Suðurgata 41, ☎ 530 2200
www.natmus.is
Planned re-opening summer 2004 after extensive renovation.

**National Gallery of Iceland**
Fríkirkuvegur 7, ☎ 562 1000
Open: 11am-5pm daily except Mondays. Closed over Christmas and New Year.

**Kjarvalsstaðir**
Miklatún, ☎ 552 6131
Gallery dedicated to artist Jóhannes S Kjarval. Open: 10am-5pm, daily all year.

**Ásgrímur Jónsson Gallery**
Bergstaðastræti 74, ☎ 551 3644
Icelandic artist, famed for his

landscape paintings. Open: 1.30-4pm, daily except Mondays 1 June-31 August; 1.30-4pm weekends only 1 September-31 May. Closed December and January.

**Sigurjón Ólafsson Gallery**
Laugarnestangi 70, ☎ 553 2906
Gallery and studio of one of Iceland's key sculptors.

**Saga Museum at Perlan**
☎ 511 1517
augusta@backman.is
www.sagamuseum.is
Recreates key events in Iceland's colourful history. Open: daily summer 10am-6pm, winter 12pm-5pm.

**Einar Jónsson Gallery and Sculpture Garden**
Njarðargata, ☎ 551 3797
Renowned sculptor whose works are on display around the city. Open: 2-4pm Tuesday-Sunday. Closed December and January. Garden open all year

Continued...

Reykjavík

47

# Places to Visit
# REYKJAVÍK

**Natural History Museum**
Hlemmur 5, ☎ 590 0500
Open: 1-5pm 1 June-31 August
and 1.30-4pm 1 September-31
May, Sunday, Tuesday, Thursday
and Saturday.

**Ásmundur Sveinsson Gallery
and Sculpture Garden**\*
Sigtún, ☎ 553 2155
Renowned sculptor whose works
are also on view around the city.
Open: 10am-4pm daily 1 May-
30 September; 1-4pm daily
1 October-30 April.

**Árni Magnússon Institute**
Suðurgata, ☎ 525 4010
The national collection of Saga
Manuscripts. Open: 1-5pm daily
1 June-1 September. At other
times by arrangement.

**Harbour House –
Reykjavík Art Museum**\*
Tryggvagata 17 ☎ 590 1201
Permanent exhibition of artist
Erró's works. Open: 10am-5pm
daily.

**The Botanical Gardens**
Laugardalur, ☎ 553 8870
Delightful park and collection
of native and introduced plants
and shrubs. Open: 8am-10pm
weekdays, 10am-10pm
weekends 1 June-30 September;
8am-3pm weekdays, 10am-4pm
weekends 1 October-31 May.

**Culture House**
Hverfisgata 15, ☎ 545 1400
various exhibitions relating to
Icelandic culture and history.
Open: daily 11am-5pm.

**Family Park and Zoo**
Laugardalur, ☎ 575 7800
Theme park and zoo containing
farm animals, reindeer, arctic
fox, mink and seals. Open:
10am-6pm daily 10 May-
1 September; 10am-5pm daily
except Wednesday 2
September-9 May.

## Entertainment

Concerts, Exhibitions, Special
Events, Theatre and Opera
performances are detailed in
the free booklet 'What's On in
Reykjavík', widely available in
the city.
whatson@whatson.is

**Cinema**
There are several cinemas in
Reykjavík and foreign films are
always shown in the original
language, with Icelandic
subtitles.

**Light Nights**
Tjarnabío Theatre
☎ 561 0280
Theatre production in English,
with audio visual displays,
illustrating folk tales, saga
scenes and history. Performances:
9pm daily, June – August.

**The Volcano Show**
Hellusund 6a, ☎ 551 3230,
Series of video films on volcanic
eruptions in Iceland. Several
shows daily in English, all year
round.

\* Free admission on Mondays. On other days one ticket is valid for
Harbour House, Kjarvalsstaðir and Ásmundur Sveinsson Gallery if used
on the same day.

# • Icelandic food – palatable or poisonous? •

Traditional Icelandic food is based on fish and lamb Throughout the centuries they have been eaten fresh as well as smoked, salted, pickled or dried for the winter months. Lamb is usually served roasted or smoked and boiled as in the national dish *hangikjöt*. A typical farming dish is *saltkjöt og baunir*, boiled lamb with split peas. Potatoes, usually boiled in their skins, have all but replaced rye bread as the main accompaniment. Fresh fish is boiled or fried and sometimes baked with cheese and sour cream. Haddock, rather than cod, is the staple with halibut, plaice, ocean perch, salmon, trout and prawns also consumed in quantity.

Famine, experienced on several occasions, breeds a 'waste not, want not' approach to food and the islanders have developed some unusual local delicacies. Try ram testicles pickled in sour whey, sheep's head jelly, sheep liver paté or cods' chins. Puffin steaks and guillemot eggs are more seasonal and were a welcome addition to the diet in spring. If you get the chance, try the infamous *hákarl*, rotten shark, washed down with a glass of local *brennivín* schnapps.

Dairy produce in Iceland is excellent. *Skyr*, a skimmed milk curd preparation is whipped with milk and sugar and served with cream and often blueberries. *Súrmjólk* is a thin yoghurt served at breakfast with brown sugar. At the bakery, try *flatkökur*, rye flour pancakes which are delicious with caraway seed cheese or thinly sliced smoked lamb.

No one should visit Iceland without trying the delicious wafer-thin Icelandic pancakes, served with rhubarb jam and whipped cream.

The new cathedral, **Hallgrímsskirkja**, is another prominent landmark that most visitors either love or hate. Few will offer it the indifference that many Icelanders show towards the creations of the State Architect, who instigated its construction in 1914, though the building was not finished until the nineteen nineties. The church's interior is light and airy and doubles as an inspiring concert venue. The tower, accessed by a lift, offers one of the best viewpoints over the city. Outside the church is a statue of **Leifur Eiríksson**, of 'Vinland' fame, a gift from the United States in 1974, on the occasion of the eleven hundredth anniversary of Iceland's settlement.

Close by Hallgrímskirkja are the

**museum and sculpture garden** of **Einar Jónsson**, whose inspirational works are displayed around the city. Another acclaimed sculptor is **Ásmundur Sveinsson**, who drew on a variety of themes including saga events and scenes from everyday life. The artist's museum and sculpture garden are near the city's main swimming pool in Laugardalur.

## European City of Culture

Reykjavík's role as 'European City of Culture' in the year 2000 was more than justified. Icelanders are passionate about the arts. Every other street corner is bedecked with sculpture. Two renowned landscape painters, Jóhannes S Kjarval and Ásgrímur Jónsson, have their own galleries. Banks, public offices, hotels and restaurants host exhibitions, but there are plenty of 'official' galleries, as well as those on the fringe, which offer the multi-talented artistic youth of the city a chance to get known.

Few European nations have hit the UK and US pop scene with as thumping an impact as Iceland. One hit wonders Mezzoforte soared to the top of the charts in the nineteen eighties, while singer song-writer Björk's successes dominated the nineties. Arriving on the pop scene since then are the alternative music band Sigur Rós, Minus, a hard core metal punk band getting rave reviews and Icelandic Italian singer/songwriter Emiliana Torrini, who has written for Kylie Minogue and sang the theme song of the Lord of the Rings 'The Two Towers'. On the classical front, tenor Kristján Jóhansson has gained international fame in opera, while Helgi Tómasson has for decades directed leading ballets in the USA. p

**Reykjavíks Arts Festival** takes place each year during the second half of May. ☎ 561 2444 www.artfest.is

## Shopping in Reykjavík

There are two main shopping areas in the city. The central part of the old town, Laugavegur and Skólavörðurstígur, has the best selection of crafts, knitwear, bookshops and souvenirs, along with some nice boutiques. Further out of town, the vast **Kringlan Shopping Mall** has the fashion shops, quality gift stores, an excellent supermarket and the city's main government-run bottle store. The January and summer sales can offer real bargains in the fashion shops, but prices overall, are higher than in the UK and North America.

Don't forget to ask for a tax refund voucher if your purchases total 4000Kr or more in one transaction.

# EXPLORING FROM REYKJAVÍK

Iceland's capital makes an ideal base from which to explore and enjoy a sample of the scenery and attractions of the island. A huge choice of excursion, by coach, jeep and air, operate from Reykjavík, while for those who prefer to do things on their own, scheduled buses and car hire are easily arranged. Several areas can be covered on a day trip from the capital: the Reykjanes Peninsula; the southern lowlands including the great sites of Þingvellir, Gullfoss, Geysir and Skálholt (detailed on the following pages; the South Shore (described in Chapter 3); and the West (described in Chapter 7).

Reykjavík

51

# • Excursions from Reykjavík •

**Reykjavík Excursions**
Bankastræti 2
☎ 562 4422 and
Hotel Loftleiðir
☎ 562 1011, Fax 552 3062
main@re.is
www.re.is
Offering the widest choice of escorted day trips from the capital. Trips can be booked through most accommodation establishments.

**Icelandic Excursions Allrahanda**
☎ 540 1313
ie@icelandexcursions.is
www.allrahanda.is
Wide choice of sightseeing and adventure excursions from Reykjavík.

**Mountaineers of Iceland Jeep tours**
Langholtsvegur 115
☎ 581 3800
ice@mountaineers.is
www.mountaineers.is
Adventurous but comfortable super-jeep day trips. Winter snowmobile and Jeep Safaris.

**BSÍ/Destination Iceland**
Vatnsmýravegur 10
(at the main coach terminal)
☎ 591 1020, Fax 591 1050
www.dice.is
Scheduled buses to places of interest for visitors, including Gullfoss, Geysir, The Blue Lagoon, Þórsmörk, Landmannalaugar and many others. A budget, unescorted option.

## The Reykjanes Peninsula

Lying south and west of the capital, the **Reykjanes Peninsula** juts 31 miles (50km) into the North Atlantic facing the full onslaught of the weather systems that drift up to Iceland, its barren landscape a grim welcome to those who arrive at Keflavík International Airport. Most people simply ignore it and head instead for Reykjavík. But the area is really worth a second glance, offering fantastic volcanic moonscapes, geothermal activity, a dramatic coastline and some excellent hiking, bird and whale watching. There is ample accommodation and visitor services include the newly revamped Blue Lagoon, the region's best known and quite unique spa attraction.

Reykjanes is entirely volcanic, indeed it sits astride the Mid-Atlantic Ridge. Activity during the Ice Age produced the tuff ridges that run its length, while post-glacial lavas and craters cover the lower lying parts. Just about every type of volcanic feature in Iceland can be found in the region but there have been no eruptions since the fourteenth century, though as Icelanders have found out to their cost in the past, this is no indication that activity has ceased.

The peninsula's south shore is battered by North Atlantic waves and fierce gales. Undeterred, many species of bird overwinter along the coast and breed on its rocky cliffs. Minke and killer whales, along with white-beaked dolphins, congregate in the offshore waters and can be spotted on whale watching trips. Traditionally, fishing and a little farming supported the local economy, now superseded by the NATO base, international airport and tourism as key employers. Unsurprisingly there are few if any trees on Reykjanes, although soft and spongy grey-green moss is quick to invade new lava and, once it gets a grip, grasses, flowers and shrub-like birch and willow take root in sheltered crevices and hollows.

Reykjanes can easily be covered on a day trip from Reykjavík, including a visit to the Blue Lagoon but more time is needed to do a whale watching trip as well. Roads to Grindavík and Sandgerði are kept open all year, but the dirt tracks beyond are often snowbound in winter and motorists should seek local advice.

## Hafnarfjörður

Leaving Reykjavík, the dual carriageway, one of the few in the country, weaves through the towns of Kópavogur and Garðabær to **Hafnarfjörður** (harbour fjord). Worth a small detour, this town of

23,000 inhabitants is Iceland's third largest and has been an important port since the fourteenth century.

Built over the 7,000 year old Búrfell lava flow, Hafnarfjörður, its cluster of wooden houses spreading up the hillside up from the harbour, includes several interesting museums, among them the Maritime Museum. The town's pride is Hellisgerði, a pleasant leafy park and gardens situated in the lava up the hill from the museums. Long the butt of the nation's jokes, the town's residents, known as Hafnfirðingar, believe that its lava cliffs are home to elves, or hidden people, living in harmony alongside the human population. To visitors, the town's claims to Viking heritage are more credible and Hrafna-Flóki, who named Iceland, is said to have landed south of here, where he found a beached whale and called the place Hvaleyri. Every two years, Hafnarfjörður hosts a summer Viking Festival but visitors can enjoy the flavour of it year round with a visit to the Viking restaurant and pub Fjörukráin.

Just before reaching Hafnarfjörður, the main road to Reykjanes bypasses the town. Turning right here leads you to Álftanes, an upmarket residential area and **Bessastaðir**, the official home of Iceland's president. Visitors can drive up as far as the church, which was built between 1780 and 1823 and contains beautiful stained glass windows by two Icelandic artists. The slightly older presidential residence was originally built as the governor's home in Danish colonial style. The view from Bessastaðir across to the capital is dramatic, particularly in winter when a dusting of snow caps Mount Esja beyond.

Outside Hafnarfjörður, in the

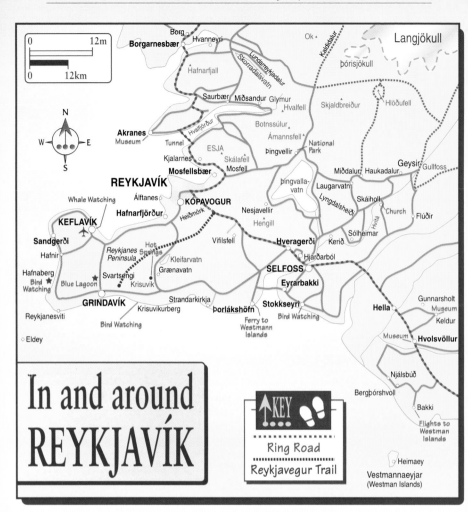

In and around REYKJAVÍK

KEY
Ring Road
Reykjavegur Trail

town's new industrial quarter, is a massive aluminium plant, a curious welcome to the cleanest capital city in Europe. It is supplied by power from the Þjórsá River hydroelectric scheme and was built as the showpiece for Iceland's attempts to attract power-greedy industries to the country as a ready outlet for its surplus energy. Opposite the plant, on the other side of the road are the remains

of a pre-Lutheran chapel, where a statue of the Catholic St Barbara was found.

## The South Shore of Reykjanes

Route 42, left off the main road, and signposted to Krísuvík, leads to the southern shore of the Reykjanes Peninsula. After a short distance it

54

Above: Reykjavík

Below: Perlan & simulated geyser, Reykjavík

Above: Statue at Strandakirkja

55

splits again, with a turn off to the Bláfjöll skiing area. Route 42 continues, with a jeep track leading to Djúpavatn and several smaller lakes where there are walking trails linked to the long-distance hiking path Reykjavegur. Lake Kleifarvatn, at 97m one of the deepest lakes in Iceland, is believed to be inhabited by a snake-like monster. The lake and surrounds have an eerie feel to them, enhanced by the frequent mist and drizzly weather conditions. Just beyond the lake is the geothermal area **Krísuvík,** with steam vents, mud pools, sulphur deposits which were once mined, and the nearby explosion crater lakes Grænavatn and Geststaðavatn.

A short distance beyond Krísuvík, Route 42 bears left and heads over beautiful moss-clad lava to Þorlákshöfn, a long and winding, but in clear weather very scenic, drive on a rough road. Stóra and Litla Eldborg are two lava ring craters to the left and right of the road. Here a 6.2-mile (10km) long walking trail takes off through the lava along the bird cliffs of Krísuvíkurberg, where guillemots, kittiwakes, fulmars and razorbills nest. **Strandakirkja**, a short detour off the road further along, is well worth a visit. The story goes that a ship ran into a storm offshore and the crew vowed to build a church if their prayers for help were answered. An angel then appeared and guided them safely to shore, where they built the church. Even today, it is said to work miracles and seamen in distress still promise donations. Consequently, the church is among the wealthiest in Iceland, even though it has no parish to serve.

Heading west from Krísuvík the dirt road twists and turns endlessly to reach **Grindavík**, a quiet fishing town of just over 2,000 people, though with a turbulent history. Sixteenth-century rivalry between English and German traders led to the murder of an English merchant named John the Broad. Then, in 1627, Barbary pirates struck, the first of several raids in which Icelanders were taken as slaves to North Africa.

## Blue Lagoon

Close by Grindavík is one of Iceland's best known attractions, the stunning **Blue Lagoon**, a quite unique bathing experience in an almost surreal setting. The Svartsengi Geo-thermal Project supplies hot water to the Reykjanes Peninsula, through a heat exchange system which allows the run-off water to feed the lagoon.

Set amidst tumultuous black lava, the distant billowing steam from the power plant forms a magnificent backdrop. The water is so rich in silica that it forms a sticky mud on the floor of the lagoon, which is said to be good for the skin. Sufferers of psoriasis and other related skin conditions find the waters beneficial and with the water temperature a tempting 30-40°C all year round, the experience is nothing short of sublime.

## The tip of the peninsula

Beyond Grindavík, a dirt road hugs the coast as far as the lighthouse at Reykjanesviti, the oldest in Iceland and dating from 1878. The offshore island of **Eldey**, formed from a submarine eruption, can be seen from here. Now a gannet sanctuary, and the third largest in the world, the island is better known as the final stronghold of the great auk which became extinct when the last of the species was clubbed to death there in 1844. In winter, harlequin ducks may be seen in the surf along the coast, while north of the lighthouse lies **Hafnarberg**, where a walking trail hugs the cliff top, allowing good views of nesting seabirds during spring and early summer. Nearby **Hafnir** has an attractive church and a marine aquarium. Just south of the village a boat was driven ashore in stormy weather in March 1940, after being adrift for two weeks in the most appalling of weather conditions. Remarkably, all the crew survived.

**Sandgerði** is the largest of a cluster of fishing villages on the tip of the peninsula. The main attraction here is The Nature Centre, a natural history museum and research centre offering guided walks for those interested in sea and shore life, bird watching and botany. Half day whale and dolphin watching trips from Keflavík are offered in conjunction with a visit to the centre. White-beaked dolphins are most commonly seen, with humpback or minke whales spotted on about one third of trips run.

Much of the north of the peninsula's tip is taken up by **Keflavík international airport** and the **NATO base**.

## Keflavík

**Keflavík**, population 7,500, has a history linked to trade and fishing, dating back to the sixteenth century. Still an important harbour and fish

## Keflavík NATO base

Three and a half thousand US servicemen and women staff the NATO base at Keflavík, established in 1951 after a much controversy surrounding Iceland's joining of the alliance two years earlier. The republic had existed for only five years, after centuries of domination as a Danish colony and occupation by Allied troops during World War II. Understandably, the prospect of a foreign military presence on home ground worried many Icelanders, knowing that they had never had an armed force of their own. Anti-NATO sentiments surface from time to time but most Icelanders are pragmatic about it all – the fact is that the base employs locals and generates important revenue for the state and businesses alike.

processing centre, the town derives most of its livelihood from servicing the NATO base and airport. For anyone planning to spend several days exploring the Reykjanes Peninsula, Keflavík, with hotels, guest houses, restaurants, swimming pool and folk museum, could be a useful base. It is also handy as an overnight stay for arriving or departing passengers at the International Airport, with some accommodation establishments offering a free transfer.

Above: Blue Lagoon
Below: Þingvellir

# The Golden Circle – Þingvellir, Gullfoss and Geysir

Iceland's 'Golden Circle', a trio of major sites of interest to visitors, draws its name from an ever-popular day excursion from the capital. The star attractions of Þingvellir, Gullfoss and Geysir, the old bishopric at Skálholt and towns of Selfoss and Hveragerði, can be comfortably toured in a day, whether by car, on an organised day trip, or as part of a longer tour. To explore the region more fully and include the Þjórsá Valley a couple of days would be ideal. The roads to Gullfoss, Geysir and Skálholt are usually open all year, but Þingvellir can be snowbound in winter.

This low-lying part of Iceland is the country's best farming district. The once extensive marshlands have been drained, and hayfields ringed by ditches and dotted with white silage bales are a common sight in summer. In clear weather, the views can be staggeringly beautiful, reaching far into the highlands to the flat dome of Langjökull, while Hekla's snowcapped cone and Eyjafjallajökull rise from the plain to the east.

## Mosfell & district

Northbound from the capital, Route 36 takes off just past the satellite town of **Mosfellsbær**. The modern church of **Mosfell**, sits on a site that dates back to saga times. The enigmatic saga hero Egill Skallagrímsson spent his last days there and is said to have plotted to dispose of his gold by throwing it over the ravine at Þingvellir to watch the assembly fight over it. His family were naturally not amused and left him at home when the Althing convened. Undeterred, Egill got two slaves to bury the gold, then killed them and to this day the whereabouts of the gold, if it ever existed, remains unknown. The nearby horse riding centre Laxness offer a variety of riding tours and operates all year round.

Reykjavík's second ski area, **Skálafell**, is off to the left as the road reaches the flat plateau of Mosfellsheiði, dotted with several small lakes. The unpaved Route 48 cuts down to Hvalfjörður from the moor, just before Þingvallavatn comes into view and you can draw off the road at a convenient point. To the south, steam rises from the **Nesjavellir** geothermal project, reached by the road that hugs the western shore of the lake. Nesjavellir supplies most of Reykjavík's water, heated by steam from 18 bore holes up to 7,218ft (2,200m) deep. The remainder comes from Mosfellsbær and from bore holes within the city. The plant also produces electricity to power the pumps that carry it, via a 15-mile (25km) long pipeline with a capacity of 1,870l per sec, to the city's storage tanks at Reynisvatn. The pipeline, most of which is above ground, is so well insulated that snow does not melt off it in winter.

## Þingvellir

The best place for a view over Þingvellir is from the main road to Reykjavík. A turning leads to a visitor centre and the edge of the ravine that overlooks the ancient assembly site, the **Althing**. Perhaps this was the view that inspired Lord Dufferin to write in a letter to his mother in 1856: "At last I have seen the famous Geysir, of which every one has heard so much; but I have also seen Thingvalla, of which no one has heard anything. The Geysirs are certainly wonderful marvels of nature, but more wonderful, more marvellous is Thingvalla". Few Icelanders would disagree, for Þingvellir is the cradle of the nation's history and independence of its people.

Þingvellir is also a site of exceptional geological interest and the ravine edge is the perfect spot for an overview of the tectonic forces that have shaped its landscape. The whole area lies on the path of the Mid-Atlantic Ridge as it passes through

Iceland from Reykjanes to Þingvellir and then northwards to Langjökull. Here, the plates of the earth's crust are moving apart. **Botnssúlur**, the highest and oldest mountain, lies to the north and is probably the remains of an ancient cone volcano. To its right is **Ármannsfell**, formed in a sub-glacial eruption during the Ice Age, behind which the flat dome of the shield volcano **Skjáldbreiður** is visible. Further right are several more sub-glacial tuff ridges and mountains, while south of them lies another, though less obvious, shield volcano **Lyngdalsheiði**.

## The Althing

Founded a little before 930, the Althing was established by chieftains who had settled the country from Norway, just over fifty years earlier. More than a formal parliament, the Althing was a council, whose members agreed to settle their disputes and be bound by the law, rather than the sword. The twelfth century historian Ari Þorgilsson tells in his history of the nation, Íslendingabók, that Þingvellir, in many respects an ideal site, was chosen by a man named Grímur. It had ample pasture for grazing, abundant fresh water and firewood and suitable space to accommodate tents for the thousands of people that attended the annual event. Importantly, it also lay on the main routes to the north, west and south of the island, which were the most densely populated.

At the annual assembly, the Lögrétta, 'Law Council', consisting of twelve members from each Quarter of the country, was the supreme authority and made and amended the laws. One of its members was elected for a period of three years as Lögsögumaður, 'Lawspeaker', whose duty it was to recite the laws and ensure that they were not forgotten. This was done from a place known as Lögberg, 'Lawrock', which today is marked by a flagpole. Curiously, some of the laws produced during this early period of Iceland's history are still in force today, including the rights to driftwood.

The second main function of the Althing was to hear and judge lawsuits at the courts, the intricate details of which are recounted in many of the Icelandic sagas. As a legal system it had its shortcomings as there was no executive body to enforce the law and carry out the sentence of the court, which could be a fine, confiscation of property or outlawry – though not capital or corporal punishment. It was up to the plaintiff to collect the fine, take the goods or ensure that the accused left the land. Only if he stayed on in Iceland, as did Gunnar of Njál's Saga, could he be legally killed by the plaintiff.

The Skjáldbreiður eruption 9,000 years ago produced a huge volume of lava, later overlain in a subsequent eruption from Tindfjallaheiði. This lava was once an unbroken plain stretching across where the lake now lies, but level with the top of the ravine and viewpoint. Over the next millennia, periodic bouts of rifting caused the land to sink and the gaping fissures which dissect the plain of Þingvellir were formed. Notice how they follow the SW-NE direction of the Mid-Atlantic Ridge. The last episode was as recent as 1789 when the land sank 20 inches (50cm), leading to the decision to suspend the Althing altogether.

In total, the land has sunk 100-130ft (30-40m) and **Lake Þingvallavatn**, at 32sq miles (83.7sq km) Iceland's largest, has slowly formed in the depression. Up to 374ft (114m) deep, the lake lies in part below sea level. Except for the Öxará River, whose course was diverted to flow over the wall of Almannagjá forming the lovely waterfall Öxaráfoss, and provide fresh water for the assemby, the inflow comes from under the lava. The outflowing River Sog is Iceland's largest spring fed river. The rather constant water temperature of 39°F (4°C) is beneficial to trout, char and stickleback, which are abundant in the lake.

The lake, plains and surrounding mountains of Þingvellir together form an area of outstanding scenic beauty, where man's impact has been negligible. Standing on the ravine edge it is hard to imagine the scene that would have met the eye when the ancient assembly was in session. What comes as a surprise to visitors is how little remains on the site – no castles or fortifications, no parliament building.

With a little imagination, you can just make out the rough outline of a turf dwelling or two. Most are fairly recent, dating from the eighteenth century and were the booths of the county officials. Booths were temporary dwellings made of turf and stone. They were occupied for a short time each year in June, when the Althing convened.

Following the old road you can walk from the viewpoint down **Almannagjá**, the largest of the gaping rifts that dissect the area, to reach the **Lawrock**. This is probably where the Lawspeaker addressed the

As power became concentrated in the hands of the most powerful Goðar, 'Chieftains', so the system of law and order broke down. It was this that prompted the nation in 1262, to sign a pact with the King of Norway, handing over legislative power. The Althing's control of internal affairs was further reduced when Iceland came under Denmark and over the following centuries ever harsher laws were brought in.

The fortunes of Iceland's beloved Þingvellir gradually dwindled but the assembly was reestablished in Reykjavík in 1844, with political reforms giving rise to a glimmer of hope for independence. Þingvellir then became the symbol of the emergent nation's struggle for self-determination. It was here, in 1930, that they celebrated the millennium of the Althing, which was attended by 30,000 Icelanders, while the independence celebration and establishing of the Republic of Iceland on 17 June 1944, was equally well attended.

# Places to Visit
## AROUND REYKJAVÍK

## Reykjanes Peninsula

### The Blue Lagoon
☎ 420 8800, lagoon@bluelagoon.is
www.bluelagoon.is
Open: daily 1 September-14 May 10am-8pm and 15 May-31 August 9am-9pm.
Buses depart Reykjavík BSI coach terminal at 10am, 11.30am, 1.30pm, 3.15pm,
5.15pm and 6pm, returning 12.40pm*, 2.15pm*, 4pm*, 6pm and 8pm.
*Services returns via Kefavík Airport for departing passengers

### The Nature Centre
Sandgerði, ☎ 423 7551
Natural history museum offering guided walks and whale and dolphin
watching. Open: 9am-5pm weekdays 1pm-5pm weekends, daily, all year.

### Marine Aquarium
Hafnir, ☎ 421 6958
Open: 2-5.30pm daily June-August; 2-4pm daily September-May.

## Hafnarfjörður

### The Icelandic Maritime Museum
Vesturgata 8, Hafnarfjörður, ☎ 565 4242
Open: 1-5pm, daily, June-September and weekends only October-May.

### Hidden Worlds Tours
☎ 565 0661
Learn about the elves, Iceland's 'hidden people' on a walking tour of
Hafnarfjörður's elf sites. Tours depart from the town's Tourist Information
Centre, daily May-September at 10am and 2pm.

## Southern Lowlands

### Þingvellir National Park
☎ 482 2660 www.thingvellir.is
Þingvellir National Park Information Centre, Toilets, caféteria, campsite and
shop. Open: daily 1 May-31 October. Interpreter visitor centre is open 9am-
5pm 1 April-1 November

### Þjórsárdalur
☎ 488 7713
Reconstructed Saga Age Farm. Based on the excavated twelfth century farm
at nearby Stöng. Open: 10-12am and 1-6pm, daily 1 June-6 September.

### Geocentre (Geysir)
☎ 486 8915 www.geysisstofa.is
Open: daily, all year
Fascinating exhibition on Geology, earthquakes, geysers and the changing
face of Iceland.

62

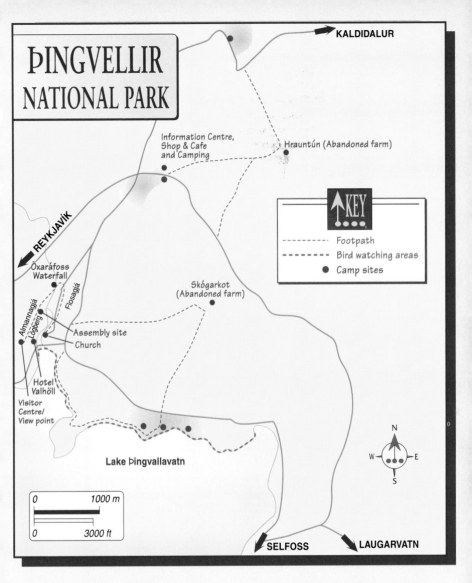

# ÞINGVELLIR NATIONAL PARK

KALDIDALUR

Information Centre, Shop & Cafe and Camping

Hrauntún (Abandoned farm)

**KEY**

- - - - - Footpath
- - - - - Bird watching areas
● Camp sites

REYKJAVÍK

Öxaráfoss Waterfall

Flosagjá

Almannagjá

Lögberg

Skógarkot (Abandoned farm)

Assembly site

Church

Hotel Valhöll

Visitor Centre/ View point

Lake Þingvallavatn

N W E S

0        1000 m

0        3000 ft

SELFOSS        LAUGARVATN

---

assembly, though evidence suggests that in the early days the site was located on **Spöngin**, the spit of land between the water-filled rifts of Nikulásargjá and Flosagjá.

To reach these fissures, cross the bridge by the drowning pool on the Öxará River, where women were put to death as recently as 1749, and take the path across the plains. Spöngin is to the left of the church by a small car park. The bridge over the rift gives a good view of the whole area and of the incredibly clear and deep water below.

Apart from the founding of the Althing in 930, the most important event to take place at Þingvellir was the conversion to Christianity in the year 1000, following which the first church on the site was built.

The **National Cemetery**, east of the church, was established in 1939 to honour distinguished Icelanders.

## Iceland's Bell

The present church at Þingvellir was consecrated in 1859 and contains a seventeenth-century pulpit and three bells, one very ancient, one from 1698 and the symbolic 'Iceland's Bell', installed for the independence celebrations in 1944. The last was made famous earlier by Nobel Prize winning author Halldór Laxness' novel of the same name. The story goes that an ancient bell, a gift from a Norwegian king, had cracked and been re-cast abroad in the eighteenth century but as the nation was too poor to pay for it, the bell was returned and disappeared. The fate of the bell seemed to mirror that of the nation, so the ringing of the new bell at the independence celebrations took on special significance to Icelanders.

It says something of the nation that the only two recipients are the poets Jónas Hallgrímsson and Einar Benediktsson. Next to the church is Þingvallabær, built for the 1930 celebrations on the site of the original farm. The older part is the home of the parish priest and national park warden, while the newer section serves as the summer residence of the Prime Minister. The hotel, across the river, is only open in summer and has a restaurant and pleasant bar with some interesting art work.

### Kaldidalur

The jeep track F550, open only in summer, leads north over **Kaldidalur**

## Þingvellir National Park

Þingvellir and its surrounds are a National Park and one of Iceland's three. The information centre, with toilets, a cafeteria, shop and campsite, is open from 15 May to 31 October and is located a few miles from the assembly site, at the crossroads where the Kaldidalur mountain track takes off to the left. A new visitor centre is located at the top of Almannagjá. A road skirts the northern shore of the lake, where there are further campsites by the water's edge. Bird watching from a marked trail that winds along this part of the lake is excellent. Varied and abundant flora is also a feature of the National Park, with around 200 species recorded.

There is plenty to see and do at and around the assembly site but for those wishing to explore further afield there are many easy walking trails in the National Park. Here are a few ideas:

**The Althing and the Ravines** (2 hours), **Hrauntún** (1.5-2 hours), **Skógarkot and the Lake Shore** (2-3 hours)

Boat trips on the lake run from Skálabrekka on the west shore of the lake 6.2 miles (10km) south of the assembly. For fishing in the lake contact the National Park information bureau.

or **Uxahryggur** to Borgarfjörður. This is a great route for those who want a taste of the uninhabited Iceland. The track passes majestic Skjáldbreiður volcano and its desert-like surounds to skirt the small ice cap Þórisjökull and the larger dome of Langjökull. The route is not especially difficult though strong winds can whip up the dust to make driving unpleasant. Allow two hours to cover the 39-mile (63km) track, which is not recommended for ordinary cars.

## From Þingvellir to Geysir

A choice of route continues from Þingvellir. Route 36 heads south to Selfoss past the hydroelectric power station Ljósafoss which is one of the oldest in Iceland and dates from 1937. Most travellers head east over **Lyngdalsheiði** on Route 365 to Laugarvatn. The dirt road, which is closed by snow in winter, gets busy on Sundays with local traffic and is winding and dusty, but it is the shortest route to Geysir. Shortly before Laugarvatn, a track to the left leads to some caves in the easily eroded tuff rock, which were inhabited up until the 1920s.

**Laugarvatn** takes its name from the hot springs which rise at the edge of the lake, now covered over to form a natural sauna. The settlement, which consists of several schools, a shop, petrol station and a few houses, is Iceland's only real holiday village. The schools convert to hotels in summer, while the mostly Icelandic visitors camp and stay in the huge caravan park and holiday home complexes. The population can swell to several thousand in summer, drawn by the water sports on offer on the lake but there is little of real interest to visitors from abroad.

## The Geysers at Geysir

**Geysir** is without doubt Iceland's star attraction but its popularity means that, unless you go out of season or in the evening and early morning, you will probably be sharing it with several hundred, even a thousand, other people. Along with neighbouring Gullfoss falls, it is possibly the only place in the country that can be called truly 'touristy' but it really is worth a visit. Only a few other places in the world can boast spouting geysers, so to have several in Iceland, along with all the other incredible natural phenomena, really is special.

Our word 'geyser' derives from the Icelandic 'Geysir', meaning 'gusher' the name given to the original and the largest of the island's spouting hot springs. According to historical sources Geysir started erupting in the thirteenth century, following a major earthquake. Since then it has gone through periods of great activity, followed by quieter spells. Following recent earthquakes Geysir has stirred and lucky visitors may witness the incredible spectacle of an eruption.

Fortunately, **Strokkur**, meaning 'Churn', a smaller geyser on the site, is incredibly active and spouts a 98ft (30m) jet of water into the air every three to seven minutes. Strokkur was first mentioned after an earthquake in 1789, but is probably much older. It was dormant for many years, when in 1963 with the demise of the Great Geysir, it was decided to clean out the shaft with a drill. This was obviously just what was needed because Strokkur has not stopped since, nor shows any sign of tiring.

Geysers differ from one another in the amount of steam and water they produce and the duration and height

Gullfoss Falls

There are many other hot springs on the site, including **Litli Geysir**, meaning 'Little Geysir', which has erupted during and after earthquakes. **Konungshver**, 'The King's hot spring', on the hill behind Blesi, was named in honour of the Danish King Christian IX, who visited the site in 1874. Nearby are three rocks, known as the Kings' Stones, which the King, and two of his successors, sat on while watch-

of the eruption. Strokkur's eruptions are short lived and produce mostly water, while the Great Geysir's can last for thirty minutes or more, ejecting water to start with and ending with a violent burst of steam. Surrounding the bowl of both geysers are beautiful, though fragile silica deposits, which take many decades to form. As the mineral-rich water cools, dissolved silica forms tiny balls which reflect blue light, giving the hot spring **Blesi**, located up the hill from Strokkur, a bluish tinge.

ing the Great Geysir erupt.

Geysir has a campsite, a hotel, interpretive geology museum, restaurant, cafeteria, petrol station and souvenir shop, which except for the campsite, are open all year round. Admission to the geysers is free. A few miles from Geysir are the ancient farm site and church at **Haukadalur**. Home to one of the most influential families in Iceland in the early centuries of settlement, it became an important centre of learning. Ari the Learned, twelfth century scholar and author of the treasured Íslendingabók and Landnámabók, studied there. A mound to the north of the nineteenth century church's graveyard is said to be the burial site of Bergþór, a troll-like figure who lived in a cave on Bláfell and whose dying wish was to be buried within earshot of the church bells.

## Gullfoss

Five miles (8km) beyond Geysir on the River Hvítá, which draws from a glacial lagoon on the eastern edge of Langjökull, is the waterfall **Gullfoss**. The 105ft (32m) high fall formed as the river carved a course following a fissure in the lava bed. It drops in two stages into a gorge, which extends for a short distance downstream. At the upper car park, there are a visitor centre, toilets and a shop and a path leads from here to a viewpoint over the falls from above. Steps lead down to the lower car park, where a path takes off down to the edge of the falls. Beware, it can be very slippery in winter.

The flow of water over Gullfoss averages 3,850 cubic ft (109 cubic m) per second. During heavy flooding it has measured almost twenty times that, but in winter it can be just a trickle, with much of the flow bound up in ice. Not surprisingly, on several occasions plans have been drawn up to exploit the hydro-electric potential of the falls. Over the years, the farmer's daughter Sigríður from nearby Brattholt fought tirelessly to protect the falls, and made many exhausting journeys to Reykjavík to plead with officials. A memorial to her stands by the lower car park. In 1979, just over twenty years after Sigríður's death, the falls and surrounding land were made a nature reserve. Brattholt now offers visitor accommodation and has a campsite.

Strokkur erupting, Geysir

Beyond Gullfoss, the paved road turns to a dirt track, marking the start of the Kjölur Mountain Track through the centre of Iceland. There is now a choice of road to join Route 1. Route 30 crosses the Hvítá at a place called **Brúarhlöð**, where the river narrows to just a few yards wide, as it passes through a canyon. The water is said to be 33ft (10m) deep where the bridge, which was built in 1959, is located. Two previous bridges were swept away in flooding in 1929 and 1930, when the water level doubled. River rafting trips run on this section of the river, an exhilarating experience, though the grade 2 rapids are a little tame for some. Over the bridge the road continues past the bed and breakfast farm at Hvítárdalur, to the village of Flúðir, a centre for greenhouse cultivation with a swimming pool and hotel.

## Þjórsá Valley

Eight miles (13 km) south of Flúðir, Route 32 takes off for the beautiful Þjórsá **Valley** which is well worth a detour as there are several interesting things to see here. The mighty River Þjórsá drains off Hofsjökull and its surrounding wetlands and at 144 miles (230km) in length is Iceland's longest glacial torrent, and among its most powerful. Islands in the river bed support dense thickets of birch, which are absent from the surrounding land and are proof of the destructive nature of sheep grazing. Introduced conifer plantations dot the hills west of the river, and there is a delightful outdoor swimming pool Þjórsárdalslaug.

Views stretch beyond the river across to the snowcapped ridge of **Hekla,** whose eruption, in 1104, destroyed most of the farms in the valley. At **Stöng**, just before the Búrfell Power Station, one of the farms was excavated, providing a useful model for the reconstructed Saga Age farm nearby. There is free access to the archeological dig and the lovely ravine Gjáin with a pretty waterfall, is just upstream from the site.

Two further waterfalls are also worth visiting in the area. **Háifoss,** Iceland's second highest waterfall at 400ft (122m), is reached by continuing on Route 32 past the intake for the power station, to a signposted track to the left. **Hjálparfoss,** the 'Helping Falls', is signposted to the right, just before the turn off left to Stöng. It is said to have been named by locals who found its pool teeming with fish, which saved them from starvation in the famine that followed the 1104 eruption.

## Skálholt

The alternative route linking Geysir with the Ring Road is Route 35, taking off just west of the geothermal area. It passes the settlement of **Reykholt**, where there are a campsite and swimming pool and a spouting hot spring, before the turn-off to **Skálholt**. Lying on the spit of land known as Biskupstungur, 'Bishop's tongue', between the rivers Hvítá and Brúará, Skálholt was for 700 years the cultural and religious focal point in what was then an entirely rural land. But for chance, Skálholt might well have developed as Iceland's capital, in place of Reykjavík.

At Skálholt a magnificent timber cathedral, equaling those of Scandinavia in size and grandeur, was built and when it burnt down in 1309, it was replaced by another. In 1550, as the Reformation swept through Iceland, the last Catholic bishop from the northern see of Hólar

## The power of religion

In the early days, Skálholt was the farm of the ambitious chieftain Gissur the White, who co-led the Christian mutiny at the Althing in the year 1000. With no school in Iceland he sent his six year old son, Ísleifur, to Germany to study for the priesthood and in doing so founded a dynasty of bishop-chieftains at Skálholt.

Gissur was dead when his son returned, so Ísleifur took over the farm and established a school for training clergy. Elected as the first Bishop of Iceland, Ísleifur was succeeded by his son Gissur, who greatly added to the Church's wealth and power base by introducing a tithe in 1096. As most of the churches were owned by chieftains, they stood to benefit enormously and a great number of new churches were built in the years following. This in part answers the question commonly asked by visitors – why are there so many churches in Iceland?

was brought to Skálholt and beheaded along with two of his sons, for having taken up arms against the Lutherans. A memorial to him stands to the left of the main road as it approaches Skálholt from the west.

By the eighteenth century, Skálholt's fortunes had sunk to an all time low. In 1797, the see was moved to Reykjavík and the cathedral dismantled and auctioned off, leaving little but the vague memory of its past glory.

The present church was completed in 1963 and has works of art by two Icelandic women artists – stained glass windows by Gerður Helgadóttir and the mosaic behind the altar by Nína Tryggvadóttir. A team of archeologists found a stone sarcophagus containing the skeleton of Bishop Páll Jónsson, who had died in 1211. The sarcophagus and beautifully carved crozier that rested by the body are on view in the crypt museum. A tunnel, which led from the medieval cathedral to the school buildings, was

restored during the excavations, which also revealed just how huge the first cathedral had been.

Back on Route 35, the farm of Sel offers accommodation, an alternative to the summer hotel at Skálholt itself. Another choice is the 'Global Eco Village' at **Sólheimar**, on a loop road east of Route 35, which runs a guest house. The community was set up for disabled and able people to live and work alongside one another, inspired by the ideas of the German philosopher Rudolf Steiner. It specialises in growing organic vegetables under glass and in the open, and produces beautiful handicrafts.

Just before crossing the River Sog, the road passes a crater row to the left and right. A parking area on the left leads to Kerið, an explosion crater or maar, with an eerie blue-green lake in it. In the 1970s, a pop group performed from a floating platform to an audience seated on the crater rim, in an unusual outdoor concert.

# 3 The Ring Road – South Coast

Opposite: Fagrifoss Falls, en route to Laki

Most first time visitors to Iceland travel some or all of the Ring Road, the circular Route 1 around the island, during their stay. Most of the 875-mile (1,400km) route is now paved and, with little traffic, driving is both safe and pleasurable. The Ring Road can be comfortably driven in a week, using a normal car, but ten days or longer allow for side trips and a more relaxed pace. For those travelling by bus the Ring Road is covered by the BSI Circle Bus Pass as well as the Omnibus Pass. Sections of the route can also be travelled by air.

## THE SOUTH COAST

### From Reykjavík to Vík

This whole section of Route 1 is paved, though between the capital and Hvolsvöllur, the traffic is heavy at times. This is one of the most populated parts of Iceland but aside from the villages and farms, there is plenty of scenic interest for visitors. Highlights include the stunning scenery of Þórsmörk, the coastal cliffs at Dýrhólaey and many beautiful waterfalls.

Leaving Reykjavík, the **Heiðmörk** recreational area, with walking and cycling trails, takes off to the right. A cluster of red-tinged hillocks on the right are the remains of pseudocraters, bulldozed during the war by the British to make the airport runway. A little further on the **Bláfjöll** ski area is signposted to

the right, in view of the mountain **Vífilsfell**, named after one of first settler Ingólfur's slaves, who was sent up to check on the approaching weather systems to see if it was safe to set out fishing.

There are few signs of habitation in these parts. A signpost reassuringly marks the fork to Þorlákshöfn but the 'sea' of rugged moss-clad lava stretching either side of the road adds to the feeling of desolation. The lava is called Kristnitökuhraun 'the taking of Christianity lava' and is said to have flowed around the year 1000 at the time the issue of conversion was being debated at the Althing. The lava was threatening the farm of one of the pagan chieftains who took this to be a sign that the gods were angry. The Christians retaliated by questioning who and what had angered the gods when the lava at Þingvellir had erupted before the settlement of Iceland.

Steam rises to either side of the road by **Skíðaskálinn**, an impressive looking restaurant where there are hot springs. The track to the left, on the sharp bend shortly before the restaurant, leads to a cluster of huts where walking trails into the Hengill volcanic area take off. Crossing Hellisheiði, the next 6 miles (10km) of Route 1 can be bleak and an orange painted emergency shelter is there for the use of motorists in trouble. Before the road was built around 1930, the bridle trail was marked by cairns, which can be seen stretching off to the left in a line.

As the road begins to descend towards **Hveragerði** in a series of wide loops, there is a viewpoint to the right. A broad plain leads to the horizon and a distant view of the icecaps and **Westman Islands**. The plain, originally the sea bed, rose at the end of the Ice Age when the weight of the ice was removed, leaving the old cliffs high and dry but giving Iceland its most productive farming land. Evidence of the former coastline can be seen the whole way along the south coast, as far as Vatnajökull.

## Hveragerði

**Hveragerði** is known as the 'Greenhouse Village' because there are more geothermally heated glasshouses here than anywhere else in the country, growing tomatoes, cucumbers, peppers, flowers and house plants. The showcase greenhouse is in a tourist complex called Eden, worth a stop for the postcards, about the best choice in Iceland. With 1,700 inhabitants, Hveragerði

is located on the edge of a massive geothermal field where as little as 33ft (10m) below the surface of the ground, the water is over 212°F (100°C). The village sprang up in the 1940s when they started growing under glass and now houses Iceland's horticultural college along with a health farm offering natural therapies. One of the village's claims to fame is that of having the first electric street lamps in Iceland, apparently erected after someone fell into a hot spring in the dark.

There is a choice of hotel, guesthouse or camping in the village, which also has a swimming pool, restaurants and fast food outlets. Wherever you go in the area, steam rises from the ground. Most of it is harnessed, but visitors can wander through the hot spring 'park' or head through the village to Gufudalur, where a small geyser **Grýla** may be coaxed into erupting. Beyond here, the road turns to a footpath, leading into the heart of one of Iceland's largest geothermal areas and linking up with the **Hengill and Nesjavellir walking trails**.

## Þorlákshöfn, Stokkseyri and Eyrarbakki

South of Hveragerði, Route 38 leads to **Þorlákshöfn**, where ferries depart for the Westman Islands. Of greater interest to visitors are the two villages of **Stokkseyri and Eyrarbakki**, a little further east along the coast and a short detour off Route 1. Eyrarbakki was for centuries the main port on the south coast though its port was far from safe. Now protecting the village is a sea wall, erected following the catastrophic flood of 1799 that destroyed

**Básendar**, further west along the coast and badly damaged Eyrarbakki. The oldest building in the village, from 1765, survived the flooding and now houses the regional museum. The church and most of the houses along the main street date from 1890-1910 and the place has a real 'old world' feel about it.

Just outside Eyrarbakki is Iceland's main prison. **Stokkseyri** has less character but like Eyrarbakki is a haven for wildlife, with seals hauled up on the rocks at low tide and abundant bird life in the wetlands surrounding the village. A great way to explore the area is on a guided sea kayaking trip, suitable for beginners and experienced paddlers alike. The shore attracts huge flocks of migrant birds, waders in particular, in mid to late May, who stop briefly en route to their breeding grounds further north, making this coast a premier location for keen birdwatchers. Þuríðarbúð is a fishermen's hut, or more accurately a fisherwoman's, as it was built to the memory of Captain Þuríður Einarsdóttir. Though such houses, built of stone and turf, were common all over Iceland, women captains were not and seamanship was, and is to this day, a man's domain.

# Selfoss

Back on the Ring Road, heading east from Hveragerði the route crosses the southern plains, passing a trio of new and rather plain towns, the first of which is **Selfoss**. Just before the town, left of the road; is **Ingólfsfjall**, a mountain named after Iceland's first official settler. Some hold that Ingólfur is buried on the flat-topped mountain, though there is no proof. The curious silvery rock near its base

is still proving a headache to geologists, at a loss to explain its origin.

The name Selfoss might suggest a waterfall in the vicinity, but there is none to speak of. The town has little of note for visitors aside from shops, accommodation and other facilities. Iceland's largest dairy is located here and produces much of the country's cheese and other dairy products. The original bridge over the **Ölfusá River** was built in 1898, one of the first bridges in Iceland. During the war, the Germans bombed a British camp at the bridge, killing three soldiers, among the only war casualties on Icelandic soil.

Ten miles (16km) east of Selfoss, Route 30 takes off for Geysir, the Þjórsá Valley, and the Kjölur and Sprengisandur mountain tracks. Route 1 crosses the muddy, swirling waters of the River Þjórsá and shortly after is the turn off for Hekla, Landmannalaugar and Sprengisandur on Route 26. Places to stay along here include **Laugaland**, a school and community centre with swimming pool offering rooms and hostel style accommodation. A little closer to Hekla is the farm **Leirubakki**, with a guest house and campsite. Near Leirubakki is the **Mount Hekla Centre**, where audiovisual presentations and displays document the history of eruptions since the settlement.

## Crossing the glacial rivers

Until the nineteen fifties, few of Iceland's glacial rivers were bridged. They were either forded on horseback, or crossed by boat on their calmer stretches. Either way, the horses often had to swim and as in this account written in 1860 by Charles Forbes after fording the Þjórsá, things were not always easy.

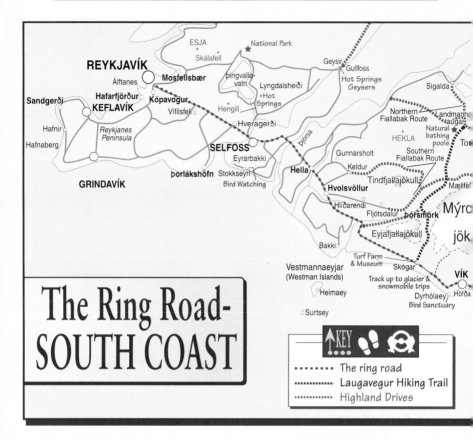

The Ring Road-
SOUTH COAST

KEY

- - - - - - The ring road
- - - - - - Laugavegur Hiking Trail
- - - - - - Highland Drives

*"Our ponies did not at all like the prospect of the half-mile swim across this black angry current, but, after many false starts under volleys of stones from the ferryman's urchins, we dragged then out of their depth, and, towing them astern with compressed nostrils and dilated eyeballs, we made for a bight nearly a mile down on the opposite side. No one could afford to be idle; the ferryman managing the ponies astern with great dexterity, the farmer and myself pulling, and the guide baling, for our bark was very leaky: altogether I was happier when we landed."*

## Saga sites

The town of **Hella,** with a choice of accommodation and a campsite, is preferred by some visitors as a base for exploring the south of the island. **Hvolsvöllur,** 21 miles (13km) to the east, is a little smaller but has similar facilities and, with views towards the glaciers, an altogether more attractive setting. Both towns are modern, giving no clue that some of the most dramatic events in Iceland's early history took place in the surrounding country. Hvolsvöllur lies in the heart of **Njáls Saga Country,**

Snowmobiling on Vatnajökull, Europe's largest icecap

## Hekla

Though **Hekla** is usually cloud-capped, Iceland's most famous volcano dominates the skyline on a clear day. The 4,890ft (1,491m) cone-shaped ridge has been built up over the last 6,600 years in successive eruptions of ash and lava. In the 1947 eruption, the last really big one, 46ft (14m) were added to its summit. It has erupted more often than any other volcano on the island since the settlement, and at least twenty times. In the twentieth century there have been six eruptions, the most recent in 2000, but it was the 1104 one which proved the greatest calamity, with a thick layer of ash burying many of the farms in the south of the island. So feared was the mountain, that medieval maps show it as the entrance to Hell. The easiest access to the summit, a full day hike, is from the north-east, where a signposted track takes off from Route F225 to Landmannalaugar. Guided tours are offered from Hella.

which the locals have used to their advantage, erecting a long overdue Saga Museum. One room focuses on the violent and tragic events of Njál's Saga, but the exhibition is worth visiting even if you haven't read the book, because there are two other halls which depict life in the Viking Age and the writing of the sagas. The museum also arranges guided tours of the saga sites in the region.

Just south of the Ring Road is the farm **Oddi**, once one of the most prosperous in the country and a seat of culture and learning. It was home to several of the most illustrious and influential Icelanders of all time: historian Sæmundur the Learned credited as being Iceland's first historian; his grandson the power-wielding chieftain Jón Loftsson and his protégé, the brilliant writer, politician and historian Snorri Sturluson.

Route 264 east off the Ring Road leads to **Gunnarsholt**, the experimental station for land reclamation and regeneration, which has been battling to control soil erosion in Iceland. The site chosen is appropriate, for drifting ash from Hekla has laid waste many farms in the vicinity. A little further on is **Keldur**, an historic turf farm, which is believed in part to date from the twelfth century, making it the oldest building in Iceland. Jón Loftsson spent his last years at Keldur, where there is now a museum, housed in the original turf buildings and an excavated tunnel, thought to date from the time of Njál's Saga, in which the farm has mention.

From Hvolsvöllur, Route 261 heads along the northern side of the Markafljót's floodplain through the fertile farming district known as **Fljótshlíð**. Waterfalls tumble down a hillside scored by deep ravines and mossy cliffs. Bathed in evening sunlight, the green of the grass is dazzling. The scenery is so lovely that as you drive past **Hlíðarendi**, where Gunnar of **Njál's Saga** lived, it is so easy to empathise with how he felt. Banished for a killing, Gunnar was about to set sail when his horse stumbled. As he dismounted he turned and looked back at his farm. He knew then that he must stay, and in doing so forfeited his life. Further up the valley, the road turns to a four-wheel-drive track, the F261, heading for the Fjallabak wilderness.

Route 1 heads from Hvolsvöllur across the floodplain. A turning off to the south leads to Njál's farm,

## The Original Bible Basher

Sæmundur was a student at the Black School in Paris when the farm at Oddi became vacant and was offered to the first man to reach it. Sæmundur asked the Devil to help him get back home quickly and pledged his soul in return with the proviso that he should stay dry during the journey. The Devil changed himself into a seal and with Sæmundur clinging to his back they set off. During the journey, Sæmundur read continually from the bible, and then, in sight of land, he struck the seal on the head with the book. The seal sank down in surprise so Sæmundur got wet. As the Devil had reneged on his part of the deal, Sæmundur then swam to shore to claim his prize.

## The Turf Farm

Turf and stone as building materials were common in Iceland until the year 1900, when reinforced concrete was introduced. The use of turf evolved because the island had no large trees. As it was difficult to build and heat large structures of turf, the typical Icelandic farm was a collection of small buildings, joined by a central passageway. In wealthier turf farms, each unit consisted of a wooden interior shell, insulated by thick walls of turf. Icelandic grass grows thickly, forming a strong and lasting mesh of roots and soil, which in areas of average rainfall, could last a century.

Turf was also used for the roof, sometimes supported by branches of birch, which spanned the beams. The angle of the roof was critical. If it were too flat, it would get waterlogged and leak. If it were too steep, it might dry out, crack and also leak. Sadly, there are very few people left in Iceland who are masters of the skill of turfing.

A typical wealthy turf farm consists of a number of store and tool rooms accessed only from the outside. From the main entrance of the house, a corridor led to the 'baðstofa', the living and sleeping quarters of the family and servants, numbering as many as twenty or thirty. Through the centuries as fuel became scarcer, it made sense for the household to live, work and sleep all in one room with the animals in the room below. Two or more household members shared a bed. During the long winter evenings stories would be told, while women would spin and do intricate embroidery work and men often carved their personal 'askur', a small wooden box with a lid, which was used as a bowl at mealtimes. Also beautifully carved were the wooden bed boards, which were used to tuck in the covers and stop you falling out of bed.

Windows were tiny, with the stomach of a cow stretched over the opening instead of glass. The other rooms leading from the corridor were the dairy, weaving room, and stores for food. Then there was the kitchen, where legs of lamb would hang to cure in the smoke from the only fire in the house. Fuel for cooking was scarce and consisted of birch twigs, sprigs of heather and often dried dung.

The homes of the poor tenant farmers were very much more basic, consisting of a tiny, single-roomed turf dwelling with a mud floor.

Bergþórshvoll, where, in the climax of the saga, Njáll, his wife, their sons and grandchildren were burnt to death in the year 1011. Excavations on the site show that a fire did take place there at around that time.

Just beyond the new bridge over the Markafljót River, the fabulous waterfall Seljalandsfoss tumbles over a former sea cliff. The falling water has eroded a hollow at the back of the falls, making it possible to walk behind them and look out through the curtain of water. Wear a rain jacket and take something to protect your camera from the spray. There is a pleasant campsite nearby.

Turf Farm Museum, Skógar

Above: Horse riders, Þorsmork
Right: Common Cottongrass (Eriophorum angustifolium), Skaftafell National Park

## Þórsmörk

Route F249 takes off here for Þórsmörk. After the glacial lagoon at **Gígjökull**, the track is for jeeps only as there are some potentially tricky river crossings. In summer a daily bus service operates from Hvolsvöllur, connecting with morning departures from Reykjavík, making it possible to visit Þórsmörk in a day though an overnight stay is more worthwhile. Because of its wooded surrounds, it is popular with Icelanders at weekends and on public holidays and can get a little crowded then.

The route in hugs the base of **Eyjafjallajökull**, a small icecap sitting snugly over an active strato volcano that has been built up over several million years. It has erupted twice since the settlement: in 1612 and

Above: Moss-covered lava, Reykjanes Peninsula

Left: Jökulsárlón, Vatnajökull

Below: Eyrarbakki

most recently in 1821-1823. The crater lies under Gígjökull, 'crater glacier', which falls in an impressive jumble of crevasses into a small lagoon approached by the right fork where the road splits. However, it really is worth a stop and with care you can walk to the edge of the glacier and depending on the conditions, even on to the ice itself.

Beyond the lagoon, huge boulders dot the flood plain, hurled down in the spectacular landslide of 1967. The base rock in this area is mostly tuff, which is unstable and easily eroded. This explains why there are so many fantastic gorges, caves and troll-like rock formations in the area. It's not hard to see why Icelanders believe in the supernatural. After fording **Steinholtsá**, which can be dangerous in flood, there are two further rivers, which are not usually problematic, before you pass a cave on your right, known as the elf church.

Continue straight on for the hut and usually quieter campsite at **Básar**. To reach **Langidalur**, where there is another hut and campsite, cross the **River Krossá** by the footbridge or ford it with care by vehicle. The third hut and campsite is at **Húsadalur**, reached by crossing Krossá earlier after fording the Steinholtsá River. Advance booking is advisable for the huts, particularly in summer and at weekends.

There were once three farms at Þórsmörk but by the nineteenth century they had all been abandoned. To protect the remaining forests from soil erosion, the land was fenced off from grazing in the 1920s and given to the Forestry Department.

Þórsmörk has some of the most dramatic hiking trails in Iceland and is a must for confident walkers who enjoy a bit of a challenge. A trail map of the area, detailing the main routes, is available from the huts. The maps are not especially accurate and some trails are indistinct and unmarked. Hikers should remember that changing river courses can wash away footbridges or make routes impassable and it is best to seek up to date advice from the hut wardens.

## 1 VALAHNÚKUR (1-1.5 HOURS)

The most popular short walk at Þórsmörk takes off on a broad trail from **Langidalur** and snakes up the hill behind the hut. The last section is a little steep but the view is well worth the effort. By descending north of the summit it is possible to make a slightly longer circular route, returning by **Húsadalur**.

## 2 TRÖLLAKIRKJA, THE RIDGES & VALLEYS (3-5 HOURS)

East of Langidalur several trails wind up the ridges and through the valleys between them. One leads to the Troll's Church, from where a steep descent leads down to the river Krossá and you can follow the valley back to Langidalur. Seek advice from the warden before doing this route as it is often difficult.

## 3 RÉTTARFELL & HVANNÁRGIL (3 HOURS)

Starting from the hut at Básar, the trail climbs through birch woods to a plateau. The trail splits and to the right climbs the peak Réttarfell, a stunning viewpoint. Bearing left, another trail leads up 2,640ft (805m) high Útigönguhöfði, which involves a scramble up the last part. The third trail descends quite steeply into Hvannárgil, a rugged gorge leading down to the main valley to return to Básar by the road.

## 4 FIMMVÖRÐUHÁLS (5 HOURS) AND SKÓGAR (10 HOURS)

This route, part of the marked backpacking trail from Landmannalaugar to Skógar, can be treacherous in high winds or low cloud. Seek the warden's advice before setting out. From the hut at Básar, follow the road up the main valley to the start of the trail, or cut across the gravel flats. The trail follows a ridge, (a short section may be tricky for those with vertigo) then climbs steadily emerging on the flat plateau Morinsheiði. Detour east to the edge of the plateau for a view of the glaciers before continuing. Heljarkambur is a tricky section, negotiated with the aid of a rope, which marks the start of the snow field between the two ice caps. A long hard slog through snow leads to the huts at Fimmvörðuháls and overnight accommodation. The old hut is now derelict but a new hut lies west of the trail. For the descent to Skógar, follow the trail, not the jeep track, and enjoy over 20 beautiful waterfalls, which culminate in majestic Skógarfoss at the end of the walk.

## 5 THE GLACIERS (4-8 HOURS)

Drive the jeep track or walk up the Krossá Valley to the end of the road where a footbridge over the river opens up walking trails to Tungnakvíslarjökull and Krossárjökull, two glacier tongues from Mýrdalsjökull. There are no easy loops here so you will need to backtrack.

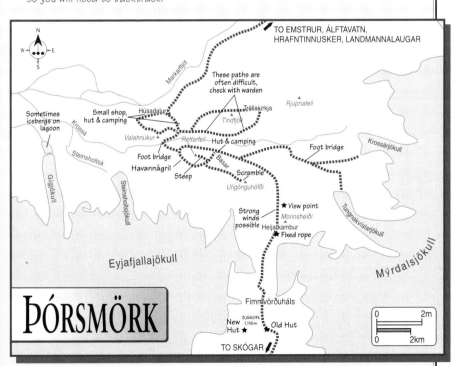

Above: Farms and Eyjafjallajökull

Below: Gígjökull on Eyjafjallajökull en route to Þorsmörk

82

Above: Campsite at Skógafoss Waterfall
Below left: Hiking at Þórsmörk
Below right: Rock stacks near Dyrhólaey

83

The great attractions at Þórsmörk are the walks, the views of the glaciers and gorges, the woodlands and wildflowers, of which there are over 150 species in the area. You could easily spend three days here and still find plenty to do. Þórsmörk lies on the route of the long-distance walking route Laugavegur which takes 4-6 days from Landmannalaugar to Skógar.

## From Seljalandsfoss to Mýrdalsjökull

Route 1 continues along the base of moss clad tuff mountains, eroded by water and wind into wonderful shapes. Camping is available at Seljavellir, where there is a swimming pool in a beautiful setting, or you can stay at Hotel Anna or Drangshlíð known for the caves, which are used as sheep pens, in a huge rock that is believed to be inhabited by 'hidden people'.

Cascading over the former sea cliffs at the foot of the Eyjafjöll range, are several spectacular waterfalls. The best known is 200ft (60m) high Skógafoss, made all the more impressive because you view it from below. You can walk to the foot of the falls, behind which the area's first settler Þrasi is said to have hidden a chest of gold in a cave. Above the waterfall, a path follows the east bank of the river past a further twenty waterfalls, not perhaps all as spectacular as Skógafoss, but some a close second. The trail continues over the glacier to Þórsmörk, a long full day walk for fine weather only.

There are a campsite, post office, bank, shop and hotel at Skógar, together with one of the best folk museums in the country, housed in original turf farm buildings.

East of Skógar is the first of the glacial outwash plains that stretch along most of the south coast between here and Höfn. Skógasandur was formed from flooding of the Jökulsá River which melts off Sólheimajökull, a glacier tongue on the southern edge of Mýrdalsjökull. There is geothermal activity underneath the glacier, which is probably linked in with the Katla volcano. As you cross the river you can

## Dyrhólaey bird sanctuary

South of the icecap and offering great views is Dyrhólaey, meaning 'door hill island'. Probably formed in a submarine eruption, similar to that of Surtsey, the 400ft (120m) high headland has been eroded to form a natural rock arch, which is so large that ships can sail through it. The area is rich in bird life, with breeding colonies of puffins, arctic terns and guillemots, and predatory great and arctic skuas nesting on the sands nearby. Dyrhólaey is signposted off the Ring Road but to protect the birds the area is closed for about 6 weeks during the May and June nesting season. Just east of the bird sanctuary but accessed via another side road off Route 1 is Reynishverfi. You can drive down to the black volcanic sand beach, where there are interesting columnar basalt formations, caves and views of Reynisdrangar, a cluster of sea stacks, off the tip of Reynisfjall.

often smell sulphur. East of the river, a track leads to the glacier and can usually be driven, with care, in an ordinary vehicle. Further east another track takes off for the edge of the icecap for those interested in trying out the exhilarating but costly sport of snowmobiling. Trips on the icecap last for an hour or more and in clear weather offer fantastic views.

## Vík

The town of **Vík** meaning 'bay' and the same word as the English place name 'Wick', shelters in the lee of Reynisfjall. It is unusual in that though it is a coastal town, it has no port. The older part of town is on the flat, while most new building has taken place on the slopes above – and with good reason. During the 1918 eruption of Katla, the plain went under water and with all the debris washed down, the coastline at Vík was extended by a further 547yd (500m). Large dykes have been built east of Vík in anticipation of future flooding, but no one really knows what will happen when Katla next erupts.

For visitors there are a couple of small hotels and guest houses and a campsite. Using an amphibious vehicle which can launch from the beach, boat trips run out to the sea stacks **Reynisdrangar** and to Dyrhólaey. Popular belief holds that the stacks are night trolls who went out fishing and got caught by the rays of the sun and turned to stone.

Just east of Vík are Reynisbrekka Youth Hostel and the delightful farm guesthouse at Höfðabrekka. The owners run jeep trips to explore the valleys behind the farm, a fantastic eroded landscape of gorges, rivers and waterfalls.

## From Vík to Höfn – white ice and black sand

The 170-mile (272km) stretch of road along Iceland's south coast is among the most scenic and interesting drives in the country and visitors should try and spend several days over it, choosing the areas of Kirkjubæjarklaustur, Skaftafell and Höfn as bases from which to explore the surrounds. Highlights of the route, which is paved throughout, are the glaciers and ice caps, the vast and empty black sands, the lavas from Laki and the impressive iceberg lagoon.

In high winds, **Mýrdalssandur** is subject to bad sandstorms, which can close the road. When this happens drivers have to wait and sit it out, a better option than having your vehicle sandblasted. As you approach the sands, what looks like an island ahead turns out to be landlocked **Hjörleifshöfði**. The 725ft (221m) high hill is named after Ingólfur Arnarson's blood brother Hjörleifur, who landed here but was murdered by his slaves shortly afterwards.

## Eldhraun

East of the sands, Route 211 does a short loop through **Álftaver**, a cluster of farms that are remarkable because they have escaped both the Katla floods and the Laki lava. Þykkvabæjarklaustur was the site of a monastery from 1168 until it was sacked and closed during the 1550 reformation.

Route 1 heads across the **Laki lava**. The 216sq mile (560sq km) **Eldhraun** is believed to be the largest flow from a single eruption, world

Above: Núpsstaður
Below: Núpsstaðaskógur
Opposite: Fjaðraglijufur Gorge on road to Laki, near Kirkjubæjarklaustur

wide, in historical times. Now clad in a soft blanket of woolly fringe moss *Racomitrium lanuginosum*, it is hard to imagine the terror the advancing scoria lava wall must have caused. The moss, in places a foot thick, is grey in dry weather but turns green when it rains. The Fjallabak mountain track, Route F208 to Landmannalaugar and Eldgjá, takes off from the west side of the lava flow. East of the lava is the settlement of Kirkjubæjarklaustur.

## Katla

The smooth dome of Mýrdalsjökull, the fourth largest ice cap in Iceland, looks innocuous enough but below the ice lurks **Katla**, one of the most active volcanic systems in Iceland. It has erupted at forty to eighty-year intervals since the settlement. When Katla blows, mostly ash and steam are erupted but the surge of meltwater which accompanies the eruption can be catastrophic. It has been calculated that the volume of water in such a jökulhlaup (glacial burst) could equal the flow of the Amazon at its mouth.

Through the ages, many farms have been swept away by Katla eruptions with that of 1311 being recorded as particularly damaging. A farmer named Sturla is said to have survived by clinging to an iceberg, which later drifted back to shore. An eighteenth century eruption killed several people, while others were stranded for days on **Hafursey** and **Hjörleifshöfði**, mountains that turned to islands as floods engulfed the plains. Katla last erupted in 1918, when icebergs the size of houses were seen floating out to sea. More recently in 1955 and 1979 there have been floods, though no eruption.

## The tale of a church, a farm and a cloister

**K**irkjubæjarklaustur, like many place names in Iceland, is composed of several elements, in this case 'church, farm and cloister'. Believed to be holy, because Irish monks were said to have lived there even before the settlement, it was little surprise that a Christian, by the name of Ketill the Foolish chose to settle there. After his death, a heathen called Hildir intended to take over the farm but dropped dead outside, fueling the belief that only Christians could live there.

A convent was established there in 1186 and it was suspected that monks from the nearby monastery at **Þykkvibær** often visited overnight. Apparently once the abbot stayed overnight though no one knew where. During the night the mother superior went to check on the sisters' conduct and found a monk and a nun sleeping together in one of the cells. She was about to issue a reprimand when the nun noticed the mother superior's unusual headdress – in horror, the mother superior discovered she had put on the abbot's underpants instead of her bonnet. She was said to have remarked as she retreated, 'We're all sinners, sister.'

The modern village (often abbreviated to Klaustur) serves the surrounding farms and has a school, health centre and swimming pool. For visitors there are a tourist information bureau, hotel, campsite, shop, post office, bank and petrol station. There are several interesting places to visit in the area. In the village itself, just beyond the hotel and school, is **Kirkubæjarstofa**. The attractive old building houses a research institute into local history, which is open to the public and has a fascinating exhibition on two of Iceland's most memorable eruptions, Laki in 1783 and Grímsvötn in 1996.

From here a walking trail (1-1.5 hours), flanked by a profusion of wildflowers, climbs steeply up the old sea cliffs past the waterfall **Systrafoss** to a small lake **Systravatn**, 'Sisters' Lake', where two nuns were said to have drowned attempting to retrieve a golden comb they saw in the water. The path continues east along the top of the cliff and descends just north of **Kirkjugólfið** 'the Church Floor' a columnar basalt formation, revealed by sea erosion. The columns are unusual in that they can be seen from above and give the impression of a hexagonal tiled floor.

Another path continues for twenty minutes past Kirkjubæjarstofa to the bluff known as **Systrastapi,** where two nuns were put to death, the one for insulting the Pope and the other for making a pact with the Devil. The nuns were buried on top of the bluff, which can be climbed with the aid of a fixed chain. From the bluff you can see where the lava came to a halt on 20 July 1783. For days it had threatened the farms and church. In despair, the local priest, **Jón Steingrímsson**, gathered the community in the church and preached a sermon imploring God to stop the lava. Apparently it worked and the place became known as **Eldmessutangi**, 'Fire Sermon Point'. On the other side of the River Skaftá, low lying hillocks suggest sand dunes, but **Landbrotsholar**, as they are known, are in fact pseudocraters.

## Laki

The fissure which produced the Eldhraun and Brunahraun lavas lies north of the Ring Road, along a 28-mile (45km) jeep track, Route F206, which takes about 2 hours to drive and makes a sensible day trip from Kirkjubæjarklaustur. A daily bus service starts running in July as soon as the road has dried out, and operates through August. The trip is well worthwhile, the drivers informative and usually a good 3-4 hour stop is made at Laki to explore and at Fjaðragljúfur and Fagrifoss along the way.

Fjaðragljúfur is a fabulous buttressed gorge, just off the route to Laki but accessible by ordinary vehicle. The best views are to be had by following the path up the east rim of the gorge and walking, with care, on to some of the buttresses from where you can gape into its shady depths. If it looks like the sun will be out, the best time for photographing it is in the morning.

Once past the last of the farms, the road climbs out of the valley and the views open up. A short stop at Fagrifoss is worthwhile. The track fords the river just above the falls, but after heavy rainfall it is advisable to take the other ford, which lies a little further upstream. In clear weather, Vatnajökull's western edge and Mýrdalsjökull are both visible and will compete for your camera's attention if you are not already distracted by the first view of the Lakagígar craters. Numbering over one hundred, the craters are spread along a 15-mile (24km) long fissure, lying SW-NE, which may be connected with the Grímsvötn volcanic system. Laki, a tuff mountain and not itself a crater, at 2,683ft (818m) high

offers the best view of the fissure and sea of lava that surrounds it. The eruptions occurred in two sequences: initially from the fissure extending south-west of Laki producing Eldhraun; later from the fissure and craters north-east of Laki resulting in the smaller flow of Brunahraun.

## Death and disaster

Dozens of farms disappeared under Laki's lava but the greatest loss of life was in the years that followed. The eruption had also produced several hundred million cubic metres of tephra and 70 million tons of sulphuric and hydrochloric acid, which hung over the island suspended in an aerosol cloud. This toxic blanket poisoned the soil, killing the grass and over half the livestock. In the terrible famine that followed one fifth of Icelanders died. The eruption affected the weather throughout the northern hemisphere and possibly caused the crop failure that preceded the French Revolution.

From the first car park, a footpath winds up to the summit of Laki taking about 30 to 45 minutes. If the weather is clear, it is worth the climb for the view of the entire row of craters. Further trails meander from the car park in among the craters. From the next parking area, a wonderfully scenic walking trail leads to a cobalt-blue lake-filled crater. The hour and a half circuit, following a lava channel, ends at the next car

Continued on page 94...

## Vestmannæyjar (Westman Islands)

### Ferry Service
Herjólfur,
☎ 481 2800 www.herjolfur.is
1 May-31 August departs
Vestmannæyjar at 8.15am and
4pm on Sunday-Friday and
8.15am on Saturday and departs
Þorlákshöfn at 12pm and
7.30pm on Sunday-Friday and
12pm on Saturday. Daily sailings
on a reduced schedule in winter
subject to weather conditions.

### Flights from Bakki to Vestmannæyjar
☎ 481 3255

### Tourist Information Bureau
☎ 481 3555

### Viking Tours
☎ 484 4884
vicking@boattours.is
www.boattours.is
Sightseeing around Heimaey
and boat tours to see the bird
cliffs and whales.

### Natural History Museum
☎ 481 1997. Open: 11am-5pm
daily 1 May-15 September; at
other times of year 3-5pm,
weekends only.

### Volcano Films
☎ 481 1045. Shown daily at
the Community Centre in
summer.

## Eyrarbakki

### Árnes Regional Folk Museum
☎ 483 1504 ,
www.south.is/husid
Open: 1-6pm, daily 1 June-31
August or by arrangement.

## Stokkseyri

### Þuríðarbúð
☎ 483 1267
A traditional fisherman's hut,
only in this case named after a
lady captain, and exhibition of
maritime artifacts. Open by
arrangement.

*Continued over page...*

Opposite: Laki lava from eruption in 1783

Above: Near Kirkjubæjarklaustur

Right: Skógafoss falls, 60m high

## Sea kayaking trips

**Kayaking Trips**
Stokkseyri ☎ 896 5716
On inland lagoons and along
the shore with abundant bird
life and seals.

## Hekla area

**Mt Hekla Centre**
Brúarlundur, on Route 26,
☎ 487 6591
Exhibition on Iceland's most
active volcano. Open: 10am-
6pm, daily, 1 June-31 August.

**Day excursion to Hekla**
☎ 487 6611
www.simnet.is/hekluf
hekluferdir@simnet.is
Departures: from Hella 10.15am
daily. Reservations necessary.

**Keldur Turf Farm and Museum**
☎ 487 8452
One of the oldest buildings in
Iceland. Open: 10am-6pm
daily, 1 June-15 September or
by arrangement.

## Hvolsvöllur

**Njál's Saga Museum
& Saga Tours**
☎ 487 8781
njala@islandia.is
Exhibition and guided tours
focused on the best known
of the great family sagas.
Museum open: 9am-7pm daily
May 15-September 15 or by
arrangement.

## Skógar

**Skógar Folk Museum**
☎ 487 8845, www.skogasafn.is
One of the most comprehensive turf farm museums in

Iceland. Open: 9am-7pm daily
June-August, May and
September 10am-5pm or by
arrangement.

## Mýrdalsjökull Snowmobiling Trips

snow@snow.is www.snow.is

## Vík

**Boat trips to Dyrhólaey and
Reynisdrangar stacks**
☎ 487 8500
info@dyrholaey.com
www.dyrholaey.com

## Around Kirkjubæjarklaustur

**Laki trips**
☎ 545 1717
Departures: 9am daily
July & August from Hotel
Kirkjubæjarklaustur.

**Núpstaðaskógur trips**
Hannes Jónsson, ☎ 487 4785
Departures: 8.30am from Hotel
Kirkjubæjarklaustur and 9am
from Núpsstaður, daily July &
August. Bookings necessary.

**Kirkjubæjarstofa**
Geology, volcanic eruptions
& natural history exhibition
and research institute in the
village. Open: 8.30-10.30am
and 2.30-9pm Monday to
Friday and 2-5.30pm at
weekends.
☎ 487 4645, Fax 487 4875,
kbstofa@isholf.is

# Skaftafell NP & Surrounds

## Skaftafell National Park Information Centre and Campsite
☎ 478 1627
Shop, cafeteria, bar and fuel station. Open: 1 June-15 September.

## Jórvík Aviation
☎ 478 2406
Sightseeing glacier flights from Skaftafell.

## Svínafell Swimming Pool, Horse Riding and Campsite
Skaftafell. Pool: ☎ 478 1765; Horse Riding: ☎ 478 1661
Located a short way off Route 1, 4 miles (6km) east of Skaftafell.

## Trips to Ingólfshöfði
☎ 478 1682/899 6488
Fantastic scenery and birds. Trips depart daily in summer on demand, leaving from 1 mile (2km) south of Fagurhólsmýri, reservations necessary.

## Glacier Trips, Skiing & Ice Climbing
☎ 894 2959
Íslenskir Fjallaleiðsögumenn (Icelandic Mountain Guides), based at the National Park Headquarters, Short and longer trips on the glaciers with equipment provided.

# Jökulsárlón

## Jökulsárlón Glacial Lagoon Boat Trips
☎ 478 2122/851 1822
Half hour boat trips run on demand, daily 15 May–15 September. The Reykjavík-Höfn bus stops here. There is a cafeteria and camping is possible here but there is no accommodation.

# Vatnajökull

## Glacier Tours
☎ 478 1000
vatnajokull@vatnajokull.com
www.vatnajokull.com
June to early September. One to two hour snowmobile and snow cat trips on Vatnajökull June to early September. Longer trips can be arranged including the 40-mile (55km) traverse to the northern edge of the ice cap at Kverkfjöll and descent on foot to the hut and road.

# Höfn

## Höfn Regional Folk Museum
☎ 478 1833
On the main road as you approach the town.
Open: 10-12am and 2-5pm, daily 1 June-31 August.

## Höfn Travel & Information Bureau & Campsite
☎ 478 1606
Also the bus terminus and excellent campsite. Vatnajökull and Lónsöræfi trips.

## GJ Lónsöræfi jeep trips
☎ 478 1717
Daily, 15 July-15 September.

## Glacier Exhibition
☎ 478 2665
Open daily June-August 1pm-6pm and 8pm-10pm. Fascinating museum on Iceland's largest icecap Vatnajökull.

Snowmobiling on Vatnajökull

park along. The track deteriorates beyond this point and doubles back in a circle to rejoin the 'main' road into Laki further south. There is no official camping nor accommodation at Laki. People do camp but fresh water can be a problem.

# From Kirkjubæjarklaustur to Skaftafell

Just east of the farm **Foss**, a parking area on the right leads to **Dvergh-amrar**, 'Dwarves' Cliffs', a jumble of basalt columns revealed by sea erosion. Beyond here the lava from the Laki eruption spreads over the plain. Notice the new course of the river **Hverfisfljót**, flowing straight over the lava. The pretty nineteenth-century church at **Kálfafell** has a seventeenth-century altarpiece but its greatest treasures, a font and Catholic cross, are in the National Museum in Reykjavík.

The impressive bluff of **Lómag-núpur**, once a sea cliff, is a landmark for miles around. A huge landslide fell from the 2,500ft (767m) high mountain in the year 1789 and hollows under the largest of the boulders that fell are still used as sheep shelters. Facing the bluff is the farm and church of **Núpsstaður** nestled at the foot of a grassy slope and overlooked by rocks that leave little doubt as to the existence of trolls. Visitors find the place enchanting, for any number of reasons, but it is the tiny turf church that is the official attraction. Part of it dates from the seventeenth century, and though extensively renovated, the original design is believed to be unchanged. During the Laki eruptions, a mass was held in the church and the priest later wrote to the bishop that, "So much ash fell that it was darker outside than inside the church".

After the intense green of most of Iceland's southern shore, the starkness of **Skeiðarásandur** comes as a surprise. The vast plain of black volcanic grit is the work of the **Grímsvötn** and **Bárðabunga** volca-

94

Skaftafell National Park

noes, lying under the **Vatnajökull icecap**. Their eruptions are often accompanied by cataclysmic floods,

## A pioneering tradition

Earlier this century the farmer at **Núpsstaður** also handled the postal service between there and Höfn, his round spanning 118 miles (189km) and taking several weeks. In those days there was no road and sometimes the rivers were impassible on horseback so he would have to cross the crevasse-ridden glaciers. This section of the Ring Road was the last to be completed, with the bridging of the Skeiðará in 1974. The postman's grandson Hannes Jónsson continues the pioneering tradition by running a daily bus service in July and August from Kirkubæjarklaustur into the inaccessible valley of the Núpsá. The attraction here is **Núpsstaðaskógur**, a pocket of relict woodland set among deep gorges with two impressive waterfalls, a campsite and toilets. An unmarked backpacking route leads further up the valley to the glacial lagoon **Grænalón** at the edge of the ice cap. This is really wild country and there are no facilities at all.

which deposit their volcanic debris to form the vast outwash plains typical of this area.

# Skaftafell

One of Iceland's foremost areas of natural beauty, **Skaftafell** and its surrounds have been a National Park since 1967, but only since the Ring Road around the island was completed has the area opened up to visitors. Until then, the cluster of farms had been completely cut off from the rest of the country by swift flowing unbridged glacial rivers. Not even rats had figured out a way of getting there.

Skaftafell's great attraction is ice – and plenty of it. Within the national park boundaries are several huge tongues of glacier that descend to the sandy outwash plains which stretch south to the coast. The glaciers spill down from the outer edge of Vatnajökull, Iceland's largest icecap, 3,244sq miles (8,400sq km) of ice which is 3,300ft (1,000m) thick in places. Vatnajökull is not an Ice Age remnant, but formed roughly 3,000 years ago when the climate started to cool again.

Towering over the Skaftafell area is Iceland's highest peak, 6,950ft (2,119m) **Öræfajökull**. It is an active strato volcano, which has erupted twice since the settlement of Iceland. In 1996, following the eruption at **Grimsvötn**, Skaftafell was once again threatened, this time by catastrophic flooding from the **Skeiðará river**, one of the chief exit points of the meltwater. Though the bridge over the river was badly damaged, the campground and National Park office escaped unscathed.

Skaftafell is famous for its flora, one reason why it was declared a national park. Sheltered by the peaks around, it enjoys more sunshine than other parts of the region. Around 210 species of vascular plant are

## Eruption of Grímsvötn 1996

Though **Grímsvötn** ranks as one of Iceland's most active volcanoes, many of its eruptions are so minor that they do not penetrate through the surface of the ice cap. When seismic reports recorded the events of 29 September 1996, Iceland and the world braced itself for a catastrophe of unknown magnitude. A 2.5-mile (4km) long fissure had opened midway between Grímsvötn and Bárðarbunga and millions of tons of meltwater were expected to burst out at any time. Yet nothing happened. The meltwater had flowed into the sub-glacial caldera of Grímsvötn and there it stayed. All went quiet when the eruption finished on 15 October and though scientists were able to get a closer look at the site, they could only speculate whether the water might escape.

The world's media had departed when the long-awaited glacial burst arrived, at 8.30 in the morning of 5 November, thirty-eight days after the eruption had begun. By noon, the power lines were down, the road gone and the bridges all but swept away. By 11pm, the discharge had peaked at 50,000 cubic metres per second, great icebergs were seen floating out to sea and the coast had extended by half a mile (almost 1km). Twenty-four hours later it was all over and Iceland breathed a huge sigh of relief as the assessment came in. Four cubic kilometres of water and a million tons of ice had wreaked less than the expected level of damage and most of the vital bridge, built in 1974 to complete the Ring Road, was still standing. Within two weeks, the road was re-opened.

found in the park. The lower slopes are covered by birch forests, up to about 850ft (260m) in altitude, though, by hugging the ground, isolated patches of birch survive as high as 2,000ft (610m). The tallest birches in Iceland are found in a small area of woodland in **Morsárdalur**, an area of the park that has never been grazed, where they reach 40ft (12m) in height. Of particular interest to botanists are the gravel flats and moraines, which have been formed this century, yet already support a significant variety of species, including birch shrub.

Skaftafell represents the westernmost limit of three flower species that are common in Eastern Iceland: harebell on wooded and grassy slopes, yellow mountain saxifrage on stony ground and the beautiful erect stems of pyramidal saxifrage, found on rocky ledges and cracks. Also found in the park are three rarities, of which the first two are protected by law: twayblade, maidenhair spleenwort and valerian.

The birch woodlands support high numbers of redwings and wrens. The wren is a separate subspecies, larger than that found elsewhere in Europe. A recent arrival is the brambling – elsewhere in Iceland it has only been recorded as a rare autumn or winter visitor.

For visitors, Skaftafell has some of the best facilities in Iceland but the popularity of the place, and its location on the Ring Road, mean that they are heavily used during the season, which runs from 1st June to 15 September. Farm accommodation is available at Bölti within the national park

# HIKING IN SKAFTAFELL NATIONAL PARK

To enjoy Skaftafell's main attractions properly you need to walk and a network of marked and well-maintained trails criss-cross the park. Be very careful near and on the glaciers. Ice and glacial debris are unstable and even if there appears to be a path on to the ice, extreme caution is needed. For those interested in exploring the glaciers, Íslenskir Fjallaleiðsögumenn, Alpine guides based at the park headquarters, offer guided walks, with instruction in the use of crampons and ice axes. For the super-fit, they offer the option to climb Iceland's highest peak, 6,950ft (2,119m) Hvannadalshnúkur. If the weather is clear, a sightseeing flight with Jórvík Aviation over the glaciers from the airstrip at Skaftafell, is well worth the expense and a less exhausting way to get the views.

Skaftafell is ideal for day walks but there are no backpacking trails and camping is only permitted at the designated sites. All the following walks start from the National Park Headquarters where detailed maps and advice are available from the warden's office. The wardens offer guided walks in the park daily in summer. Walking times are for the return trip but do not include stops.

## 1 SVARTIFOSS (1-1.5 HOURS)

A popular and easy walk to a beautiful waterfall framed by basalt columns.

## 2 SKAFTAFELLSJÖKULL (1-1.5 HOURS)

An easy walk on the flat to the snout of the glacier. Follow the base of the cliffs through the woods and return over the moraines to complete the loop. Many plant species can be observed during the walk. Take great care at the edge of the glacier, where the terrain is very unstable.

Opposite: Jökulsárlón glacial lagoon formed as the glacier has retreated

Right: Svinafellsjokull, Skaftafell National Park

## 3 KRISTÍNARTINDAR (6-7 HOURS)

A full day walk climbing to 2,300ft (700m) which is best done in clear weather. From the camp ground the trail ascends through the birch woods to Svartifoss. It continues on to a plateau and then climbs the ridge overlooking the Morsá Valley with great views of Skeiðarájökull, Morsárjökull and the rhyolite peaks and volcanic plugs of Kjós. The route then skirts the base of Kristínartindar, a cluster of peaks rising to 3,700ft (1,126m), to the eastern rim of the plateau and a viewpoint called Gláma. To climb the peaks take the indistinct trail up the valley to a saddle and scramble to the summit. Descend the same route back to the saddle then continue along the ridge to take an alternative descent on scree to Gláma. From here there are stunning views across the crevasses of Skaftafellsjökull to Öræfajökull. To complete the loop follow the well-marked trail along the eastern rim of the plateau for a gradual descent back to the campsite.

## 4 MORSÁRJÖKULL (6-7 HOURS)

Mostly on the flat, this walk leads to a lagoon at the foot of the glacier Morsárjökull, which tumbles down steep cliffs from the ice cap. Even from a distance the rumble of the crashing ice can be heard. Roughly half way there a side trip across the valley leads to Bæjarstaður, where warm springs emerge by a pocket of birch woodland that boasts the tallest and straightest trunks in Iceland. (Check that the bridge over the Morsá River is intact).

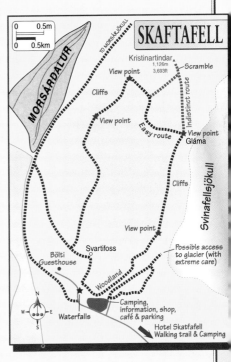

or the spacious and idyllically located Hotel Skaftafell is another option. A huge campsite at the National Park headquarters is equipped with hot showers with a shop, cafeteria and information bureau on the site. Camping is also possible by Hotel Skaftafell, with toilets but no showers, and at the farm Svínafell, which has the area's only swimming pool. Here lived Flosi Þórðarson whose quarrel with the sons of Njáll led to the tragic burning in Njál's Saga.

# From Skaftafell to Höfn

East of Skaftafell lies the abandoned farm site of **Sandfell,** dating back to settlement times and marked by a lone tree in a hayfield. The 'Book of Settlements' relates that Þorgerður, a widow whose husband had died on the voyage from Norway, farmed here. As a woman she was entitled to claim only as much land as she could lead a young heifer around on a spring day. Following the Öræfajökull eruptions of 1362 and 1727, much of Sandfell's land was laid waste by flooding though it continued to be worked until 1945. From here starts the easiest route up Hvannadalshnúkur, a strenuous 11-14 hour ascent for properly equipped and fit hikers. Hiring an alpine guide from Skaftafell is strongly recommended.

A beautiful turf church, dating from 1884, sits among a cluster of farms at **Hof** where visitors can stay. Glacial rivers made travel between communities hazardous and farms found in groups are typical of this region of Iceland, which is known as **Öræfi.** Meaning 'wasteland', it replaced the original name of Litla

Hérað after eruptions on the glacier devastated the area. East of Hof, the route crosses a rock-strewn wasteland, dotted with giant boulders and other debris from the catastrophe.

Another group of farms, together with an airstrip, shop and fuel station, is found at **Fagurhólsmýri.** This is the starting point for Öræfaferðir's trip by tractor-drawn hay wagon to **Ingólfshöfði,** a headland formed in a submarine eruption, but now joined to the mainland by glacial outwash plains. Its 330ft (100m) high cliffs are a breeding site for sea birds. Below the cliffs, seals may be spotted and occasionally minke whales further out to sea. The headland and the plains below are the hunting ground of the area's chief predator, the impressive great skua. During the breeding season these magnificent birds perch on grassy knolls, by their preferred nesting sites, which they defend fiercely. Öræfaferðir runs the tractor trips daily in summer.

Ingólfshöfði is named after Iceland's first official settler, Ingólfur Arnarson, who is believed to have landed there in the year 874. A memorial, commemorating the event and his sojourn during the following winter was erected there in 1974. Also on the headland are a lighthouse and an emergency shelter, one of the first to be built in Iceland, erected following a spate of shipwrecks in which seamen died needlessly of exposure. Orange-painted shelters like these are found along all uninhabited stretches of coast and are equipped with blankets, food, a heater and radio – for use in genuine emergencies only.

By the small hydroelectric scheme and farm accommodation at **Smyrlabjörg,** midway between

## Iceberg Lagoon

The glaciers are currently in retreat, and have been for the last decades. As they recede they leave behind deep lagoons of glacial melt water. The largest of these is **Jökulsárlón,** translating as 'Glacial River Lagoon', which lies at the foot of **Breiðamerkurjökull,** one of the broadest glacier tongues on Vatnajökull's south side. Several miles long and wide, the lagoon has been formed since the end of the nineteenth century and is now one of Iceland's deepest lakes. Icebergs the size of a football field break off from the glacier that spills into the lagoon. Boat trips take visitors on a thrilling ride among the icebergs, which can be gleaming white, mottled with sediment, cobalt blue or jade green, depending on their size and age, and on whether they have flipped over. The trips run from early June to early September. At other times, a walk along the edge of the lagoon can be equally rewarding and seals, eiders and other birds may be spotted from the shore.

Jökulsárlón and the town of Höfn, a track leads up to the edge of Vatnajökull. The jeep route is steep and rough but visitors with ordinary vehicles can leave them at the bottom and pick up the scheduled bus which makes the hour long trip up and back down each day from Höfn. There is a restaurant and bar at **Jöklasel** on the edge of the icecap. Apart from the views along the way, the only reason to make the trip is to take one of their snowmobile or snowcat trips onto the ice. The snow cat is a heated vehicle seating 10-15 passengers, which is used for glacier excursions, with greater comfort, though less excitement.

East of the town of Höfn, the broad valley of the river **Hornafjarðarfljót** attracts abundant birdlife to its marshes and ponds and in April and May reindeer can often be observed from the road. Once summer is underway, the reindeer migrate to higher pastures, north-east of the ice cap.

# Höfn

**Höfn** means port and is close to the English word 'haven'. With possibly the most scenic location of any town in the country and a population of 1,800 it is the only sizeable community in the south-east of Iceland and the only port. As such it is not a very safe one and swift tidal currents, coupled with frequent storms, have often brought tragedy to ships returning to port. The town dates from 1897 when rowing boats were being replaced by diesel powered vessels, which could cope with the currents at the port entrance, so the new settlement was an obvious choice as a base for a budding fishing industry. Höfn now draws its livelihood from herring and lobster fishing as well as serving as a focal point for communities in the surrounding region.

For visitors, there are a hotel, guesthouses, a youth hostel and a campsite that is among the best equipped in Iceland, with a laundry as well as hot showers. The campsite is also the bus terminal and has

Surtsey eruption, July 1964

an information and travel bureau. Several shops, a swimming pool, regional museum, **Glacier Exhibition** and a choice of restaurants complete the range of facilities, which make the town a sensible base for exploring the region. The popular daily bus service to Vatnajökull, which includes a stop at the iceberg lagoon, starts at Höfn. Several local companies offer jeep trips in the area, including trips on the ice cap and visits to Lónsöræfi, a wilderness area for hiking north of Höfn.

# VESTMANNAEYJAR
## (WESTMAN ISLANDS)

Fifteen islands and dozens of rocks and skerries make up Vestmannaeyjar, the archipelago off Iceland's south shore. Entirely volcanic in origin, the islands are believed to have been formed within the last 10,000 years. The presence of so much volcanic activity is down to the position of the Mid-Atlantic Ridge, which the islands straddle. According to Landnámabók, when Iceland was first settled, a group of Irish slaves killed their master and fled to the rocky and inhospitable islands to hide. The slaves were discovered, put to death and the islands named after these 'Men from the West'.

Continued over page...

Westman Islands: 1973 eruption wall of lava engulfed a house but spared another

# VESTMANNAEYJAR (WESTMAN ISLANDS)

Continued...

Once the mainland had become fully settled, it was the islands' turn and their grassy flat tops, fertilised by the guano of seabirds, produced exceptionally fine ewes. Moreover, the fishing was good, and the birds a welcome addition to the diet so it is not surprising that even several hundreds of years ago, the islands supported a healthy, though defenceless population. This made them an obvious target for the Algerian pirate raids that marked the darkest chapter in the islands' history.

Only **Heimaey**, the largest of the islands, is inhabited. Most visitors fly in from Reykjavík or take the shorter hop over from the tiny airstrip at **Bakki** on the mainland. An alternative is the three-hour ferry trip from **Þórlákshöfn**, sheer bliss on a dead calm day, but otherwise utter misery. The town of Heimaey, has 4,600 inhabitants and is one of Iceland's leading fishing ports.

The half day sightseeing tour of the island gives a good overview of what there is to see and do and includes a drive to the base of **Eldfell**, the new volcano. Here, steam still hisses from the ground, said to be is warm enough to bake bread in. Most people visit Heimaey on a day trip, but staying overnight gives time to climb the volcano for the stunning views.

From May to early August, Heimaey's star attraction are its thousands of puffins. Once the young are able to fend for themselves, the parents stop bringing food, encouraging them to leave their burrows. Doing this at night for safety, the chicks can get disoriented by the lights of the town. Each morning, the local children scoop up the birds, before the cats and gulls step in, and release them in the sea

Heimaey's austere stone church is the third oldest in Iceland, built in 1778. Also worth a visit is the small **Natural History Museum and Aquarium**. The best way to appreciate the wildlife is on the excellent boat trip around the island, which runs during the summer. The boat sails under the towering bird cliffs, with chances to observe not only puffins but all the other auk species except the little auk.

Sheltered **Klettsvík Bay**, near the entrance to Heimaey's port is the temporary home to **Keiko**, star of *Free Willy*, brought here from Oregon in September 1998. Housed in a large sea pen, initially, Keiko was later released and made his way to Norway following a group of wild killer whales. He died there in Taknes Fjord in December 2003

# Fire on Heimaey

Few Westman Islanders imagined that several thousand years of calm would end as abruptly as they did on the night of January 22, 1973. Within hours, a mile-long fissure had opened up along Heimaey's eastern flank and the inhabitants found their homes bombarded. By an extraordinary coincidence, virtually the entire fishing fleet was docked that night due to fierce storms the day before. So, the 5,000 plus inhabitants were evacuated instantaneously.

Most eruptions in Iceland are over in a matter of days but not this one, which was already building a sizeable volcanic cone, the new mountain of **Eldfell**. In a desperate bid to halt the flow of lava which threatened the port, millions of gallons of sea water were pumped onto its front. A simple solution, never tried before, it worked. Now the entrance to the port is tighter than before but better protected. As a touching reminder of the event, a house, partly engulfed by lava, has been left standing.

# Surtsey

When a thin plume of steam was spotted rising several miles off Iceland's south coast, in November 1963, scientists flocked to the site to observe the birth of Vestmannaeyjar's sixteenth island. Many submarine eruptions are short-lived but three years on, it was still going strong. Measuring just 0.7sq miles (1.9sq km), **Surtsey** is now a nature reserve with restricted entry. Scientists have been presented with a unique opportunity to monitor how life forms establish themselves on new terrain. For visitors, the only option is to take a nerve-testing sightseeing flight.

Opposite: Djúpivogur fishing fleet

North of Höfn, the change in landscape is immediate and dramatic. The glaciers are gone from view, replaced by steep-sided mountains rising from sheltered fjords.

Geologically, this is one of the oldest parts of Iceland, where ancient volcanic systems were active before the onset of the Ice Age three million years ago. The immense **Breiðdalur volcano**, erupted multiple sheets of basalt that formed the foundations of the island. Then when the Ice Age took over, its glaciers cut through many thousands of feet of rock layers, in a process of erosion taking millions of years. This has given the coastal mountains of the east their typical stepped appearance, each step or layer representing a single lava flow. Corries, hanging valleys and u-shaped valleys are typical features of the glaciated landscape.

## Stokksnes & Vesturhorn

Just before Route 1 heads north up the steep hill of **Almannaskarð**, a turning takes off following the coast to **Stokksnes**, where an offshoot of the NATO installations at Keflavík was located. For those interested in wildlife, a couple of offshore islands are a popular haul out for seals, while eider ducks and black guillemots can be observed swimming off the rocks and noisy arctic terns nest onshore.

The majestic mountains **Vesturhorn**, **Brunnhorn** and further to the north, **Eystrahorn**, show distinct banding, in muted shades of grey-green and beige-pink. They are probably the remains of the magma chambers of ancient volcanic systems that have been revealed by glaciation and uplifting. Such rock is known as intrusive – it differs from the surrounding rock, and because it cooled more slowly, became harder and more resistant. Two types are visible here – granophyre (a lighter acidic rock) and gabbro (a darker basic rock). Gabbro is one of the only rocks in Iceland hard enough to be successfully engraved, so is often used for gravestones and monuments.

## Papafjörður

The uninhabited bay north of Höfn gets its name from the 'Papar', the name given by the early Norse settlers to the Irish monks they found living in Iceland on their arrival. **Papós,** near the mouth of the fjord, housed a trading post until the late nineteenth century, when it was moved to Höfn. Aside from the place names and mention of the monks in early manuscripts, there is no further evidence of their stay but it is said that they left Iceland rather than live among heathens.

107

# Lón

The district of **Lón**, is fed by the milky **Jökulsá í Lóni**, the only glacial river to drain from the eastern edge of Vatnajökull. Shifted by wind and wave action, its sediments have formed a broad spit across the bay, so making it unsuitable for fishing vessels, but forming a flat coastal plain and grazing land for the farm **Stafafell**. This ancient farm dates back to settlement times and was visited by the Christian missionary Þangbrandur, on his tenth century crusade. Unwilling to be converted, the farmer at Stafafell challenged him to a duel. The cleric is said to have defended himself with a crucifix before killing the farmer. The attractive timber church on the site dates from 1866 while its pulpit and altarpiece are seventeenth century.

The youth hostel at Stafafell offers accommodation and has a campsite. It also arranges transport into the **Lónsöroefi** wilderness that lies further up the valley, nestled under the eastern extremity of Vatnajökull. With its gaudy rhyolite mountains, this remote and rugged area is reminiscent of the better known Landmannalaugar region. A footbridge over the Jökulsá river makes much of it accessible for hiking. To get there use the transfer service arranged through the hostel at Stafafell. Day trips, with a three hour guided hike in the area, depart from Höfn and Stafafell. Before setting out, seek advice from the warden at Stafafell on the state of the trails and the availability of space in the hut if you plan to stay overnight. Note that the overland trail to Snæfell is only for very experienced hikers and a tent and GPS are recommended. It involves river and glacier crossings.

Below the peak of **Eystrahorn**, just before the lighthouse, are the remains of what looks like a turf farm in miniature, which were actually built as a set during the filming of a Halldór Laxness novel. The next stretch of road heading north, is among the most dramatic in Iceland. Hugging the granophyre and gabbro screes of Eystrahorn, it winds above a coastline of steep cliffs and sandy bays, pounded by the Atlantic breakers. Rafts of moulting eider ducks can often be observed from a number of viewpoints where it is safe to draw off the road. In spite of its name, **Álftafjorður** 'Swan Fjord' usually has fewer whooper swans than Lón to the south. Its beautiful glaciated valleys are an invitation to explore to adventurous hikers.

## Roman remains

**B**ragðavellir, a farm in Hamarsfjörður, achieved fame when, in the early twentieth century, two Roman coins were unearthed. Dating from AD 270-305, they led to the supposition that a Roman ship might have been blown off course and landed on Iceland's eastern shore, long before the Norse settlers. The theory has now been largely refuted and it is thought that the coins were picked up as trinkets and brought to Iceland after the settlement.

# Djúpivogur

The fishing village of **Djúpivogur** has among the most dramatic settings of any in the region. The pleasant Hotel Framtíð, once the village shop,

## A literary legacy

More books are published per capita in Iceland than anywhere else in the world. They are beautifully bound hardback volumes, and there is hardly any market for paperback editions. Several daily and regional newspapers and countless popular and special interest magazines fill newsagents' shelves, while libraries lend more books per capita than anywhere else on earth. Iceland can boast, as it has done for centuries, almost full literacy.

The nation's love affair with the written word goes back to the beginning. The early settlers brought with them from Norway the tradition of poetry as entertainment, themed on mythology and heroic deeds. Then the fledgling nation took on the task of writing its own brief history, documented in the 'Book of Settlements' and 'Book of Icelanders'. These were followed by the greatest achievements of all, the great family Sagas of the thirteenth century.

The Icelandic word 'saga' means both 'history' and 'story', which is interesting because the Sagas are just that, a blend of fact and fiction. Some hold that they were based on oral tradition, passed down through several generations before being written down. Others believe, probably more accurately, that they were composed as works of fiction, loosely based on historical events and persons. What is remarkable is that they are anonymous and that they have survived. Their survival is largely due to the efforts of eighteenth century scholar Árni Magnússon who travelled the length and breadth of his country hunting them down. Many manuscripts were rotting away, or in some cases had been cut up and used for shoe leather. Árni took them to Copenhagen and set about copying them word for word. Before he had finished, a great fire swept through the city and some, though it may never be known how many, were lost.

Whatever their historical accuracy, the Sagas are, above all else, a good read. Skilfully crafted, meticulously detailed and at times, astonishingly humorous, they are a fascinating account of how people may have lived, thought, felt and behaved at the time they were written. Many have been translated into English and published in popular paperback editions.

---

overlooks the port. There are a museum, boat trips to Papey Island and some beautiful coastal walks out on the end of the peninsula, which is also a bird sanctuary.

A few miles north of Djúpivogur, the farm **Teigarhorn** is famous for it zeolites. Over sixteen different types of this mineral are found in Iceland. The finest have clusters of elongated, spindly crystals that resemble magnified snowflakes. Zeolites and other secondary pore minerals are formed

by rainwater seeping down through porous bedrock to a depth where it hits hot layers. Absorbing minerals from the surrounding rock, the hot water rises. Once it reaches cooler layers it fills crevices and cavities, forming crystals of zeolites, quartz and calcite, also known as Iceland spar. The site is now protected but the farm has a collection of specimens on display in a small museum.

**Berufjörður** at the head of the

*Continued on page 112...*

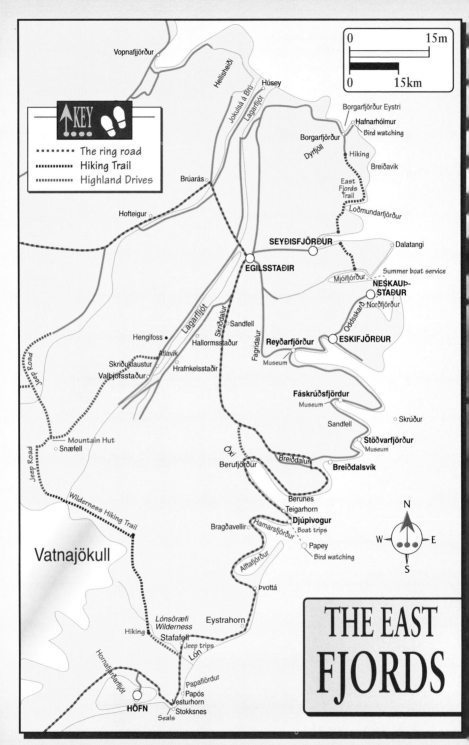

THE EAST FJORDS

**KEY**

- - - - - - - - The ring road
··········· Hiking Trail
··········· Highland Drives

Vopnafjörður
Húsey
Hellisheiði
Jökulsá á Brú
Lagarfljót
Borgarfjörður Eystri
Hafnarhólmur
Bird watching
Borgarfjörður
Dyrfjöll
Hiking
Breiðavik
East Fjords Trail
Brúarás
Loðmundarfjörður
Hofteigur
SEYÐISFJÖRÐUR
Dalatangi
EGILSSTAÐIR
Summer boat service
Mjóifjörður
NESKAUP-STAÐUR
Norðfjörður
Oddskarð
Lagarfljót
Skriðdalur
Sandfell
Fagridalur
ESKIFJÖRÐUR
Hengifoss
Hallormsstaður
Reyðarfjörður
Museum
Atlavik
Skriðuklaustur
Hrafnkelsstaðir
Valþjófsstaður
Fáskrúðsfjörður
Museum
Sandfell
Skrúður
Jeep Road
Stöðvarfjörður
Museum
Mountain Hut
Snæfell
Öxi
Berufjörður
Breiðdalur
Breiðdalsvík
Jeep Road
Wilderness Hiking Trail
Berunes
Teigarhorn
Djúpivogur
Bragðavellir
Hamarsfjörður
Boat trips
Papey
Bird watching
Vatnajökull
Alftafjörður
Þvottá
Lónsöræfi Wilderness
Eystrahorn
Hiking
Stafafell
Jeep trips
Lón
Hornafjarðarfljót
Papafjörður
Papós
Vesturhorn
HÖFN
Stokksnes
Seals

110

Above: Near Hvalnes, south-east Iceland
Below: Reyðarfjörður

fjord was birthplace to nineteenth-century Cambridge scholar Eiríkur Magnússon, who translated many of the Icelandic Sagas into English. From the farm the jeep track **Öxi** takes off, climbing steeply to the open moors above the fjord. It may look like a short cut but the route is very rough and slow.

At the mouth of the fjord, on its north shore, is the farm of **Berunes**, where there is a scenically located Youth Hostel and campsite. Along the next stretch of the road, many volcanic dykes are exposed in the mountain side as vertical bands of rock, perpendicular to the horizontal layers. Dykes are fissures which were once deep inside the earth. They filled with intrusive magma which hardened slowly, because it was at a depth, and became more resistant to erosion. That is why dykes often protrude from the surrounding rock, or become sea stacks.

Route 1 continues to **Breiðdalsvík**, a village which has sprung up over the last decades, based around the fishing industry. It has a scenic location and the popular Hotel Bláfell and adjoining campsite. The road splits at Breiðdalsvík with Route 96 continuing around the fjords, while Route 1 heads inland over a pass to Egilsstaðir.

Taking Route 1, the road turns to gravel as it heads up the valley, which cuts through the centre of the extinct **Breiðdalur volcano**. Driving further up the valley you pass a row of tables by a track leading to a farm. On display and on sale are rock specimens, including calcite, chalcedony, quartz, jasper and zeolite, gathered by local children. They may also have Icelandic sweaters for sale, hand-knitted on the farm.

The road climbs steeply to the pass, where in early summer the beautiful purple saxifrage blooms

freely. West of the pass the jeep track **Öxi** winds down over the moors to Berufjörður. Route 1 follows the valley **Skriðdalur**, passing a small lake that was formed when a huge landslide blocked the course of the river. The sheltered valley supports patches of birch woodland, where an attractive campsite is located at the farm **Stóra Sandfell**. From here it is a fifteen-minute drive on a paved road to Egilsstaðir, the main town of the region.

# The fjords and fishing villages

The alternative, and longer, route to Egilsstaðir follows the fjords, past the fishing villages of Stöðvarfjörður, Fáskrúðsfjörður and Reyðarfjörður. **Stöðvarfjörður**, with a population of 270, is worth a stop for a visit to the rock and mineral museum **Steinasafn Petru**, a private collection of specimens gathered from the region. **Fáskrúðsfjörður** has slightly more of the feel of a town about it. In the late nineteenth and early twentieth centuries it became the base for the French fishing fleet. The French built a hospital and chapel there and 49 French and Belgian seamen are buried in the graveyard at Krossar. The village has many poignant reminders of the era and hosts a "French Festival" each July.

Rising from the south shore of the fjord is the laccolith Sandfell, a dome-shaped mountain formed of intrusive acid rock, connected with an extinct volcano to the north. From the head of the fjord, two tracks lead up the valley, turning to bridle trails which cross the mountain ranges north and south. These were the old routes connecting the fjords before the coastal road was built.

## Tragedy at sea

Just offshore at the mouth of the fjord, is the island of **Skrúður**, which has one of Iceland's five gannet colonies. On Christmas Day 1986, the Liberian registered vessel *Syneta* went down in heavy seas off the island with the loss of all on board. When the 'May Day' call came through, the rescue helicopter was 300 miles out at sea, picking up survivors from the Icelandic vessel *Suðurland*, which had also gone down. It has since been suggested that the *Suðurland* may have run into a Soviet submarine.

The site of a proposed massive aluminium plant, twenty-two-mile (30km) long **Reyðarfjörður**, the longest of the East Fjords, was the site of an allied base during World War II. The village of Reyðarfjörður, also known as **Búðareyri**, has opened a museum of war memorabilia. A hotel offers accommodation. Perhaps the fjord's greater claim to fame is as landing place to a Viking named **Naddoddur**, who was blown off course in the year 850. Washed up on Iceland's east coast, he named the island Snæland.

From Reyðarfjörður, there is a choice of route. Paved Route 92 heads inland through Fagridalur to Egilsstaðir. A 13-mile (21km) detour leads to remote **Mjóifjörður**, considered by some to be the most beautiful of the East Fjords. Locked in by steep-sided mountains, there is little land for farming and only a handful of people live there year round, though a century ago it attracted hordes during the fishing season. From the settlement of **Brekka**, which has a guesthouse runs boat transport to **Norðfjörður**, the track continues out along the shore of the fjord to **Dalatangi**. Ruins of Iceland's first lighthouse can be seen here, alongside the modern one.

The other road from Reyðarfjörður leads to **Eskifjörður**, a fishing village which began as a trading post in 1786. A hotel, campsite and maritime museum are among the facilities for visitors. Beyond here a track follows the fjord, leading to a choice of hiking trails through the uninhabited fjords to the north. The main road continues over Iceland's highest mountain pass, 2,312ft (705m) Oddskarð and through a tunnel to descend to **Neskaupstaður**, commonly referred to as **Norðfjörður**.

With a population of over 1,500, it competes with Egilsstaðir as the largest town in the east, which is something of a surprise, given its isolation. The town owes its prosperity to herring but now the herring is long gone, replaced by large stern trawlers bringing in a catch of cod for the quick freezing plants. The few visitors that make it here comment on the town's open aspect and the broad valley behind the fjord. However, Neskaupstaður is backed by a steep and forbidding range, which in the winter of 1974 sent a massive avalanche down on the town, killing twelve residents and sweeping away one of the fish factories. South of the town, the fjords are deserted, offering good hiking for those prepared to carry all their own food and gear.

*Continued on page 116...*

Above: Eastern fijords, near Borgarfjörður
Below: Neskaupstaður

Above: Lónsöræfi, hiking among rhyolite mountains
Below: Reyðarfjörður

# Places to Visit
# EAST FJORDS AREA

## Lónsöræfi

**Stafafell Guesthouse, Hostel, Campsite and Lónsöræfi trips**
☎ 478 1717
stafafell@eldhorn.is
www.eldhorn.is/stafafell
Located 18 miles (28km) north of Höfn on Route 1. Jumping off point for Lónsöræfi trips.

## Djúpivogur

**Papey Boat Trips**
☎/Fax 478 8183
Daily, May-September, on demand.

**Langabúð**
☎ 478 8220
Handicrafts and folk museum.

## Stöðvarfjörður

**Steinasafn Petru**
☎ 475 8834
Interesting private mineral collection in home and garden of Petra Sveinsdóttir. Open: all year by arrangement.

## Fáskrúðsfjörður

**French sailors' Museum**
☎ 475 1525
Nostalgic and Poignant reminder of an era when French fishermen out-numbered Icelanders in these parts. Nice café with homebaked cakes.

## Reyðarfjörður

**Stríðsárasafnið**
☎ 470 9090
Museum of World War II memorabilia. Open: 1-5pm, summer only.

## Neskaupstaður

**Natural History Museum**
☎ 477 1606
Open: 1-5pm, weekdays, 17 June-31 August.

## Mjóifjörður

**Mjóifjörður Boat trips**
☎ 476 0005/853 3004
Departs Mjóifjörður Monday 10am and Thursday 9am and from Neskaupstaður Monday at 2pm and Thursday at 5pm. Useful transport for walkers. Guesthouse accommodation at Mjóifjörður
☎ 476 0007  mjoi@simnet.is

## Seyðisfjörður

**Tourist Information Bureau**
☎ 472 1551, Fax 472 1315,
www.sfk.is

**Technology Museum**
☎ 472 1596
Interesting exhibition of local memorabilia housed in the old telegraph office, built in 1894. Open: 2-6pm, daily 15 June-31 August.

## Borgarfjörður Eystri

**Álfasteinn Crafts & Information Bureau**
☎ 472 9977, Fax 472 9877,
alfasteinn@eldhorn.is
www.alfasteinn.is
Artifacts made of local stones and minerals.

**Guest House Borg**
☎ 472 9870, Fax 472 9880,
Accommodation and jeep transfers for hikers.

## Egilsstaðir & Surrounds

**East Iceland Heritage Museum**
☎ 471 1412
Open: daily except Monday 1 June–1 September 11am-5pm. Local history museum for the region.

116

**Information Bureau**
☎ 471 2320, Fax 471 1863
www.east.is
By the fuel station, campsite and
shopping complex.

**Tanni Travel**
☎ 476 1399, Fax 476 1599,
tanni@eldhorn.is
Transportation arranged for those
planning to hike to Snæfell and
Lónsöræfi. Wednesday &
Saturday.

## Egilsstaðir

All the roads in the east of Iceland converge on **Egilsstaðir** making it a convenient base for exploring the region. With the main airport for the east of Iceland, there are daily flights to Reykjavík, as well as weekly flights to the Faroe Islands. Bus services to Akureyri, Höfn and the East Fjord villages run out of Egilsstaðir. There are hotels, an attractive outdoor pool, well-equipped campsite and a range of shops including a large supermarket. Anyone heading west on Route 1 towards Lake Mývatn or into the highlands by car should fill up with fuel and supplies here.

## Exploring from Egilsstaðir

Egilsstaðir sits in the broad valley of the river **Lagarfljót**, a glacial torrent fed from the northern edge of Vatnajökull. The region has a rather more extreme climate than the rest of the country with colder winters but warmer summers and the valley supports a thriving farming community. Visitors without their own transport can reach many places by public bus. Transport to Mount Snæfell and the Kárahnúkur power project runs twice weekly and can be booked through the information bureau at Egilsstaðir's campground.

## The monster of Lake Lögurinn

The icy waters of the lake are said to be inhabited by a serpent-like monster that became the scourge of the local people during the Middle Ages. As there are no reptiles in Iceland, its origin is something of a mystery but folklore tells of a young girl who was given a gold ring by her mother and told to put it in a chest with an adder. Checking up on it later, the girl was frightened to see that though the gold had grown in size, so too had the snake. The chest was cast into the lake and shortly after the monster began to appear, snatching its unwary victims as they fished. Eventually, the chest and monster were chained to the bottom of the lake, but every so often it manages to rear its ugly head.

Fifteen miles (24km) long and 368ft (112m) deep **Lake Lögurinn**, Iceland's third largest lake, sits in a basin scoured out by Ice Age glaciers. The shores of the lake support the largest remaining tract of natural

*Continued on page 120...*

# DAY WALKS FROM BORGARFJÖRÐUR EYSTRI

The area makes a great base from which to explore on foot with marked hiking trails into the mountains and deserted bays east of the town, and to Dyrfjöll to the west. Those with four wheel drive transport can drive as far as Loðmundarfjörður or Breiðavík, opening up further options for hiking. Guesthouse Borg offers jeep transport to and from the start and end of trails.

## 1 BORGARFJÖRÐUR-BRÚNAVÍK (4 HOURS CIRCULAR WALK)

The trail takes off from the east side of the fjord, to the isolated bay of **Brúnavík**, which was farmed until 1944. A moderate walk with great views from two passes 1,312ft (400m) and 1,053ft (321m) in height.

## 2 BORGARFJÖRÐUR-BREIÐAVÍK (7-9 HOURS CIRCULAR WALK)

A circular route starting with a 3-4 hour walk over 1,571ft (479m) Gagnheiði on a jeep track to the bay of **Breiðavík**. The return walk, taking 4-5 hours is via the 1,177ft (359m) high pass Súluskarð and 1,053ft (321m) Hofstaðaskarð. A long day, but a fairly easy walk.

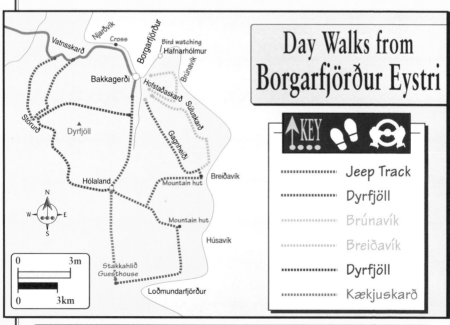

Day Walks from Borgarfjörður Eystri

KEY

............... Jeep Track
............... Dyrfjöll
............... Brúnavík
............... Breiðavík
............... Dyrfjöll
............... Kækjuskarð

**Opposite top:** Dyrfjoll

**Opposite inset:** Arctic Riverbeauty (Epilobium latifolium)

118

## ↑3 DYRFJÖLL (4-5 HOURS OR MORE)

There is a choice of four routes to the prominent notched mountain. The easiest access is from the saddle at Vatnsskarð, on the road from Egilsstaðir, and the trail takes 2-3 hours to the landslip **Stórurð**, looping round to return via a path lower down, a further 2 hours. From Borgarfjörður a more difficult route, taking around 5 hours, crosses a 2,040ft (622m) shoulder on the northern flank of the mountain, joining the trail to Vatnsskarð. An easier approach is from **Hólaland**, 5 miles (8km) south of Borgarfjörður, taking 4 hours to Stórurð.

## ↑4 KÆKJUSKARD (6 HOURS)

6 hour hike over a 700 metre pass, offering great views. Several river crossings.

forest in Iceland, **Hallormsstaðas-kógur.** Protected since 1905, when it was chosen as the site for early forestry experiments, the forest has been enlarged with the planting of around 50 imported tree species from 177 different sources world wide. It is not hard to see why Icelanders love the place and many visitors too will appreciate the quiet walks on easy forest trails. A network of paths starts from the hotel which has a leaflet and map on the walks.

Recommended is the walk around the arboretum. The Icelandic word 'Trésafn' translates as 'Tree Museum', which is quite appropriate in a country as short of trees as Iceland. From here, a trail leads south above the lake shore to a viewpoint, where the impressive summit of Snæfell can be seen up the valley. The trail ends at the beautiful campsite at **Atlavík,** which is popular with families and best avoided at weekends.

Beyond Hallormsstaður the road continues to the head of the lake, now rapidly silting up, where the farm and church of **Valþjófsstaður** stand. The church, dating from 1966, has a beautiful carved wooden door, a replica of the original church's thirteenth-century door, which is now in the National Museum in Reykjavík and is considered one of its most valuable items.

On the lake's west shore a walking trail leads up the hillside, following the course of a river and gorge to the waterfall **Hengifoss.** It is Iceland's third highest, plummeting 387ft (118m) into a glacially eroded valley and gorge, where individual lava flows, intermingled with reddish sediments form a curious striped effect. It takes an hour to reach the falls, with a stop at **Litlanesfoss,** a smaller waterfall

framed by impressive basalt columns.

A few miles north of Skriðuk-laustur and before the trail to Hengifoss, Route F910 takes off up a steep hill, leading to the mountain **Snæfell.** At 6,012ft (1,833m), the extinct central volcano, formed during the late Ice Age, is the highest mountain in Iceland outside of Vatnajökull. Much of the land west of it may be flooded to make way for a controversial hydroelectric power scheme. Reindeer are often seen in the remote and beautiful surrounds of the mountain, where there is a hut for visitors to overnight and possibilities for hiking.

The climb up Snæfell starts from the hut and can be done in a day. Crampons may be needed. South of Snæfell a 4-5 day wilderness hike leads to Lónsöraefi for experienced, self sufficient hikers. It is necessary to cross a glacier along the way. In fog the route is hazardous and a GPS is essential. There are 3 huts along the way but it is advisable to take a tent as well.

In clear weather, the views of Iceland's vast interior are awe-inspiring. A jeep track continues to the edge of Vatnajökull, while a second loops round to Hrafnkelsdalur.

The 17-mile (27km) paved Route 93 heads from Egilsstaðir over a dramatic mountain pass to **Seyðis-fjörður,** a beautiful town of brightly painted wooden houses, situated at the head of the fjord of the same name. A century ago it was among the largest in Iceland and a prosperous trading post. Until the nineteen eighties its status was enhanced by being one of only a handful of towns to boast a liquor store. Though best known as the terminus for the Norræna ferry, which sails weekly in summer linking Iceland, the Faroe

Islands, Norway, Denmark and Shetland, the town is worth a visit for its scenic location and fine walks in its surrounds. A hotel, guesthouse, campsite and youth hostel, as well as a range of shops, cater to visitors' needs. A pleasant day walk leads to **Vestdalur**, while a backpacking route heads both north to **Loðmundarfjörður** and south to **Mjóifjörður**.

# Borgarfjörður Eystri

The northernmost of the East Fjords is off the beaten track yet those who make the effort to visit are rewarded with the region's most stunning mountain scenery. A landmark from miles around, the cleft peak of **Dyrfjöll**, meaning 'Door Mountains' offers fine hiking on marked trails. Its complex geology is still a puzzle, but experts believe it may have formed in an eruption under an ancient lake-filled caldera. Acid rhyolite mountains are abundant in the area, in many shades of brown, pink and beige. The flanks of **Hvítserkur**, one of the most striking, are criss-crossed with darker basalt dykes. The mountain is situated south of Borgarfjörður Eystri, on the jeep track to Loðmundarfjörður.

The approach road to the village of **Borgarfjörður Eystri**, passes the bay of **Njarðvík**, hugging a steep scree where travellers, even as recently as 1909, have been swept to their death by avalanches and rock falls. In the fourteenth century, such happenings were blamed on a creature, half-man, half-beast, who lived in a cave on the scree. In an effort to stop the tragedies, a cross was erected with the Latin inscription *Effigiem Christi qui transis pronus honora*. Translating as 'Those who pass here, honour the image of

Christ', it seems to have been only partly effective, because though the beast has not been seen since, the accidents continued. The cross has been replaced several times, most recently some fifty years ago.

Also known as **Bakkagerði,** the village (population 108) has a guesthouse, campsite and a pretty church, which holds a painting by Jóhannes S Kjarval, who was brought up there. Many interesting rocks and minerals are found in the region and there is a craft shop selling rock specimens in the village. Birdwatchers can head along the east shore of the fjord to **Hafnarhólmur**, where puffins, fulmars and kittwakes nest and can be observed from a viewing platform. During the breeding season the area is closed before noon, to avoid disturbing the birds.

Guesthouse Borg and the community centre offer visitor accommodation. For hikers the region has much to offer and with mountain huts (contact Álfasteinn to book) at **Breiðavík** and **Húsavík** you can stay overnight in the wilds. A map of the hiking trails is available locally or on the Álfasteinn website.

Located on the spit of land that separates the rivers Lagarfljót and Jökulsá á Dal, at their estuaries 37 miles (60km) north of Egilsstaðir, the horse riding farm and hostel **Húsey** deserves special mention. Guests are welcome to join in the farm work or bring in the salmon and trout nets. It's a great place for birdwatching with some forty species commonly observed. Seals are abundant in the area, though be warned that the farmer exercises his traditional right to hunt them. This said, the place is a wonderful spot to unwind for a few days and learn about life in rural Iceland.

# 5 North-East Iceland

*L*acking waterfalls, high mountains or volcanic features of note, few visitors make the effort to explore the far north-eastern coast of Iceland.

## THE NORTH-EAST COASTAL ROUTE

For those travelling between Húsavík and Egilsstaðir, either by car or using the three times a week bus service, the coastal route offers an alternative to the desert tract followed by Route 1.

Though the route is longer and mostly unpaved, the small fishing villages and farms have a sort of timeless feel about them. This is the northernmost part of mainland Iceland, just a few miles short of the Arctic Circle, and probably the best place for serious midnight sun-seekers. Coastal fog can be a problem, but on the whole, the region has a higher than average sunshine record. A rocky coastline, indented by sheltered bays is home to thousands of seabirds while inland there are key breeding grounds for wildfowl and waders.

Heading north from Egilsstaðir, Route 917 passes **Brúarás**, a country guesthouse, before following the course of the Jökulsá á Dal river to its estuary. It then heads over **Hellisheiði**, a summer route which is often very rough and only just passable to normal vehicles. The alternative faster Route 85 to Vopnafjörður, takes off further west, traversing desolate valleys and ridges before dropping to the **Hofsá Valley** and turf farm museum of **Burstafell**. Dating in part from 1770 the buildings contain farm implements, furnishings and artefacts gathered from all over the region.

The Hofsá is one of a number of rivers in the area which offer excellent, though expensive, salmon fishing. **Hotel Tangi**, named after the spit of land on which the village of **Vopnafjörður** sits, offers visitor accommodation, along with **Skjól guesthouse** and campsite, and the farm of **Syðri Vík,** situated on the bay south of the village. With a population of just over 600, it has the best, although still limited, range of shops and facilities along the coast.

Heading north, the road passes a turn off to the swimming pool at Selárlaug, while to the east a track follows the coast to the bird cliffs at **Fuglabjarganes**. Route 85 climbs over the plateau to the tiny village of **Bakkafjör›ur**. Beyond here the road hugs the shore of the bay before reaching **Langanes**, the remote and exposed peninsula north-east of

## The Northern Lights

Nature's own light show, the Aurora Borealis, or northern lights, is one of the most awe-inspiring of natural phenomena. Most commonly observed between November and February, they are occasionally witnessed even in late August. To see them at their best, you need a clear, moonless night and no other sources of light around. Late evening often gives the best displays and the 'show' can last from several minutes to hours, as rippling curtains of light dance across the night sky, in shades of green, pink and yellow.

They appear to be caused when solar wind particles collide with air molecules in the earth's atmosphere and their energy is transferred into light. The phenomenon is only found in the polar regions because the magnetic field lines, which accelerate the particles down to earth, are open here, but locked at lower latitudes.

Þórshöfn. The village has a nice guesthouse, Lyngholt, and swimming pool. High clearance four wheel drive vehicles can drive the 31 miles (50km) of dirt track to the uninhabited tip of Langanes, which is famous for its abundant seabirds. West of Þórshöfn is the peninsula of Rauðanes where a 3 hour marked hiking route follows a dramatic coastline of cliffs, basalt columns and a dozen natural rock arches and sea stacks.

Iceland's northernmost mainland is low-lying **Melrakkaslétta**, which translates as 'Fox Plains' though the chances of spotting the elusive arctic fox are no better here than in most other inhabited parts of Iceland. In June and early July, the air throngs with arctic terns, noisily defending their nesting sites against intruders. At the northernmost tip of the peninsula, the lighthouse of **Hraunhafnartangi** stands behind a driftwood-strewn beach. It was a sheltered landing spot in Saga times and in Fóstbræðra Saga, hero Þorgeir Hávarsson was slain here but not before doing away with fourteen of his adversaries. A heap of stones is said to mark his burial place.

Farm accommodation is available at **Ytri Áland** on the south-western shore, while **Raufarhöfn** has a rather pleasant hotel, the Norðurljós, which arranges boat trips to the Arctic Circle, as well as kayaking, canoeing, trout fishing and bird watching trips.

## DESERT ROUTE – EGILSSTAÐIR TO LAKE MYVATN

The 116-mile (180km) stretch of road through the interior of the north-east is still largely unpaved and crosses one of the most desolate tracts of uninhabited Iceland. It marks the northern boundary of a vast desert extending south to the ice cap and west as far as the Skjálfandfljót River. The huge expanse of black sand, lava and Ice Age moraines sits in the rain shadow behind Vatnajökull. Add to this the porous nature of the ground and there is simply not enough moisture for vegetation to survive. Another problem is that most of the desert lies at over 1,640ft (500m) in altitude, so the growing season is shorter. In the few places where there is surface water, grass and moss will grow freely to create oases that are islands of green in a sea of black.

From Egilsstaðir, Route 1 passes the hot water pipe that pumps hot water to the town, from one of the few geothermal sources in the east of Iceland. The road crosses the mighty **Jökulsá á Dal**, a powerful glacial torrent that dumps 100 tons of sediment an hour at its estuary, as such the most laden river in Iceland. You can drive to a parking area by the bridge with picnic tables and a view over its gorge and murky waters below. The river flows out of **Brúarjökull**, a glacier tongue on the northern edge of Vatnajökull that is prone to surging. This happens when a glacier has been in retreat and a bulge of ice develops higher up forming a kinetic wave which prompts the ice to surge forward. In its last major surge in the 1960s, the glacier moved forward 5 miles (8km).

The road follows the river valley for 21 miles (33km), passing several small waterfalls that cascade down its slopes. Soil erosion is a major problem in the valley, and many farms are struggling to keep their grazing land intact, not helped by the herds of hungry reindeer that graze here in spring. Nearby the farm Hofteigur are indistinct remains that may have been a temple in pagan times. A rocky promontory named Goðanes, juts into the river and was believed to be a site of sacrifices, held if the Norse god Thor was insulted. At **Skjöldólfsstaðir**, there is a small guesthouse, café and craft shop selling items produced by local communities, which include hand-knitted sweaters. There are a swimming pool and campground on the site as well.

# Upper Jökuldalur

The side Route 923 continues up the valley to **Brú**. Meaning 'Bridge', the farm was the site of a ferry point over the river Jökulsá á Dal mentioned in Saga times. In the eighteenth century, a shepherd went missing here one Christmas Eve. His body was found beside the river the next day alongside the tracks of a four legged beast. The foreleg tracks were those of an eagle's claw, while the hind legs were hoofed, like a horse.

Beyond Brú, the road continues up the side valley of **Hrafnkelsdalur**, named after the enigmatic protagonist of Hrafnkel's Saga. His farm Aðalból is now a guest house, beyond which the jeep Route F910 heads south to Snæfell. The saga is centred on the east of Iceland and so accurately are places described and events related that it is not hard to bring it all alive. Those making it as far as Brú can return to Route 1 by taking Route 907, or continue along the jeep track F910 west to the **River Kreppá**, joining the main track to Askja and Kverkfjöll. Note that there are several unbridged streams and the route is designated for four wheel drive high clearance vehicles.

# Jökuldalsheiði – the edge of the habitable world

Route 1 climbs steeply to **Jökuldalsheiði** a moorland plateau strewn with the remains of some 16 farms. Farming started here in the year 1840, prompted by shortage of land elsewhere but many farms were abandoned after the Askja eruption

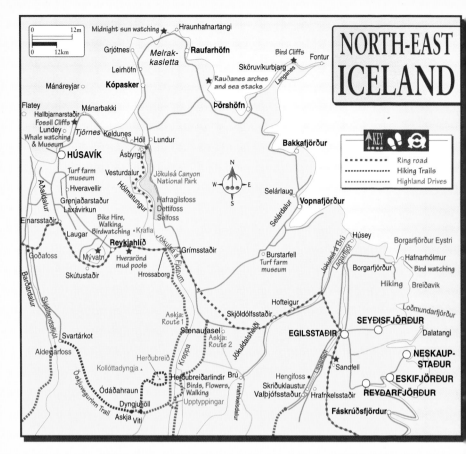

## NORTH-EAST ICELAND

**KEY**

- ---- Ring road
- ······ Hiking Trails
- ······ Highland Drives

of 1875. Facing famine, many of the inhabitants emigrated to the USA and Canada, forming the close knit communities of 'Vestur Íslendingar', (Western Icelanders) which continue

to this day. Sænautasel, on route 907, a short detour away, is a restored farm from the era, with pet farm animals and a nice café.

There is now a choice of route.

## A harsh reality

It is believed that author Halldór Laxness was inspired by the tenacity of the people of Jökuldalsheiði to base his novel *Independent People* on the area and its inhabitants. Protagonist of the epic is Bjartur of Summerhouses, whose stubborn independence borders on stupidity, a character who inspires not only anger and frustration, but also compassion and pity. His obsession and single-mindedness leave a trail of destruction which envelops his whole family in needless tragedy and suffering.

Laxness, in his youth an ardent communist, championed the cause of the working man and woman. A prolific writer, his early novels focused on the appalling poverty of many Icelanders during the early twentieth century. Laxness was awarded the Nobel Prize for Literature in 1955.

Hafragilsfoss Falls, Jökulsa Canyon National Park

The old road continues over Jökuldalsheiði to the start of the desert. From the pass at the top of the last ridge, a breathtaking view of the route ahead unfolds. In really clear weather it is possible to see 50 miles (80km) towards Lake Mývatn and over the Ódaðahraun lava desert to the south. The viewpoint is a wild and desolate spot, with the odd snow flurry even in summer, so it is something of a surprise to find a picnic table there.

On the plain below, sits the farm and church of **Möðrudalur**, an unexpected and incongruous sight. At 1,538ft (469m) above sea level, the farm is the highest and most isolated in the country, yet it is excellent grazing land for sheep. Möðrudalur's church was completed in 1949 by the local farmer, Jón Stefánsson, who built it in memory of his wife. Determined to complete the job single-handed, he even painted the altarpiece, which depicts the Sermon on the Mount.

Just south of Möðrudalur, Route F905 takes off for Askja and Kverkfjöll. The track is for four wheel drive high clearance vehicles only and there are several unbridged rivers to be forded, with the further hazard of drifting sand on sections of the route.

The new section of Route 1 cuts north-east of Möðrudalur, linking up with Route 85 to Vopnafjörður. Just before the bridge over the Jökulsá á Fjöllum Route 864 to Dettifoss takes off. This route, which follows the east bank of the river, is usually open by the middle of June and is easier than Route F862 to the west, which is a rough jeep track. By the junction is the farm **Grímstunga**, which offers visitor accommodation and camping. Isolated Grímstunga clings

on, while others in the area have given up, faced with severe winters, drifting sand and the ever-present battle against soil erosion.

# Jökulsá á Fjöllum

At 129 miles (206km) long this is Iceland's second longest river and one of its most powerful. Fed almost entirely by glacial meltwater, the river's flow varies enormously, but is greatest in summer. The average flow of 183 cubic metres per second can swell to four or five times that, following prolonged rainfall, a hot sunny spell or volcanic activity under the ice cap. After the Ice Age glaciers retreated around 10,000 years ago, the river began to follow roughly its present course. Then, several bouts of catastrophic flooding, probably caused by eruptions under Vatnajökull, eroded its canyon downstream and left scars all along its course. On a smaller scale, such floods still occur, most recently in 1995.

The river has always been considered hazardous and impassable on horseback, except near its source. It was first bridged near its mouth in 1905 but the bridge at Grímstunga dates from 1947. A few miles west of the bridge, Route F88 takes off for Herðubreiðarlindir and Askja, a jeep track for four wheel drive high clearance vehicles only.

Just off Route 1, but accessed from the Askja track, is the drive-in crater **Hrossaborg**. An explosion crater, rising 131ft (40m) above the surrounding land, those with the energy can walk the trail up its rim for a fine view over the uninhabited highlands. The 20-mile (28km) stretch of road between Hrossaborg and Mývatn skirts the northern boundary of Óðaðahraun. With an area of around 2,163 sq miles (5,600 sq km), this is the largest expanse of lava in Iceland, though it originates from several eruptions during the last 10,000 years. Midway between Mývatn and the Jökulsá, the jeep track F862 takes off to Dettifoss, 16 miles (25km) of very dusty single track road, suitable for high clearance four-wheel-drive vehicles only. Beyond Dettifoss the road improves and can be driven by all vehicles.

# LAKE MYVATN

Mývatn deserves its reputation as one of Iceland's most fascinating areas of natural beauty. Its abundant birdlife, incredible variety of volcanic and geothermal features and wealth of walking trails, make it a particularly rewarding place for visitors. It is also very popular, and from June to August it can be difficult to get accommodation unless

## The bird life of Mývatn

For the naturalist, Mývatn's bird life is the star attraction. No less than fourteen species of duck breed around the lake and the numerous ponds adjacent to it. In a good year, numbers can swell to 25,000, making it one of the greatest concentrations of wildfowl in the world. The commonest species are the tufted duck and the scaup. Red breasted merganser, Barrow's goldeneye, and wigeon each have between 400 and 700 pairs. The Barrow's goldeneye breeds in few other locations in Iceland, which is its only European breeding ground. The harlequin duck, long-tailed duck, mallard, common scoter and teal are fairly common, while pintail, gadwall, shoveller and goosander are rare. Goldeneyes are occasionally spotted but do not breed in Iceland, while pochards are also very rare but have been known to breed.

Most species of duck are already paired up at their nesting sites by the end of May. Once mating has taken place, the drakes leave the nesting site and most head out to the lake to lose their conspicuous breeding plumage. The exception are the harlequin drakes, which make their way back down to the coast.

Other birds found at Mývatn include Slavonian grebe and the great northern diver or loon, one of Iceland's largest and most spectacular birds. Numerous non-breeding whooper swans gather on the lake each year, along with a few breeding pairs. Another important, and rare, breeding bird at Mývatn is the gyrfalcon. Though it may be seen in flight, its nesting sites are a closely guarded secret.

To protect the nesting ducks, the area bordering the north west shore of the lake is off limits to walkers from 15 May to 20 July each year. Bird watching can still be rewarding from the road, which is open to traffic. Other spots include the lake shore at Reykjahlíð, the area around Höfði, the pseudocraters at Skútustaðir and the River Laxá.

you book in advance. As the lake and surrounds are a protected area, camping is only allowed at designated sites but there are several of these in the area so finding space is not usually a problem.

The main and best equipped campsite is at the village of **Reykjahlíð**, behind Hotel Reynihlíð and it has a laundry service and unlimited free hot water. The wardens' office is also a tourist information bureau though the main one is at the supermarket. A quieter campsite is on the shore of the lake by the **Eldá Travel Bureau**, which also arranges excursions and private bed and breakfast accommodation in local homes. A third site is located a few miles out of the village on the road to Skútustaðir.

Of the two hotels, the Hotel Reynihlíð is the larger and has more in the way of facilities, while Hotel Reykjahlíð has a more inspiring setting. Sleeping bag accommodation is available at Hlíð, by the airport, while the Guesthouse Birkihraun is a further option. The village has grown up around employment provided by the area's two main industries, the Krafla power station and the diatomite plant. It has an excellent swimming pool with hot pots and a sauna, bank, post office, general store and souvenir shop. Adjoining Hotel Reynihlíð is the pub and café Gamli Bærinn, which turns into quite a lively nightspot at weekends in summer. The food is good, if a little pricey. Down the road, the café Hverinn is also good and more reasonably priced.

**Skútustaðir**, Mývatn's second village, which is located on its south shore in an altogether quieter and more scenic setting, has a good hotel and a campsite in a sheltered hollow beside the pseudocraters. There are also a general store, a café and restaurant, sleeping bag accommodation and an indoor swimming pool.

Mývatn is on the main bus route linking Egilsstaðir and Akureyri, with a daily service in summer. Mýflug, 'Midge Fly' operates sightseeing flights around the lake, to Krafla, the Jökulsá Canyon, Grímsey Island, Askja and Vatnajökull. If you get a clear day, the twenty-minute flight over the lake is well worth the money for its stunning photographic opportunities.

## Midge madness

The lake is remarkably shallow, just (4.5m) in depth at its deepest point, letting light penetrate to the floor throughout. This allows midge larvae to thrive along with other important organisms, which are a key food source for trout and wildfowl. The name Mývatn in fact means 'Midge Lake'. At times during the summer, particularly in spells of calm, sunny days, they multiply and swarm to reach plague proportions but, they do not usually bite. Those that do are the black flies congregating around the River Laxá, where it exits the lake and then it is only the females which bite and only at certain times during the season. The shops at Mývatn sell head nets, which may look silly but make a lot of sense!

Above: Lake Mývatn, near Höfði and Kalfaströnd
Below: Ásbyrgi, wooded gorge, Jökulsá Canyon National Park

Mývatn and its surrounds have been protected as a conservation area since 1974. The lake, which is 14.5 sq miles (37sq km) in area, lies 911ft (278m) above sea level. Though away from the moderating influence of the coast, its climate is surprisingly mild in summer. The lake was formed in two stages which are linked to geological developments in the region. The Ice Age left behind an open moorland, dotted with moraines and surrounded by a number of rhyolite ridges and tuff mountains formed in subglacial eruptions during the Ice Age.

About 8,000 years ago the moon-like crater **Lúdent** was formed east of the lake. Then, 3,800 years ago, an eruption began from **Ketildyngja**, 15 miles (25km) south-east of Mývatn, pouring out lava and damming the course of a river, to form a shallow lake. The lava eventually spread out on the plain south of Húsavík. Some 2,300 years later, one of the geological gems of the Lake Mývatn area, the imposing crater **Hverfjall**, was formed, heralding the start of a new round of activity. Explosive steam jets, trapped under the layer of molten rock, created many of the fine pseudocraters and lava pillars that are characteristic of Mývatn.

In historical times activity has focused on the Krafla area. The devastating 'Mývatn Fires' lasted five years, starting in 1724 with an explosive eruption in the Krafla area that formed the crater **Víti**. From the fissures that opened up in its wake, flows of lava ran, engulfing much of the farming land and even threatening the settlement at Reykjahlíð.

# EXPLORING AT MÝVATN

Most visitors spend at least two days in the area, though there is easily enough to see and do to fill a week. Those without their own transport can opt for a range of coach day excursions which visit the lake, Krafla area, the Jökulsa Canyon and further afield to Askja and Kverkfjöll. Bike hire is available from the main campsite and Hotel Reynihlíð and there are plenty of marked walking trails in the surrounds of the lake.

## Around the Lake

The 23-mile (37km) route around the lake can be done in half a day with your own vehicle, though a full day will give more time to enjoy the

## Hot pool

Opposite Vogar, a gate marks the track to **Grjótagjá**, which can be driven in an ordinary vehicle. Grjótagjá is a cave and fissure, with several openings, filled with hot water. It was once a popular bathing spot for locals but after 1975 the water temperature rose to (140°F/60°C) and, though steadily cooling down, it is still too hot to swim in. Beyond the fissure, look out for an iron rod to the left of the road, which spans a crack in the lava. It was put up during the Krafla eruptions to monitor the extent of rifting in the area, shown by the gap between the two sections of the rod.

incredible array of natural curiosities. Those without a car can cover the route on an excursion, or hire a bike and cycle it. If you have the choice don't do the trip on a sunny day unless there is a wind, because of the midges.

Along the east shore **Vogar** was home to the extraordinary Jón Jónsson, who farmed here during the first half of the nineteenth century. He was well known for his hospitality to visitors from abroad, who repaid him with books, for an Icelander the most precious of gifts. Using these, Jón taught himself English and later wrote his own autobiography – in English! Vogar has a nice campsite and cowshed café Vogafjós, with its dairy herd.

The road along the lake continues past a gate, marking the track to the foot of **Hverfjall** (also spelt Hverfell). This impressive crater, with a diameter of 3,280ft (1,000m), is technically known as a tephra ring. It was formed in an explosive eruption, which ejected tephra and fragments of bedrock. From the car park at the base of the crater, a trail leads to its rim from where there is a fine view.

The next turn-off leads to **Dimmuborgir**, which has a slightly spooky feel to it, especially in half light. A geological formation that is probably unique in the world, it formed when lava filled a broad basin. Water, trapped underneath, escaped through steam vents and hardened the surrounding lava. Abruptly, the lake drained and its crust collapsed, leaving behind the hardened vents as pillars. Two circular trails, a longer 1 hour route and shorter 20 minute loop, lead to some of the most bizarre of the features. 'Gatklettur' is a keyhole formation

that you can walk through and 'Kirkjan' with a little imagination can be likened to a Gothic cathedral in miniature, complete with arches and three altars.

**Höfði** is a private park and woodland by the **Kalfaströnd pillars** which offers the classic Mývatn shot with the lava pillars and lake in it. There is an entrance charge. An alternative (and free) place for a similar view is a hundred yards south at the next pull out. You can also walk out along the **Kalfaströnd peninsula** for further views. The small river **Grænilækur** is practically the only surface water flowing into the lake. All other water enters from under the lava.

The small settlement of **Skútustaðir** at the southern end of the lake has an hotel, guesthouse, shop, restaurant, swimming pool and campsite. For visitors, the attraction is the **pseudocraters**, which are grouped in clusters around a small lake. They are formed when lava flows over water or marshy ground and traps steam underneath. In explosive bursts the steam escapes through a vent, blasting the lava into ash-like fragments which accumulate, in much the same way as they would in a real eruption, around the vent. There are several trails through the craters and if you have time it is well worth taking the one hour walk around the lake.

The **Laxá** is undoubtedly Iceland's most beautiful spring-fed river. Flowing out of the lake, it leaps exuberantly along a youthful course, following the route taken by Mývatn's lava on its 31-mile (50km) journey to the sea. On its many islets grow huge stands of wild angelica, giving cover to nesting ducks, in particular the harlequins, of which several hundred pairs breed along the river. From the old bridge over the river, the ducks and their chicks can often be seen playing in the rapids. The Icelandic name of the species is 'Straumönd' meaning 'current duck'.

Though there are fewer volcanic features along the west shore, the bird life is abundant. The ponds north-west of the lake are the chief breeding ground for many of Mývatn's ducks and are closed to foot traffic during the nesting season. Once the chicks are hatched, they make their way to the main lake. Egg collecting has been a traditional supplement to a farmer's income and for centuries the ducks have been exploited in this way. Farmers were careful to take just one or two eggs from a nest but such were the numbers of nests that, at times, a single farm could harvest six to eight thousand in a season.

Another important resource is the lake's trout. Early in the twentieth century, up to 100,000 fish a year were caught and smoked. The traditional curing method involves the use of animal dung as fuel, which gives the fish a unique taste. It is popularly eaten with the dark and slightly sweet rye bread that is baked in the warm ground of nature's own bakery, by the breeze block factory opposite the road from the diatomite plant.

The north shore of the lake was engulfed by lava from the 1729-29 eruptions. Typical of ropy lava are its dome-like structures cut through by gaping fissures. A walking trail leads along the shore of the lake from Reykjahlíð.

## Bjarnaflag & the diatomite factory

Diatoms are minute single-celled algae that live in Lake Mývatn. Their skeletal remains, rich in silica, build up as a silt deposit on the lake floor providing the region with a lucrative industry. The diatomite is sucked up and pumped to the factory, where it is dried using steam from the **Bjarnaflag geothermal power station** nearby. The resulting powder is used as a thickener in several industries, as well as a filter in the making of wine and beer. The plant was badly damaged during the 1975-84 eruptions. In the face of growing concerns about the fragile ecosystems of the lake, the management is looking into ways of extracting the diatomite from beneath the lake bed.

## EXPLORING FROM MÝVATN

**Krafla,** pronounced 'Krapla', is a 2,683ft (818m) high mountain that has given its name to the surrounding volcanic area and series of nine eruptions between 1975 and 1984. Typical of a long-lived central volcano, underlying the area of Krafla is a magma chamber and caldera. Calderas form when the magma chamber empties suddenly, causing the land to subside. Krafla is one of Iceland's most recent and most accessible eruption sites, its volcanic features easy to see and very beautiful.

The site lies 5 miles (8km) off Route 1, beyond the Kröflustöð power station north-east of Lake Mývatn and most people visit it as part of a day trip during their stay at the lake. For those without their own

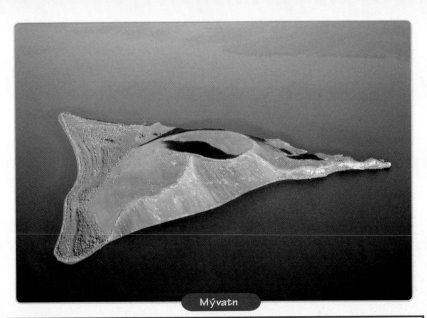

Mývatn

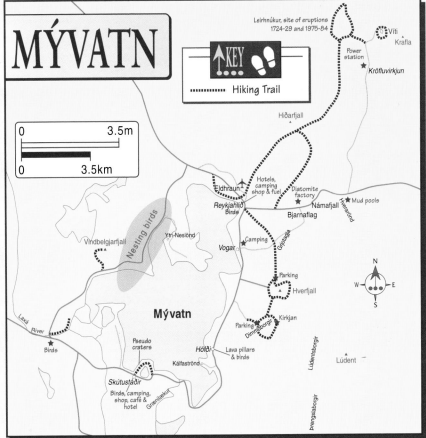

# MÝVATN

KEY

·········· Hiking Trail

0      3.5m

0      3.5km

Leirhnúkur, site of eruptions 1724-29 and 1975-84

Víti

Krafla

Power station

Kröfluvirkjun

Hiðarfjall

Hotels, camping shop & fuel

Eldhraun

Diatomite factory

Reykjahlíð
Birds

Námafjall

Mud pools

Bjarnaflag

Hverarönd

Nesting birds

Ytri-Nesiönd

Vindbelgjarfjall

Vogar

Camping

Gnúpagja

Parking

Hverfjall

N

W   E

S

Laxá River

Mývatn

Kirkjan

Parking

Dimmuborgir

Birds

Pseudo craters

Höfði

Lava pillars & birds

Kálfaströnd

Lúdentsborgir

Lúdent

Skútustaðir

Birds, camping, shop, café & hotel

Grænilækur

Prengslaborgir

135

## The power station

The idea of harnessing power from Krafla's steam fields was conceived in the early nineteen seventies, before the start of the eruptions. No one really expected it to blow so soon but the first of the eruptions came while they were still drilling bores and building the power house for the **Kröflustöð power station**. More problems followed, not least the rising and sinking of the land, causing bore holes to block and steam pressure to drop. Eventually the first of two 30 megawatt turbines was up and running but it was many years before the plant was operating near its full potential. One of the more positive things to emerge from the project is the immense bank of knowledge in the field of geothermal technology, which has been put to good use on other projects in the country. Iceland has also established a school of geothermal technology, attended by participants from all over the world.

transport, the options are to take an escorted excursion, to hire a bike or to walk there. There is a marked trail from the village of Reykjahlíð, a 7-mile (12km) walk, following the lava flows from the 1724-29 eruptions and taking around 3 hours each way.

## Víti

To reach the eruption site, continue on the road past the power station

Though it was once possible to roam anywhere, to protect the fragile natural features, strict conservation measures now limit hiking to marked trails. This all makes good sense because the vegetation is very vulnerable to erosion and the scars left by errant hiking books can take decades, if not centuries, to heal.

## 1 GRJÓTAGJÁ-HVERFJALL-DIMMUBORGIR (4-5 HOUR CIRCULAR WALK)

Start from Reykjahlíð, by the fissure Stóragjá, where Route 1 takes off for Egilsstaðir. The path crosses the lava to reach Grjótagjá, then continues to the foot of Hverfjall. Climb up the crater wall and walk clockwise around the rim (anti-clockwise for a shorter route). The view from the top gives a birds eye perspective on the volcanic features of the area. It is a steep descent down the south-west slope of the crater. At its base an option is to follow the track east to the fissure of Lúdentsborgir and crater Lúdent, 4 miles (6km) away for a longer walk. Otherwise follow the trail and cross the stile to reach Dimmuborgir. Walk through the lava formations. Just past the

and up a steep hill. The embankment to either side of the road is a good place to look for volcanic bombs. At the top of the hill bear right and follow the road for a short way to the parking area by the crater **Víti**. Meaning 'hell', Víti was formed in a short and explosive eruption in

'keyhole', the trail divides. Turn left and complete the hike with a circular walk to the car park, via the 'church'. Turning right takes you straight to the car park. From here you can walk along the road to the lake shore and back to the village, a further 4 miles (6km).

## ↑2 VINDBELGJARFJALL (1.5-2 HOURS UP AND DOWN)

The rhyolite mountain on the west side of the lake rises 820ft (250m) above the surrounding land and it's a long hard slog to the top. It is worth it for the incredible view of the whole lake, and of the ponds where many of the ducks nest.

## ↑3 REYKJAHLÍÐ-KRAFLA (3-4 HOURS ONE WAY)

The trail starts from the campsite by the airport and heads over the 1724-29 lava to Hlíðarfjall. There is more lava to cross to reach the foot of Leirhnjúkur and the new lava and craters from 1975-84.

## ↑4 REYKJAHLÍÐ-HLÍÐARFJALL (3-4 HOURS CIRCULAR WALK)

The same route as above but climbing the summit of Hlíðarfjall for a fine view. The circular walk continues to Brunaborgir, craters from 1724-29 and ends by the swimming pool in the village.

### EASY SHORT WALKS

**Skútustaðir** $-1\frac{1}{2}$ hours around the small lake and through the pseudocraters.

**The lake shore at Reykjahlíð** – the trail starts from Hotel Reynihlíð and leads west along the lake shore.

**The moraines behind Reykjahlíð** – a trail leads from the campsite to the swimming pool over the moraines left by retreating Ice Age glaciers. There is a good view from the summit of the moraines.

1724, which marked the onset of the notorious Mývatn fires. Unlike other craters where the eruptive material builds up around the vent, such craters, known as maars, create a hole blasted out of the ground. Where it lies deeper than the groundwater table, a lake is formed.

On a clear day, the water is a stunning shade of cobalt blue and the walk around the crater rim, taking around 45 minutes, lets you appreciate its beauty from all angles.

**Continued on page 141…**

## Vopnafjörður

### Burstafell Turf Farm Museum
☎ 473 1466
Open: 10am-6pm, daily 17 June-15 September.

### Angling
The region has some of the best salmon and trout fishing in Iceland.
River Hofsá ☎ 473 1508, Heiðarvötn Lakes ☎ 473 1124,
River Selá ☎ 473 3752, River Vesturdalsá ☎ 473 1475.

## Raufarhöfn

### Arctic Circle Boat Trips, Kayaking & Fishing
☎ 465 1233, Fax 465 1383

## Lake Mývatn

### Reykjahlíð
Hlíð Campsite, Cabins & Bike Hire
☎ 464 4103, Fax 464 4305
Main campsite, with laundry, information office, hot tub and free
showers.

### Cowshed Café Vogagjós
vogar, ☎ 464 4303
Camping and guesthouse. Open daily in summer. Milking times 7-8am
and 5.30-7pm

Dimmuborgir lava formations; 'The Church'; Lake Mývatn

Viti explsion crater 1724 eruption 'Mývatn Fires'

## Elda Travel Service
Bjarg, ☎ 464 4220, e-mail info@elda.is, www.elda.is
Excursions in the Mývatn area, boat and bike hire, campsit and guesthouse

## Sightseeing flights
Mýflug
☎ 464 4400, Fax 464 4341, myflug@mmedia.is   www.myflug.is

## Snowmobiling and other winter activities
Hotel Reynihlíð (Reykjahlíð) ☎ 464 4170, www.reynihlid.is.
Hotel Sel (skútustaðir) ☎ 464 4164, www.myvatn.is

## Askja Tours
☎ 464 4196, Fax 464 4380, myvatntours@isholf.is
www.isholf.is/myvatntours
Guided tour to Herðubreið and Askja. Day trip or stay overnight at the
hut or camp and take next day bus.

## Kverkfjöll & Askja Trips with SBA
☎ 550 0700,  sba@sba.is  www.sba.is
3-day trip to the uninhabited interior, departing Mondays and Fridays,
July and August, from Akureyri, Húsavík and Mývatn.

## Lake Mývatn Conservation Area Visitor Centre
☎ 464 4390, Fax 464 4378
Interesting natural history and geology exhibition and Information
Bureau. By the swimming pool. Open: 9am-10pm, daily 1 June-
31 August.

Continued over page...

Continued...

## Húsavík & Surrounds

### Húsavík Whale Centre
☎ 464 2520, abbi@icewhale.husavik.com   www.icewhale.is
One of the best museums in Iceland, also an information bureau.
Open: 9am-9pm, daily 15 June-15 August; 9am-6pm daily 1-14 June
and 16 August-1 September. By arrangement outside these times.

### Whale watching and boat trips to Lundey Island
(see FactFile).

### Húsavík Museum
☎ 464 1860
Open: 10am-6pm, daily in summer, or by arrangement.

### Fjallasýn Excursions
☎ 464 3940, fjallasyn@fjallasyn.is   www.fjallasyn.is
Jeep trips to Askja, Kverkfjöll and the wilderness surrounds of Mývatn
and Húsavík.

### Grenjaðastaður Turf Farm Museum
☎ 464 3688
Located on Route 856 south of Húsavík. Open: 10am-6pm, daily
June-August.

## Tjörnes Peninsula,
## Ásbyrgi and Jökulsá Canyon

### Ásbyrgi Shop, Café and Service Station
On Route 85. The only service for visitors in the vicinity of the
National Park.

### Jökulsá Canyon National Park Information Centre & Campsite
At Ásbyrgi, ☎ 465 2195
Among the best equipped campsites in Iceland with laundry and
drying cupboard. Open: 1 June-15 September.
A second campsite and information centre in Vesturdalur closes
31 August.

### Hallbjarnastaðir Fossil Museum
☎ 464 1968
Marine fossils collection located on Route 85, 9 miles (14km) north of
Húsavík. Open: 9am-8pm daily, 1 June-15 September.

### Þórshamar Folk Museum
☎ 464 1957
A fascinating private collection of local memorabilia at Mánarbakki, on
Route 85, 15 miles (24km) north of Húsavík.

# Leirhnjúkur

In the distance, the beige-brown clay mountain of **Leirhnjúkur** is reached after a 20-minute walk from the parking area back along the approach road. About half way along the path, the land dips abruptly just before you reach the first lava. This was the result of subsidence during the 1975-84 eruptions and the surface cracks formed at the time are clearly visible as gaping holes in the ground. Leirhnjúkur itself was formed under ice but on its south side are craters that produced much of the lava from 1724-29. Running north of the mountain is the 5-mile (8km) long fissure, **Gjástykki**, from which the more recent lavas flowed. The following walk through the area takes about two hours at a leisurely pace. The trail leads past the sulphur-encrusted flank of the mountain to a sizzling, stench-laden bowl of mud pools and steam vents that could be anyone's vision of hell. Special care is needed here and stepping off the path and brown clay areas carries the risk of breaking through the thin crust and getting badly burned.

Above the mud pools, the path splits. Head over the tortured black lava, following the trail of mud left by others' hiking boots, to the foot of the crater in the distance. This crater dates from the 1724-29 eruptions but opened up again in the more recent ones, ejecting a river of viscous iron-laden lava, tinged red by oxidation. With care it is possible to follow the lava river and climb to the crater rim. Here you can sit on ground warmed by steam rising through the lava and enjoy an awe-inspiring view over the sea of basalt. Scramble down the other side of the crater to a gaping circular vent,

complete with stalactite-like drips, which was formed by rapid escape of gas. From here head over an indistinct path through the lava to the fissure, which is easily identified by the steam rising along its entire length. The path follows the fissure, along which are dotted numerous small craters and patches of brilliant yellow sulphur deposits. Back at the foot of Leirhnjúkur is the largest of the new craters, which in 1981 erupted much of the lava you have walked over.

It is worth climbing Leirhnjúkur and looking at some of the older craters as well as enjoying a last view down the full length of the fissure. From here a trail descends to loop around the southern side of the mountain and join the path back to the car park. The marked trail to Reykjahlíð takes off before reaching the main path.

# Námaskarð

This is the name popularly given to Iceland's best known area of mud pools, which is more correctly known as **Hverarönd**. Situated 4 miles (6km) east of the lake behind the pastel-shaded mountain **Náma-fjall**, it can be reached by car, on the official coach excursion, by bike or on foot, following Route 1. Anyone walking there can first climb Námafjall for a wonderful view of the pools from above and then walk down a marked trail to the site itself.

The mud pools cover an area of several acres and it takes about an hour to see them. You can walk among the pools here, but for visitors' safety, the pools themselves have been roped off. In broadest terms, the brown clay areas are safe

## Mud pools

Mud pools are a bit like a primitive chemical plant. The steam and water, percolating upwards through porous rock to the surface, contain dissolved chemicals and gases, mainly hydrogen sulphide and carbon dioxide. When they react with oxygen in the air, mineral deposits, like sulphur and gypsum, are formed. Iron sulphide, commonly called pyrite, forms in the mud pools, giving them a dull blue-black hue. Also present is sulphuric acid, which breaks down the surrounding soil and rocks, forming the sticky clay mud. The red and rust-brown clay is tinged by iron oxide.

Mud pools at Leirhnúkur Krafla

to tread on but avoid the buff, white, red or yellow patches. The most active mud pools are those with a crater rim around them, formed from the spatter caused by escaping gas bubbles. The pools are not static but evolve over a period of time, with new pools starting up and old ones dying out as the years pass.

## FROM MÝVATN TO HÚSAVÍK

This barren stretch of road was built to transport the diatomite to Húsavík for export. In few other parts of Iceland has soil erosion been so devastating and final as here. Yet, where the land has been fenced off from grazing and sown with seed, miraculously it is green again. Coming down from the windswept plateau past a small lake, a road takes off to **Laxárdalur** and a small hydro-electric power station, dating from 1938, which can be visited if arranged in advance. Close by is the old turfed parsonage at **Grenjaðar-staður**, now a museum. There are two pleasant country guesthouses in the area, **Rauðaskriða**, on the banks

Above: Krafla eruption site 1975-84, sulphur deposites on new lava
Below: Whale watching – humpbacks

of the Skjálfandafljót and **Hraunbæ** by the Laxá River. Either would make a good base for a few days. North of here the 39 sq mile (100 sq km) **Aðaldalshraun** lava, which flowed down the Laxá valley from Mývatn, occupies most of the plain. Birch thickets thrive in the lava, concealing often hazardous fissures. In 1946 a local farmer went missing and was found alive after two days, having fallen into a 25ft (7m) deep chasm.

With a population of 2,500, **Húsavík** has the feel of a town about it that is lacking in so many of Iceland's coastal settlements. Its setting, overlooking **Skjálfandi Bay** to the uninhabited peninsula of **Fjörður** and snowcapped **Viknarfjöll**, is to many visitors, the most dramatic of any town in Iceland. Húsavík means 'Bay of Houses', and it lays claim to being the oldest place name

## Whale watching

**N**orður Sigling (North Sailing) offer whale watching trips on beautifully restored fishing vessels with ample deck space for viewing. The whale watching focuses on **Skjálfandi Bay**, where minke whales, white-beaked dolphins and harbour porpoises are regularly seen. Occasionally, larger cetaceans like humpback, sei, fin and blue whales arrive on fishing forays, if the pickings in the bay are particularly good. Over 95 per cent of trips encounter one or more of the above species. Sightings of minke whales can be particularly memorable because they often approach very close. Some, are as curious about us as we are about them, sometimes lifting their heads out of the water for a better look. At other times they swim around and under the boat providing wonderful photographic opportunities. In early summer, evening trips are run, so you can go whale watching under the midnight sun.

in Iceland, bestowed by Viking Garðar Svavarsson, who spent a winter here some years before the permanent settlement began. Now a busy commercial and fishing port and a service hub for the outlying districts, it has also gained a reputation as a superb whale watching destination.

Anyone who goes whale watching should also visit Húsavík's fascinating **Whale Museum**, located down by the port. The first of its kind in Iceland, the award-winning museum has interpretive displays on the cetacean species found around Iceland, several whale skeletons and a library and video collection. One of the warehouses below the museum is used for curing shark by the traditional method of hanging in the open air. You will probably be guided by the smell as the meat is allowed to rot naturally, before being eaten.

Húsavík has a hotel, a pleasant guesthouse in an old timber building and a campsite. Its **local history museum** is worth a visit and has the dubious glory of housing a stuffed polar bear, which was shot on the island of Grímsey in 1969, after

drifting over from Greenland on pack ice. By far the most striking feature of the town is its church. Built in 1907, when the town's inhabitants numbered 500, the church was among the largest in the country, seating 450 people. A light on the tower guides boats to port, while the large windows at the rear look out to sea, so that the locals could watch the boats return and offer up prayers in times of bad weather. The painting behind the altar is of Lazarus. The work of a local artist, it was considered quite controversial at the time because the scenery of the Jökulsá Canyon forms the backdrop to the painting and its figures were modeled on local people.

There are pleasant walks in the area around Húsavík. The mountain behind the town offers an impressive view of its surrounds while along the cliffs, wooden racks that are still used to dry fish, can be seen. Sea angling and bird watching trips to the island of **Lundey**, which means 'Puffin Island', operate from the harbour and boats are also available to take walkers across the bay to the uninhabited Fjörður peninsula.

Bus services link the town with Mývatn, Akureyri, Ásbyrgi, the Jökulsá Canyon and the north-east coastal towns between Raufarhöfn and Egilsstaðir.

# AROUND TJÖRNES

The road around the peninsula ranks among the most scenic coastal drives in Iceland and there are several worthwhile detours and stops to be made. The first is the track by the farm Ytritunga. Shell fossils are exposed in the cliff face along the road that leads down a steep slope to the jetty. You can park at the top and walk down. The fossils are known as the **Tjörnes layers** and are embedded in marine sediments, which alternate with river, glacier and lake deposits and bands of lava and ash. The oldest layers date from three to three and a half million years ago, before the onset of the Ice Age. Some of the fossils are of a type of shell that can only survive in water temperatures between four and six degrees warmer than found around Iceland at present. What has fascinated geologists is the clear evidence of climatic upheaval showing at least ten warm phases, or inter-glacial periods, alternating with colder spells during the Ice Age. And if further proof is needed, the lignite beds are of tree species like beech and oak, which no longer grow in Iceland.

On the beach below the fossil layers, there is a large chunk of dark green soapstone. It is the only example in Iceland of this rock, which however is common in Greenland, and must therefore have floated over on drift ice at some stage.

Several offshore islands can be seen along the route. Low-lying **Flatey** once supported a community of 120 fisherfolk and farmers but its isolation and periodic earthquakes have now left it deserted. Curiously, **Grímsey**, which is 25 miles (40km) out to sea, is still inhabited and can be seen from the coast on a clear day. **Mánáreyjar**, a couple of miles offshore, were formed during submarine eruptions.

**Mánárbakki**, the farm at the tip of the peninsula, has a cluster of masts on its land, which are part of an ongoing Japanese research project into the northern lights. As **Öxarfjörður Bay** comes into view, the road follows the cliff top where puffins nest between late May and early August. A few miles further along, you can draw off the road and walk to a viewpoint over the estuary of the Jökulsá á Fjöllum. The black sand beach is littered with driftwood mostly from Siberia, where logs are floated down the rivers. An ancient law gives the farmer on whose land they wash up, the rights to collect the driftwood

Trout and salmon farming are big business in this area. The enclosures where the young fish are raised are parked in the small lakes that can be seen as you drive down the long hill to the plain. The farm of **Keldunes** was birthplace of eighteenth century sheriff Skúli Magnússon, the first Icelander to be given an office of importance under the Danish administration. He fought for free trade and was instrumental in getting the Danes to revoke their trade monopoly and economic stranglehold on the nation. The statue of an eagle at Keldunes was erected to commemorate Skúli because it was said that on the day he was born, an eagle was seen at the farm.

The community centre **Skúlag-arður** offers accommodation, meals and camping, while nearby **Hóll** farm does horse riding and accommodation. Just north of the farm is a substantial lake, called **Skjálftavatn**, meaning 'Trembling Lake', which was formed by the land sinking during the Krafla eruptions of 1975-84. A few hundred yards beyond the farm, there are gaping fissures to either side of the road, which opened up during the tectonic upheaval. Further on, Route 862 to Dettifoss and the Jökulsá Canyon National Park takes off, following the west bank of the river.

# JÖKULSÁ CANYON NATIONAL PARK

The National Park headquarters are at the campsite at **Ásbyrgi**, at the entrance to the huge horseshoe-shaped gorge, which lies west of the Jökulsá Canyon, where the river spills out on to its floodplain. Legend has it that Odin's eight-legged horse Sleipnir, while roaming the skies, touched down with one hoof and marked the spot. Geologists are unconvinced and suggest that it formed during cataclysmic flooding, the result of volcanic activity under Vatnajökull after the end of the Ice Age.

There are clear signs that an enormously powerful river has at some stage flowed through the gorge, yet today it is completely dry. At its head, where a spectacular waterfall may once have been, a trickle of water flows over 328ft (100m) high cliffs, which shelter a delightful area of woodland. Here, birch, willow and rowan trees achieve quite respectable heights while wood cranesbill and bilberry shrubs carpet the forest floor. Since 1970 a colony of fulmars has been nesting on the gorge's cliffs and in the pond below the waterfall there are tame wigeon. Several easy walking trails lead from the car park to a natural spring, the lake and a viewpoint. There is also another campsite here, though with only cold water.

The main campsite, among the best equipped in Iceland, has hot showers, a washing machine and drying cupboards, which are good news

## • Ásbyrgi walking trails •

### THE HEAD OF THE GORGE (2 HOURS EACH WAY)

From the main campsite walk across the floor of the gorge to the base of the east wall. A fixed rope helps you scramble up to follow the cliff-edge trail to the head of the gorge, for some awe-inspiring views. To avoid the rope, walk to the shop and take the longer trail that links up with the other at the top of the rope.

### EYJAN (40 MINUTES EACH WAY)

From the warden's office a trail leads to Eyjan, 'The Island' and heads south to the top of the wall for a view up the gorge.

146

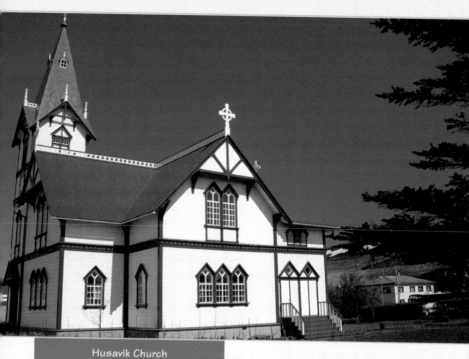

Husavik Church

for wet hikers, cyclists and campers. A shop and fuel station are located back on the main road, a 15-minute walk from the campsite. Two walking trails start from the campsite.

The **Jökulsá Canyon National Park** protects the 16-mile (25km) long gorge of the **Jökulsá River**, a mighty glacial torrent, which has its source on the northern edge of Vatnajökull. The star attractions of the park are its waterfalls, still cutting back and lengthening the gorge to this day. The largest, **Dettifoss**, is 150ft (45m) high; just downstream is **Hafragilsfoss**, smaller but in some ways every bit as impressive, while upstream lies horseshoe-shaped **Selfoss**, just 33ft (10m) high. Dettifoss, though far from being the highest in Iceland, is undisputedly the country's most impressive fall, and may even deserve the title of Europe's most powerful waterfall.

The gorge is densely wooded in places and supports an interesting flora including several orchids, serrated wintergreen, the rare herb paris and fungi, including the edible *Boletus scaber*. In late summer it is a popular spot for gathering edible berries, especially delicious bilberries. These are a preferred food for ptarmigan that abound in the park, which is also one of the best places in Iceland to see the gyrfalcon.

## Exploring the National Park

The park and campsites are officially open from 15 June to 1st September. The road along the west bank is closed before 15 June though may be open into September. East of the river, the road may open earlier, allowing access to the waterfalls.

Many of the interesting features of the park can be accessed by vehicle. In a day, you could fit in Dettifoss, Hólmátungur, Vesturdalur and Hljóðaklettar with short walks from

147

# • Hiking the Jökulsá Canyon Trail •

This well-marked and signposted hiking trail runs between Dettifoss and Ásbyrgi, along the west bank of the river. It can be walked in one very long 11-hour day, but to spend time looking at the canyon's features, you will need two days. It makes little difference whether you start the trail at Dettifoss or Ásbyrgi as the gradient is very gentle throughout, but wind direction should be your deciding factor. As camping is only allowed at designated sites, you will need to overnight at **Vesturdalur**. There is no shop there so carry food for two days as well as your tent.

Starting at Ásbyrgi, walk along the eastern rim of the gorge to its head. Then continue over the smooth rocks of the old riverbed until you meet the present course of the Jökulsá. Head for the red craters in the distance, from where you descend through Hljóðaklettar to the campsite at Vesturdalur (4-5 hours).

The second day is longer and more challenging. Walk past the rock pinnacles Karl and Kerling, 'Troll and Trollwife'. Take a detour to the cliff at Kallbjörg and cave Gloppa, where you can scramble through a natural rock arch and descend to the river Hólmá (the official route by-passes this excitement). Follow the river along to the waterfall and Katlar before reaching the car park. Continue high above the river to a spectacular view of the deepest part of the canyon. Just before you get to Hafragil, the path splits. The longer route, for those wishing to avoid the rope, is a rather tedious walk around the gully. The shorter route descends rapidly into Hafragil. Beyond the gully you contour round a scree slope and boulder field to reach the waterfall Hafragilsfoss. Continue at the same level until you reach the next gully where the path begins to climb. The last part is a scramble up, using a fixed rope for support. Walk over the plateau until you hit the river again and Dettifoss comes into view. (6-7 hours).

each area, but two days would allow you to walk the entire length of the canyon and see all the these places and much more. A daily summer bus service goes from Húsavík to Ásbyrgi, Vesturdalur, Hólmatungur, Dettifoss, Krafla and Mývatn, returning along the same route later in the day. It only allows a short stop at each place but is useful as transport to and from the start and end of the two-day hike down the canyon. Alternatively, an escorted day tour from Lake Mývatn covers the major sights, but leaves little time to explore.

## The waterfalls

**Dettifoss** can be viewed from the west or the east bank of the river. From the east bank car park it is a 10-minute walk to the falls and there is a good view down the canyon along the way. The west bank gets most of the spray off the falls, so photography can be trickier, but it is much greener on this side and some say the view is better. It takes 25 minutes to the falls from the car park. To reach **Selfoss**, follow the river upstream for about 30 minutes from either bank.

**Hafragilsfoss** is most easily seen by taking the signposted track just north of Dettifoss on the east bank. It is a few minutes' walk from the car park to the viewpoint but you cannot get down to the falls from here. To do this you must approach from the west bank, following the trail along the side of the canyon from Dettifoss, taking about an hour. This walk involves a rope-assisted descent, just an easy scramble, though not recommended for anyone with vertigo. You can also drive to a car park above Hafragilsfoss and go down from there, again using a rope. Once down in the canyon, the waterfall is stunning and for many people, more beautiful than Dettifoss. North of the falls a gully cuts into the wall of the canyon. At its base, fresh water seeps through the lava, forming a cobalt-blue pool, which contrasts with the muddy water of the river. This is the deepest, most rugged and spectacular part of the canyon, where the river has cut through a crater row, exposing a feeder dyke in the gorge wall.

# The central canyon

**Hólmatungur**, the central section of the canyon is reached by a signposted detour off the road on the west side of the river. Numerous streams emerge from under the lava, among them the energetic Hólmá, which tumbles down the hillside in a series of foaming rapids, called **Hólmarfossar**. From the car park a track leads down towards the river. Where it crosses the first stream, a trail takes off to the left leading to the waterfall.

Continuing on the main path, another trail takes off to the right and descends through the woods to the narrowest part of the Jökulsá River, called **Katlar**. Here the river has abandoned its original course over a small waterfall and is busy carving a new channel through a shallow gorge. The swirling, murky water looks threatening as it hurtles through the channel. Sensibly, rope barriers have been erected where the river is undercutting the cliff.

**Vesturdalur** is a grassy valley, edged by cliffs, and an offshoot of the main canyon. There is a National Park warden and information office on the site as well as a campsite, with basic facilities, though a beautiful location. The real attraction here are **Hljóðaklettar**, the 'Echo Cliffs'. Several thousand years ago, a violent fissure eruption produced a crater row along the bed of the Jökulsá. Then, when the river flooded, the loose material surrounding the volcanic vents was washed away, leaving behind the plugs. The chaotic jumble of caves and columnar formations at Hljóðaklettar suggest complex forces at work during the cooling phase.

A 20-minute walk from the car park leads to a circular trail through the formations. You could walk the trail in 30 minutes, but that would leave little time to appreciate the supernatural feel of the place. If you have time, walk on further up the hill to the summit of **Rauðhólar**, 'Red Hills', which are part of the same crater row, but still intact. There's a wonderful view from the top and the red and black ash stands out against the lush green vegetation on the other side of the river, providing an excuse for yet more photographs.

# 6 The North of Iceland

*I*n this region, some of the most blood-curdling events in Iceland's history were played out against a backdrop of dramatic scenery. At its heart, and enjoying a better than average sunshine record, is the town of Akureyri. Those with time to explore away from the Ring Road will discover a wild coastline of columnar basalt cliffs, sandy spits and sheltered fjords where villages sit snugly at the base of forbidding mountain ranges.

## FROM MÝVATN TO AKUREYRI

Leaving the lake, paved Route 1 climbs over open moorland, with good views in clear weather down into the highlands. **Laugar**, is a school and summer hotel, whose main claim to fame is that it has the oldest indoor swimming pool in Iceland, dating from 1925. Nearby **Einarsstaðir** has an attractive church built in 1862. A recent priest, Einar Jónsson, was a renowned faith healer.

**Bárðardalur** is the longest inhabited valley in Iceland, bordered on its eastern side by the huge **Ódáða-hraun** lava desert. Bárðardalur marks the start of the **Sprengisandur mountain route** across central Iceland, which takes off west of the river. East of the river is the trail head for the long-distance path Öskjuvegurinn (see Chapter 9: The Uninhabited Highlands).

**Goðafoss**, the beautiful horseshoe-shaped waterfall on the Skjálfanda-fljót river is one of Iceland's most

### Early milestone

The year 1000 brought waves of unrest to the nation, as Christians sought to break away from the pagan Althing, and form their own assembly. The pagan chieftain Þórgeir of Ljósavatn, a farm near Goðafoss, was Law Speaker at the time. He understood that if a quick solution was not reached, then civil war would be inevitable. In an historic speech he proclaimed that 'if we divide the law, we also divide the peace'. He declared that all should be christened but that some of the pagan practices would still be tolerated, though not in public. To show his commitment to the new law he took the carved images of his gods and cast them into the waterfall Goðafoss.

admired and easily accessed. At this point, the river cuts through lava from the **Trölladyngja** shield volcano, which erupted over 7,000 years ago, sending a flow of molten material 63 miles (100km) north along Bárðardalur. Meaning 'Fall of the Gods', the waterfall's name emerged from a ground-breaking milestone in Iceland's early history.

The scheduled buses make a short stop at the falls but it is worth staying longer if you can and walk down the path following the river to the bridge. There is another small waterfall, along with some impressive rock arches. By the bridge, there is a café, shop, fuel station, post office, bank, craft stall and guesthouse, while there is a summer hotel at **Stóru Tjarnir**, just beyond Ljósavatn.

The landscape changes dramatically as the road enters the steep-sided, wooded valley of Fnjóská-dalur. Now well out of the present day volcanic zone, the mountains and valleys here show all the scars of intense glaciation. Further up the valley lies **Vaglaskógur**, one of the best preserved pockets of relict woodland in the country with 30ft high birch trees. There is a campsite, though it is best avoided on weekends, as it is popular with the locals.

There is a choice of route here. Paved Route 1 heads straight for Eyjafjörður while a jeep track goes over **Vaðlaheiði**, the most direct but roughest route, which used to be the main road. The third, Route 835, which is unsurfaced, continues north up the valley. Before it turns west, there are wonderful views into the uninhabited **Fjörður Peninsula**. Snow lies lower and longer here than in the surrounding areas, which is why these valleys and fjords, though once farmed, are now deserted. The jeep

track F899 leads to the tip of the peninsula, over **Flateyjardalsheiði**, a wonderful area for walking. Horse riding trips, are arranged by Polar Hestar at the farm **Grýtubakki**, but there are no facilities for independent visitors on the peninsula.

The road ends just beyond the fishing village of **Grenivík**, leading to the remote **Látraströnd** coast, which offers possibilities for adventurous hikers. Before the turn off to Grenivík, head south along Eyjafjör-ður to rejoin Route 1. En route you pass the restored nineteenth century parsonage at **Laufás**, which is one of the nicest turf farm museums in Iceland. The church dates from 1865 and contains a valuable seventeenth century pulpit. Behind it, an impressive mountain ash tree lays claim to being the oldest in Iceland, planted by the church's builder on the grave of his father in 1855.

One of the longest and most scenic fjords in Iceland, Eyjafjörður

## Irish forbears

Settlement in the region dates from around 980 when an Irishman, Helgi the Lean arrived with his wife Þórunn Hyrna at the head of the fjord. Here Þórunn gave birth to a baby girl, on an island on the estuary of the Eyjafjarð-ará River. Ancient belief suggests that this gave the parents the right to claim all land from which the river drained on its journey to the sea. In the event, Helgi and Þórunn settled up the valley and named their farm **Kristnes**, because they were Christians.

was etched out by Ice Age glaciers. Its flat-topped mountains, rising to 4,920ft (1,500m) in height, are the highest in the north of the country and are snow-capped all year round. Steep-sided, they offer poor grazing land for sheep, so farming in the region focuses on cattle rearing and, with a warmer summer than other parts of the country, the growing of the staple potato.

# Akureyri

With a population of 15,000, **Akureyri** is Iceland's largest town outside of the Reykjavík area and one of its most pleasant. Its beautiful location near the head of the fjord, pleasant tree-lined streets and reliable sunshine record make it popular with visitors. There is enough to see and do in and around the town to fill two or three days, though Akureyri is often passed over as a base for a stay, in favour of Lake Mývatn. Local travel agencies, Nonni Travel and SBA run guided excursions, and by using scheduled buses, visitors can also reach quite a few places of interest in the outlying areas, including Mývatn.

Akureyri means 'Cornfield Point', showing that there was once a farm on the site but there are no clues as to who lived there until 1562, when trade first began in the area. In 1787, when the Danes revoked their monopoly on trade, the settlement was granted municipal status, though effectively the Danish influence continued. One of the oldest houses in the town, **Laxdalshús**, was built as a merchant's home in 1795 following the Danish tradition, as were many other early buildings. Though still an important commercial hub, the town now thrives on its

manufacturing industries as well as fishing.

The oldest part of town spreads along Aðalstræti following the shore of the fjord towards the airport Aðalstræti 4 was the original pharmacy, a grand building with carved wooden surrounds to its doors and windows. Number 14, the old hospital, is among the oldest two floor buildings in the land. At number 54, stands **Nonnahús**, the childhood home of Jesuit priest Jón Sveinsson (1857-1944), who wrote a series of children's books under the pen name Nonni. Built in 1850, the house is open to the public as a museum and is worth a visit for its insight into the spartan life of most ordinary Icelanders at the time. Further along at number 58 is the **Municipal Museum** and timber church that was moved here in 1970 from its original site across the fjord.

The present town centre revolves around the pedestrian precinct of the northern end of **Hafnarstræti** and the square of **Ráðhústorg**. Here, a number of shops entice visitors with the usual range of knitwear and beautiful, though pricey books on Iceland. There are several nice cafés and bars in the area, though, as in the capital, the night life tends to be a bit slow getting started and many places are empty until midnight. **Kaupvangsstræti** has several galleries and craft shops and **Akureyri's Art Museum**.

Several flights of steps lead from the main street to Akureyri's modern church. Part way up is the home of Reverend Matthías Jochumsson (1835-1920), one of Iceland's greatest poets and writer of the National Anthem. It is open to the public. The church commands an impressive view of the fjord and was completed

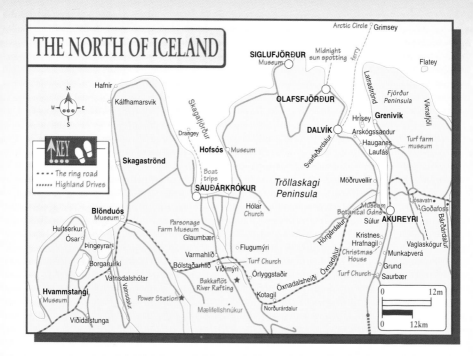

THE NORTH OF ICELAND

KEY
- - - The ring road
..... Highland Drives

in 1940 by the same architect as Hallgrímskirkja in Reykjavík. Inside, the church houses an impressive 3200 pipe organ and beautiful contemporary stained glass windows, which depict scenes from the history of Christianity in Iceland. Of particular interest to visitors from the UK is the central stained glass window behind the altar. Part of a set, destroyed when Coventry Cathedral was bombed during World War II, the surviving stained glass mysteriously found its way to Copenhagen, from where it was purchased by a dealer on behalf of the town of Akureyri.

**Eyrlandsvegur** leads from the church to the Botanical Gardens. This tree-lined street, of brightly painted homes and carefully tended gardens, is typical of the old Akureyri. Just before you reach the grammar school, a statue titled 'The Outlaw' by sculptor Einar Jónsson is worth a stop. There is a look of grim determination, or perhaps resigna-

tion, on the man's face as he carries his dead wife over his shoulder, child in his arms and dog by his side.

It is hard to believe that this is Iceland, such is the profusion of blooms in the town's public park and **Botanical Gardens**. Established in 1912, the gardens consist of imported trees, shrubs and plants, with particularly vibrant stands of delphinium, aquilegia and meconopsis. A section of the gardens is devoted to arctic and Icelandic flora, with examples of most species of flowering plant found on the island, including clumps of lovingly nurtured stinging nettles, docks and dandelions.

Akureyri has a choice of several hotels and guesthouses, a youth hostel and well-equipped campsite. In winter it offers some of the best downhill skiing in Iceland. There are air connections to Reykjavík and Ísaförður and bus services to Reykjavík and Egilsstaðir, via Mývatn and Grímsey.

Above: Akureyri 'The Outlaw'

Below: The school at Akureyri

# EXPLORING FROM AKUREYRI

The uninhabited valleys, precipitous mountains and ice fields of the **Tröllaskagi Peninsula**, separating Eyjafjörður from Skagafjörður to the west, are a tempting prospect for adventurous backpackers. There are traces of old bridle trails but those wishing to explore the area are advised to contact the Touring Club of Akureyri for advice and to book space in any of their huts.

The broad and fertile valley south of Akureyri has several places of his-

## Hiking

**V**aðlaheiði, across the fjord from Akureyri, has a number of marked walking trails, detailed on a map produced by Ferðafélag Akureyrar (Touring Club of Akureyri). The club owns several mountain huts in the region around Akureyri and in the uninhabited interior, and arranges day and weekend hikes, which visiting non-members may join. An easy 8-mile (13km) trail follows the banks of the **Eyjafjarðará River**, starting at the airport and ending at **Hrafnagil**. Around the river estuary the bird life is excellent, with 25-30 species breeding and many others coming to feed there.

The **Glerá Valley** and its gully, behind the town, also has hiking trails and is popularly believed to be inhabited by elves, the 'hidden people'. From the valley, a long slog leads to the 3,978ft (1,213m) summit of **Súlur**.

torical interest. **Hrafnagil** was home to Iceland's last Catholic bishop, Jón Arason and there is now a hotel here, along with the gimmicky, but for children quite enchanting, **Christmas House**, open all year round. South of here, **Grund** was a major estate in Saga times and has an ornate and impressive church, built in 1905 by the farmer. **Saurbær's turf church**, built in 1858 is one of only a handful remaining in the country. On the east bank of the river, **Munkuþverá** was site of a monastery from 1155 until the Reformation in 1550 and was birthplace of Saga hero Killer-Glum. The road continues to the head of the valley, where it turns to dirt, becoming the F821 track, which joins the highland route south over Sprengisandur. **Öngulsstaðir** is a country guesthouse which is well placed for day walks on Vaðlaheiði.

## Grímsey

The island of **Grímsey** lies 25 miles (40km) off Iceland's north coast. On a clear midsummer evening, with its green meadows and black basalt cliffs bathed in the mellow light of the midnight sun, the place is quite idyllic. Bisected by the **Arctic Circle**, it is the only place in Iceland which can truly claim to be arctic. It attracts a fair share of certificate seekers, who fly in with Air Iceland from Akureyri or with Mýflug from Mývatn, stopping for just an hour. An alternative is the ferry that sails twice a week in summer between Dalvík and Grímsey, taking three and a half hours each way, with three hours on the island. The ferry links in with the bus service between Akureyri and Dalvík.

There is a small guesthouse and café by the airstrip on Grímsey, where visitors may also camp. If you have the time, it is worth spending a day there to try and seek out the last few pairs of little auk to breed in Iceland, as well as enjoying the company of hundreds of thousands of puffins, guillemots, kittiwakes and fulmars. Arctic terns also breed on the island, so take a stick to ward them off as they are fiercely defensive of their nesting sites. By holding the stick above your head, the terns will attack it, rather than your scalp.

The 2 sq mile (5 sq km) island has a population of 93, which is remarkable given its isolation. They live from fishing and farming and the village has its own primary school, swimming pool and a small chess library. Hearing of the locals' skills at the game and their lack of resources, an American benefactor, Willard Fiske, donated a sum of money to buy chess sets and books, even though he had never visited the island. Tourist literature on Grímsey lists a filling station as one of the services though there is barely a mile of navigable road.

# Tröllaskagi Peninsula

This 163-mile (261km) loop could be done in a day from Akureyri, taking in the towns of Dalvík, Ólafsfjörður, Siglufjörður and Hofsós, with a detour to the old bishopric at Hólar, and the option of returning to Akureyri, via Öxnadalsheiði or staying in historic Skagafjörður to explore further. The road is paved for much of the way, but by allowing two days, you would cover it at a more relaxed pace and you could include a whale watching trip from Hauganes, or a visit to the island of Hrísey. Stunning fjord scenery, breathtakingly beau-tiful mountains and plenty of cultural and historical sites make this a drive with something for everyone and highly recommended.

Heading north from Akureyri on Route 1, turn off on Route 82 and follow the fjord. **Hauganes** is a small fishing village and starting point for whale watching trips around the island of **Hrísey**. Minke whales, white-beaked dolphins and harbour porpoises are commonly seen on the trips, which can also include sea angling for cod, while humpback whales are occasionally sighted. The next village **Árskógssandur** is the jumping off point for trips over to Hrísey. The ferry takes 20 minutes and runs several times a day between the island and the mainland. Hrísey has a thriving fishing village, abundant sea bird and eider duck colonies and easy walking trails.

# The midnight sun

From early May to late July, there is practically no night in Iceland. But the country is not bathed in perpetual sunshine because, except for the offshore island of Grímsey, it lies south of the Arctic Circle. The midnight sun can be observed from this tiny island and from the north coast of mainland Iceland during late June. Other popular viewing points include Melrakkaslétta, the Tjörnes Peninsula and Olafsfjarðarmúli in Eyjafjörður.

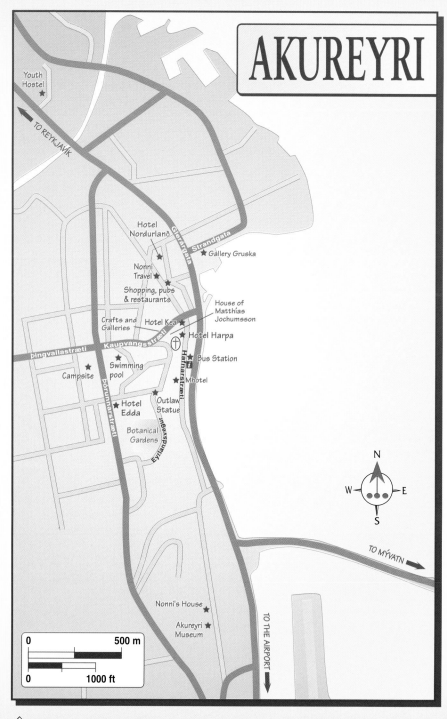

AKUREYRI

Youth Hostel

TO REYKJAVÍK

Hotel Nordurland

Glerárgata

Strandgata

Gallery Gruska

Nonni Travel

Shopping, pubs & restaurants

House of Matthías Jochumsson

Crafts and Galleries

Hotel Kea

Kaupvangsstræti

Hotel Harpa

þingvallastræti

Hafnarstræti

Bus Station

Campsite

Swimming pool

Mhotel

þórunnarstræti

Hotel Edda

Outlaw Statue

Botanical Gardens

Eyrarlandsvegur

N
W        E
S

TO MÝVATN

TO THE AIRPORT

Nonni's House

Akureyri Museum

0 ——— 500 m
0 ——— 1000 ft

Above: Hraun Farm, Öxnadalur

Below: Goðafoss Falls

The road continues to **Dalvík** and the headland before you reach the town is a good place to view the midnight sun. Dalvík's history goes back to settlement times and it has achieved notoriety on several counts. A pernicious ghost named Klaufi plagued the area in the tenth century. Despite exhuming his body and beheading it he continued his violent rampages, only now appearing with his head under his arm. In 1934 the town was rocked by a powerful earthquake, which damaged all the buildings in the area. Lastly, the area was home to the Bakkabræður, characters from Iceland's rich folklore, known for their incredible stupidity.

Today, Dalvík prefers to be known as a prosperous fishing town with a gorgeous outdoor swimming pool, a summer hotel and several guesthouses in the area. Behind the town, the valley of **Svarfaðadalur** is a nature reserve, protecting the breeding grounds of some thirty bird species. Traces of old bridle trails lead over a challenging route to Hólar and might appeal to adventurous backpackers.

The road climbs gradually to **Ólafsfjarðarmúli**. A 2-mile (3.4km) tunnel now bypasses a spine-chilling section of road, which hugged the cliff. The old road is an awesome midnight sun watching spot, with the waves crashing on the rocks at the base of the cliff. **Ólafsfjörður** used to be locked in during winter and with no sun for months on end because of its high mountains, had a chilly feel to it. With a recently refurbished hotel, it is a possible overnight stop for those exploring the **Tröllaskagi Peninsula**. Beyond the village the road turns to gravel, cuts inland and crosses a low pass to reach the coast just south of Siglufjörður.

Until 1946, the town of **Siglufjörður** could only be reached by sea. Then a track was bulldozed over the 1,968ft (600m) pass Siglufjarðarskarð, but was later replaced by the road around the coast. The track to the pass is now a walking route and once up there you can continue along the ridge for some great views.

The town was born of the sixties' herring boom and continued as a major base for the herring fisheries until 1970, when fish stocks abruptly disappeared. Predictably, Siglufjörður has a **Herring Museum**, which recreates the incredible atmosphere of the herring years. The town has a hotel, guesthouse and campsite, and with a population of 1,600, several shops.

Route 76 follows the coast to the delightful village of **Hofsós**, population 197. An eighteenth-century timber warehouse houses the **Skagafjörður Regional Museum**, which has interesting exhibits on the island of **Drangey**, including the techniques used for harvesting sea birds from the cliffs. There is another museum in the village dedicated to the emigration of Icelanders to the New World between 1870 and 1914. The museum traces the factors that led to their departure and the life they shaped for themselves abroad. It also functions as a Genealogy Data Base for descendents of the immigrants. The village has a guesthouse and campsite and a nice café, **Sólvík**.

South of Hofsós the farm **Gröf** was birthplace in 1614 to the celebrated religious poet Hallgrímur Pétursson. A small turf chapel on the site is believed to be the oldest place of worship in the country.

Ten miles (6km) south of Hofsós, Route 767 is signed to **Hólar**. Iceland's northern bishopric was established in 1106 and for almost 700 years served

160

as a focal point for religion, education and culture in the north of the country. In 1798 the seat was abandoned, when the bishopric at Skálholt in the south was moved to Reykjavik. The impressive eighteenth century church still on the site has a separate tower, built in 1950 to mark 400 years since the death of Jón Arason, the last Catholic bishop at Hólar. Of the Lutheran bishops, sixteenth-century Guðbrandur Þórláksson was notable for printing the first Icelandic edition of the bible.

Hólar has something of a holiday camp atmosphere in summer with all sorts of facilities for visitors, including swimming, horse riding, guided walks, exhibitions, as well as accommodation and camping. A challenging backpacking route leads over Heljardalsheiði to Svarfaðadalur and Dalvík.

Back on the main road, the route splits at the **Héraðsvötn Estuary,** where important wetlands are a key breeding ground for whooper swans and other waterfowl. Route 75 follows the coast round to the town of **Sauðárkrókur,** the regional centre for the **Skagafjörður district,** and a town famous for its equestrian events and prowess. There is the usual range of hotel and guesthouse accommodation and a campsite in the town. North of here, the farm at **Reykir** has

## Iceland's Civil War

The thirteenth century brought troubled times to Iceland, which until then had enjoyed centuries of relative peace and prosperity. Under a flawed judicial system and with the church building huge wealth from its tithe, conflicts between church and chieftain became commonplace. To counter the church's power, the common farmer's allegiance was directed at those chieftains influential enough to defend his interests. Slowly but surely, power became concentrated in the hands of six major family clans. Bickering among themselves, they also pandered to King Hákon of Norway. The king was quick to take advantage of this, playing one chieftain off against another until the stage was set for the greatest bloodbath a nation with no national armed force had seen.

**Örlygsstaðir**, just above Route 1, near the farm of **Miklibær** was the site of the battle, which took place on 21August, 1238. Almost 3,000 people, from three family clans were involved. At a decisive moment, those on the losing side took refuge in the church at Miklibær. Threatening to burn the church down, the victors forced them out, slaughtering them as they emerged. All told 110 people were killed. The Haukadalur clan, victors on this occasion were losers on the next, when chieftain Gissur Þórvaldsson lost his entire family in a vicious arson attack on his farm **Flugumýri**, just to the north. Gissur himself escaped the flames by hiding in a barrel of sour whey.

It was Gissur who was eventually branded with the title of traitor, by delivering his country into the hands of the Norwegian King in 1262. By then most of the country was tired of the feuding and an oath of loyalty plus a few taxes seemed a small price to pay for peace.

Grímsey Island, looking towards the mainland

a hot spring, known as **Grettislaug**. It was said that outlaw Grettir thawed out in the hot pool after his epic four mile swim from Drangey.

Sauðárkrókur is the jumping off point for boat trips to **Drangey**, a 558ft (170m) high flat topped island teeming with bird life, which became the last stronghold of the ill-starred hero of Grettir's Saga. He took refuge here with his younger brother to wait out the last year of his outlawry. Grettir was known for his incredible strength and the Saga tells of how, when his fire went out on Drangey, he swam to the mainland to fetch glowing embers. The island's steep cliffs made it easy to defend but Grettir was no match for sorcery. Enlisting the help of a witch, his enemies were able to attack, wound and kill him.

# FROM AKUREYRI TO VARMAHLÍÐ

Leaving Akureyri Route 1, now paved the whole way to Reykjavík, follows the glaciated **Hörgá** and **Öxnadalur** valleys, passing the country hotel at Þelamörk. The next 50 miles (80km) are highly scenic, with uninhabited valleys and majestic mountains that are an invitation to explore for adventurous and well-equipped hikers.

The pretty church at **Bakki**, is typical of churches in Eyjafjörður, in that it has a separate bell tower. As the road begins to climb there is a pull out to the right, where it is worth stopping for a view of the jagged peak known as **Hraundrangi**. Long believed impossible to scale, legend had it that hidden treasure awaited those to first reach the summit of the 3,526ft (1,075m) pinnacle. This was finally achieved in 1956, though the three climbers came down none the richer. The farm of **Hraun**, nestled below the peak, was birthplace of nineteenth century poet Jónas Hallgrímsson. There is evidence here of a huge landslide, where the whole side of the mountain collapsed, blocking the valley and forming the pinnacle Hraundrangi. From the end of the road on the other side of the river, there is a pleasant walk up to a small lake, **Hraunvatn**.

Herds of semi-wild horses graze the upper valley and pass beyond where the road drops to **Norðurádalur**. Just past the first farm, the gorge **Kotagil** is worth exploring. Bands of lignite, including 20-inch (50cm) tree trunks, are exposed in its cliff faces and interesting rock specimens litter the floor of the gorge. With care, you can boulder hop to the head of the gorge, where there is a small waterfall. It takes about an hour there and back from the road.

The broad valley of **Skagafjörður** is excellent farming country and an important breeding area for horses. Many of the most dramatic events of the turbulent thirteenth century, which led to Iceland ceding legislative power to Norway, were played out here. The settlement of **Varmahlíð** has grown up around the hot springs found in the area and its café and fuel station are a popular stopping place for motorists. There are also a hotel, swimming pool, shop, bank and post office on the site, and a craft shop, with attractive ceramic work and paintings.

Just north of Varmahlíð on Route 75, is the turf parsonage of **Glaumbær**, probably the best known of all

Hrísey Island, Eyjafjörður

163

the farm museums. From the early twentieth century many turf farms were abandoned and without proper upkeep, they simply disintegrated. A visiting Englishman, Mark Watson, came to Glaumbær and fearing that it might suffer the same fate, donated a sum of money for its preservation. The farm is now in the hands of the National Museum of Iceland. The buildings date from the eighteenth and nineteenth centuries and contain an impressive collection of memorabilia gathered from all over the region. There is a very nice café, serving wonderful cream pancakes, which is housed in a traditional timber family home, moved to the site in 1977.

One of Iceland's most famous women in history, lived for a time at Glaumbær. Guðríður Þorbjarnardóttir gave birth to the first white man to be born in North America on an eleventh century voyage of discovery to Vinland.

The farm of Viðimýri, near Varmahlíð was the base of the thirteenth century Ásbirningar clan. Its lovely restored turf church is open to visitors. Past the church, Route 752 leads to the farm guesthouse **Bakkaflöt**, which also has a swimming pool and a well equipped campsite, with indoor cooking facilities, which are a real bonus to wet campers. River rafting trips on the nearby Jökulsá Vestari and Jökulsá Austari rivers, as well as canoeing, can be arranged from the farm. Those with the energy can climb 3,732ft (1,138m) **Mælifellshnjúkur**, the highest peak for miles around. The peak's name means 'measuring mountain'. By the amount of snow remaining on it in late spring and early summer, it was said that the farmers could gauge if it was safe

to set off to cross Iceland by the highland routes. The path takes off from the track that lies west of the mountain. Route 752 continues up the valley, turning to the jeep track F752, which joins up with the **Sprengisandur** route, deep in the highlands.

# FROM VARMAHLÍÐ TO BLÖNDUÓS

From Varmahlíð Route 1 crosses **Vatnsskarð**, a low-lying pass. On the way up is a monument to the Icelandic-Canadian poet Stephan G Stephansson, who was born in the area. There is a great view of the midnight sun from here, with the island of Drangey in silhouette. Beyond the pass, the farm of **Bolstaðarhlíð** has an impressive sheep pen, used by farmers during the autumn round-up. Beyond here Route 731 takes off for the **Blandá Hydroelectric Power Station**, which went on stream in 1991. Just beyond the powerhouse, is the start of the F35 mountain route.

Route 1 follows the Blandá river to its mouth and the town of **Blönduós**. It's a fairly ordinary town that has developed as a commercial base for the surrounding communities. For visitors it has the usual range of facilities including a hotel, guesthouse, campsite and an interesting **handicraft museum**.

From Blönduós, a pleasant circular drive can be taken around the **Skagaströnd Peninsula** to the north. The village of the same name is one of Iceland's oldest trading posts. **Hildebrandshús**, built in 1733, is the country's oldest surviving commercial premises. At various times during its history, the village found

## A powerful issue

Iceland's mighty glacial rivers offer enormous potential for hydroelectric power generation. The country has for a number of years been self-sufficient in power, and no electricity is generated from burning fossil fuels. Environ-mentalists in Iceland are therefore questioning why the National Power Company, Landsvirkjun, continues to research and commission massive new schemes, amoung them the controversial Kárahnúkur project in the east, which involve the flooding of sensitive and pristine wilderness areas in the uninhabited central highlands.

The answer lies in part in Iceland's over-dependence on export earnings from fish products. By producing surplus cheap electricity, the government attracts power-hungry industries to set up in the country. Selling energy could generate important revenue and Landsvirkjun are quick to point out that they have funded land reclamation studies. However many Icelanders are deeply disturbed by what they see as wanton and irreversible destruction of their country's natural heritage.

itself the attention of English, Danish, Dutch and Hanseatic merchants, whose business was not always peaceful trade. North of the village at **Kalfhamarsvík**, there are impressive columnar basalt cliffs and the remains of a fishing settlement abandoned in 1940, while at **Hafnir**, on the tip of the peninsula, is a seal colony. The land is flatter here and dotted with small lakes which support abundant bird life.

## HÚNAVATN AND VATNSNES

**Húnavatn** is the name given to the district of north-western Iceland bordering **Húnaflói Bay**. Typical of the landscape are valleys bordered by ridges of low hills, and though less dramatic than other parts of the country, the scenery is still pleasing to the eye. Ample low-lying land but rather few safe anchorages, mean that farming, rather than fishing is the main economic activity. Many of the region's rivers are rich in salmon, providing excellent, though costly, recreational fishing.

South of Blönduós, lies the fertile valley of **Vatnsdalur**, where the family chronicle Vatnsdaela Saga, took place. Less well known than some of the other sagas, the story follows the fortunes of the dynasty founded by the patriarch Ingimundur the Old. It is hard to imagine the blood-letting and violent feuding that took place, so green and peaceful is the valley today. Those familiar with the saga may head up the valley to **Hof**, the family farmstead where the murder of Ingimundur by a quarrelsome nearby farmer took place.

The mouth of the valley is studded with many hundreds, if not thousands of cone-shaped hillocks, known as Vatnsdalshólar. They were formed when the waterlogged mountain above collapsed at the end of the Ice Age, sending down a huge

*Continued on page 169...*

165

## Grenivík

### Fjörðungar
☎ 463 3236,  joning@nett.is www vip.is/fjordungar
4 day hiking trips from Grenivík to the uninhabited Fjörður Peninsula, using pack horses to help carry the luggage.

### Laufás Turf Farm Museum
☎ 463 3106
Attractions & Activities, dating from 1840, located on Route 83.
Open: 10am-6pm,
daily 1 June-15 September.

## Eyjafjarðará Valley

### Christmas House & Garden
☎ 463 1433
At Hrafnagil on Route 821,
5 miles (8km) south of Akureyri
Open: 10am-10pm, June-August;
2-10pm September-December;
2-6pm January-May; daily.

## Hrísey Island

### Hrísey Ferry Sævar
☎ 466 3544, eyfar@eyfar.is
Sailings depart all year from Árskógssandur every two hours 9.30am-9.30pm and from Hrísey every two hours 9am-9pm.
Additional sailings in summer.

### Whale Watching
Whale watching around Hrísey.

## Akureyri

### Tourist Information
☎ 462 7733
info@eyjafjordur.is
www.eyjafjordur.is
At the Bus Station,
Hafnarstræti 82.

### Akureyri Church
Open: daily 10-12am and 2-5pm.
Services 11am Sundays.

Whale watching, Eyjafjörður

Vidimyri Turf Church, Skagafjörður

## Sigurhæðir – Reverend Matthías Jochumsson's House
Eyrlandsvegur 3
(entry from Church steps)
Open: 2-4pm, daily,
15 June-1 September

## Nonni's House
Aðalstræti 54, ☎ 462 3555
Childhood home of children's author Jón Sveinsson.
Open: 10am-5pm daily
1 June-1 September.

## Akureyri Municipal Museum
Aðalstræti 58, ☎ 462 4162
Open: 11am-5pm daily 19 June-15 September; 2-4pm Sundays 16 September-31 May.

## Botanical Gardens
Eyrlandsvegur
Open: 8am-10pm weekdays,
9am-10pm weekends,
1 June-31 October.

## Skiing at Hlíðarfjall
☎ 462 2280  www.hlidarfjall.is
Lifts and groomed slopes
4 miles (6km) from Akureyri.

## Golf

**Akureyri Golf Club & Arctic Open Championship**
☎ 462 2974, Fax 461 1755
gagolf@nett.is
The most northerly 18-hole golf course in the world.

## Tours from Akureyri

**Nonni Travel**
Brekkugata 3, ☎ 461 1841
nonni@nonnitravel.is
www.nonnitravel.is
Guided tours, boat trips, horse riding.

**Sport Tours**
82 Hafnarstræti ☎ 461 2968
email: sporttours@sporttours.is
www.sporttours.is
Super Jeep and Activity Tours

**Akureyri Bus Terminal**
Hafnarstræti 82, ☎ 550 0700
www.sba.is
Guided tours to Mývatn,
Skagafjörður and Kverkfjöll.

## Art and Craft Galleries

There are several in Kaupvangsstræti and Galleri Gruska on Strandgata.

*Continued over page...*

# Places to Visit
# NORTH REGION

## Grímsey

**Ferry to Grímsey**
Sæfari sails Monday, wednesday and Friday at 8am from Dalvík to Grímsey and back the same day, with a connecting bus from and to Akureyri. The journey takes 3.5 hours and allows a three hour stop on the island. Book through nonni Travel ☎ 461 1841 www.nonnitravel.is

**Flights to Grímsey**
With Air Iceland from Akureyri Airport www.airiceland.is, daily or with Mýflug from Mývatn www.myflug.is.

## Siglufjörður

**Herring Era Museum**
☎ 467 1604, Fax 467 1888 herring@siglo.is, www.siglo.is/herring
Herring salting, music and dancing on Saturday July to early August.
Open: 10am-6pm daily 20 June-15 August and 1-5pm in spring and autumn.

## Hofsós

**Skagafjörður Regional Museum**
☎ 453 7935
Housed in an eighteenth century Danish warehouse. Open: 11am-6pm, daily 10 June-10 September.

**The Icelandic Emigration Museum**
☎ 453 7935, Fax 453 7936 hofsos@hofsos.is
www.hofsos.is
Of special interest to descendents of Icelanders who emigrated. Genealogy and information service. Open: 11am-6pm, daily 10 June-10 September (office open all year round).

**Hólar Travel Service**
☎ 455 6333 tourist@holar.is
Summer accommodation, cabins, camping, horse riding and other activities, based at the former bishopric of Hólar, on Route 767.

## Sauðárkrókur

**Sauðárkrókur Folk Museum**
In Aðalgata, ☎ 453 6870
Open: 2-6pm daily, June-August.

**Drangey & Malmey Boat trips**
☎ 453 8245/855 5000
www.skagafjordur.com/eyjaskip

## Varmahlíð and surrounds

**Ash Ceramics**
☎ 453 8031
Pottery, paintings and crafts.

**Glaumbær Folk Museum**
☎ 453 6173
Located 4 miles (7km) north of Varmahlíð on Route 75. Fascinating collection of memorabilia in a well-preserved turf parsonage. Open: 9am-6pm, daily 1 June-20 September, or by arrangement.

**Víðimðri Turf Church**
☎ 453 8167/453 6173
One of few remaining in Iceland, located just off Route 1, 0.5 mile (1km) south of Varmahlíð.
Open: 9am-6pm, daily 1 June-31 August, or by arrangement.

**River Rafting**
see FactFile

## Blönduós and surrounds

**Blönduós Handicraft Museum**
☎ 452 4067
Open: 2-5pm, weekdays, 20 June-20 August or by arrangement.

landslide. To the north of the main road is a monument marking the site of the last public execution in Iceland, which took place on January 12, 1830. The block and axe used are now in the National Museum in Reykjavík.

Four miles (6km) north of here, Iceland's first monastery was built in 1112 at Þingeyrar, which became an important educational and cultural hub prior to the Reformation. It is believed, though there is no conclusive proof, that many of the Icelandic Sagas may have been written there. The present church, a sober and imposing edifice, was built of local stone, transported by sledge across the frozen **Lake Hóp**.

A short detour south of Route 1 is the church and farm of **Viðidalstunga**, where the priceless Flateyjarbók manuscript was written in the year 1400. Bishop Brynjólfur Sveinsson later made a gift of the book to the Danish King. It remained in the royal library until it was brought back to Iceland in 1971, an important event which paved the way for many other national treasures to be returned. South of the farm, the river Viðidalsá plunges over two waterfalls into a mile long gorge, **Kolugljúfur**. There are several guesthouses in the area, at Kolugil, Dæli and Viðigerði.

North of Route 1, Routes 716 and 717 lead to a puzzling feature called **Borgarvirki**, just east of Vesturhópsvatn. Meaning 'Fortress', Borgarvirki is a columnar basalt rock formation standing 30-50ft (10-16m) above the surrounding land. Inside it is a depression containing the remains of some huts, while stone walls line the top of the basalt cliffs. No one really knows who made the fortress, if indeed it was such, nor why.

Continuing on the same road brings you to **Hvítserkur**, on the west shore of **Húnafjörður** and east side of the **Vatnsnes Peninsula**. This curious 50ft (15m) high rock stack is the remains of a volcanic dyke, eroded by wave action. Local folklore claims that a troll intent on bombarding the monastery of Þingeyrar with rocks, was distracted and turned to stone by the rays of the sun. From one angle, it looks more like a musk ox, or overladen packhorse. There is a nice youth hostel at nearby **Ósar** overlooking a river estuary where hundreds of seals have but to breed. At the tip of Vatnsnes at a place called **Hindisvík**, is one of Iceland's largest seal colonies. On the same side of the peninsula is the town of **Hvammstangi**, with a museum dedicated to trade. South of the ring road stands the farm of **Bjarg**, where Grettir of saga fame was born. A jeep track, the F578, starts further up the valley and leads across **Arnavatnsheiði,** whose many thousands of tiny lakes and ponds are an angler's dream.

169

Opposite: Mount Esja

*T*he west of Iceland may not boast Iceland's most dramatic scenery but its landscapes are steeped in the history and drama of the sagas and the mystique and legend of the island's rich folklore. Pristine salmon fishing rivers, fertile valleys, the country's highest waterfall and largest lava caves and hot springs are some of the highlights. The Snæfellsnes Peninsula has a lure of its own and in some respects is a microcosm of the whole island. Its landscapes are extraordinarily varied and it offers some of the best bird and whale watching in Iceland.

## Across Holtavörðuheiði

Hrútafjörður is at the crossroads of several routes but scenically is rather dull. Heading north takes you to Hólmavík and the West Fjords region, while Laxárdalsheiði leads to Snæfellnes. Route 1 heads over Holtuvörðuheiði to the district of Borgarfjörður. In winter, the route can be snowbound, making for challenging driving conditions and there is little shelter from drifting snow on the top. By contrast, clear weather can bring wonderful views of Langjökull ice cap and the smaller dome of Eiríksjökull.

South of the pass, Route 1 follows the beautiful Norðurá River, renowned for its fishing. A prominent landmark in the valley is the cone-shaped laccolith, Baula, pronounced 'boiler' and formed from an intrusive acid eruption. Route 60 takes off here for the West Fjords region. Many holiday cottages dot the val-ley, which is a popular weekend and summer retreat for Icelanders. The crater Grábrók, stands by the road at the turn-off to Hreðavatn and Bifröst Hotel. Its shapely cone was formed in an eruption two to three thousand years ago.

## Borgarfjörður

One of Iceland's most extensive lowland areas, Borgarfjörður is a fertile farming district of abundant geothermal activity and steeped in historical intrigue. Its gentle landscapes were hugely appealing to land-hungry settlers. The region's most famous early settler was the enigmatic warrior and poet Egill Skallagrímsson, whose story is told in the skillfully crafted Egils Saga. Arguably, one of the finest sagas, it may have been the work of Snorri Sturluson, another illustrious resident of the area. The lowland areas give way to valleys, which in turn lead to an uninhabited

171

wilderness bordering the glacier **Langjökull**.

The region's main town is **Borgarnes**, which sits on a rocky spit of land on the northern shore of Borgarfjörður. Powerful tidal currents in the fjord have always made fishing difficult, so Borgarnes is primarily a service town. With the new tunnel under Hvalfjörður and bridge over Borgarfjörður, it takes barely an hour to drive from the capital. The town has two hotels, a youth hostel, campsite, swimming pool and the usual range of shops. A small park in the town is believed to be the burial site of Saga hero Egill's father, Skallagrímur Kveld-Úlfsson, while a statue in the park shows Egill carrying the body of his beloved son Bödvar, who drowned in the river and is also buried there.

The beautiful church at **Borg**, just outside Borgarnes at the turn-off for Snaefellsnes was site of the settlement farm of Skallagrímur. With his father Kveld-Úlfur, he set sail from Norway but on reaching the coast of Iceland, father and son got separated and Kveld-Úlfur fell ill. He asked his men to make a coffin for him, cast it overboard when he died, and tell his son to settle where the coffin washed up. The coffin was soon found and Skallagrímur made his home on the site.

Kveld-Úlfur had a dark and sinister side to his character that passed down the line, inherited by his son, and also his grandson Egill, whose violent temper took grip at the tender age of six, when he killed for the first time. Yet Egill's character also had a soft and melancholy side to it. When his son Bödvar drowned in a storm, he went into a deep depression refusing to eat or drink. His daughter-in-law tricked him into

drinking some milk and suggested he might compose a poem in Bödvar's honour before he died. Egill then got so involved in writing, that he forgot his vow to die. The poem, 'Sonatorrek' meaning 'Lament for my Sons' is a lyrical masterpiece and the statue outside the church of Borg, by twentieth century sculptor Ásmundur Sveinsson is named after it.

For those interested in finding out more about Egil's Saga, the tourist office arranges guided walks around Borgarnes, tracing its history and the events of the Saga.

Hvanneyri, Iceland's main agricultural college, recently upgraded to university level, is situated at the foot of the sinisterly named **Skessuhorn**, 'Troll Wife's Horn', an impressive peak rising to 3,171ft (967m), across the fjord from Borgarnes. There is a collection of agricultural machinery on the site, which is open to visitors.

## Deildatunguhver

The largest hot spring in Iceland, pumps out 180 litres of boiling water per second, which is pumped to heat the towns of Borgarnes and Akranes. The hot water is also used to heat glasshouses here and is piped through the soil of the outdoor vegetable plots to speed up the growth process. A subspecies of hard fern *Blechnum spicant fallax* grows around the hot springs and is peculiar to this location and one other. The hot spring is located just off Route 527, south of the River Hvítá.

# The valleys

Reykhóltsdalur is a pleasant and fertile valley, which lies south of the Hvítá River. The main attraction is **Reykhólt**, a place of huge historical importance to Icelanders. The thirteenth-century historian, politician and writer Snorri Sturluson lived there. As a child, Snorri was fostered by the eminent Jón Loftsson of Oddi and grew up well versed in the history and literature of Scandinavia. To further his political aims, Snorri married to acquire the wealthy estate of his forefathers at Borg. The marriage was not a success and shortly after the birth of his children, he moved to Reykhólt. Snorri's career, his rise and fall, have all the drama and tragedy of a Shakespeare play. A key protagonist in the political chaos of the thirteenth century, Snorri made more enemies than friends and eventually met his death at the hands of power-hungry chieftain Gissur Þórvaldsson.

Snorri was murdered in the cellar of his house at Reykhólt, from where a tunnel led to his naturally heated bathing pool. Though the house is long gone, the tunnel and bathing pool have been restored and are a poignant reminder of these events. Reykhólt has a summer hotel, museum and literary research institute. Outside the old school is a statue of Snorri by the Norwegian sculptor Gustav Vigeland. It was a gift from Norway in recognition of Snorri's historical masterpiece Heimskringla, a history of the Kings of Norway. Snorri also wrote the Prose Edda, a work dedicated to Norse mythology, as well as a handbook for aspiring poets.

Meaning 'White River', the **Hvítá**, which drains off Langjökull and Eiríksjökull, is often a pastel shade of blue, rather than the muddy brown of Iceland's other glacial rivers. Its upper reaches support quite extensive birch woodlands, where at **Húsafell,** a kind of holiday village has sprung up, with wooden chalets, a campground, swimming pool and shop. It caters mostly to Icelandic families but is open to everyone. With much to see and do in the area, it makes a good base for a few days.

Beyond Húsafell, the jeep track F550 takes off for Þingvellir, via Kaldidalur. Rough in places, it is not suitable for ordinary cars. You can access Iceland's second largest ice cap **Langjökull** from a side track off the F550 16 miles (24km) from Húsafell. Snowmobile and skidoo trips operate here onto the ice cap. The view from the top of its icy dome is breathtaking.

Hraunfossar & Barnafoss are neither particularly high, nor have a great volume of water, yet they are enchanting. West of Húsafell, the river leaps through a narrow channel in a series of rapids, known as **Barnafoss**. Below Barnafoss, the river widens and on the north bank numerous fresh water streams emerge from under the lava and cascade over the side of the gorge into the river, forming the cascades known as **Hraunfossar**.

The highest summit in the west of Iceland 5,494ft (1,675m) **Eiríksjökull** is a tuff table mountain, formed in a sub-glacial eruption during the Ice Age. It is named after the outlaw Eiríkur, who lived in Súrtshellir. Fleeing from pursuers he climbed a pinnacle on the side of the mountain. One of his pursuers reached up with an axe and chopped off the outlaw's foot. He is said to have lived to tell the tale.

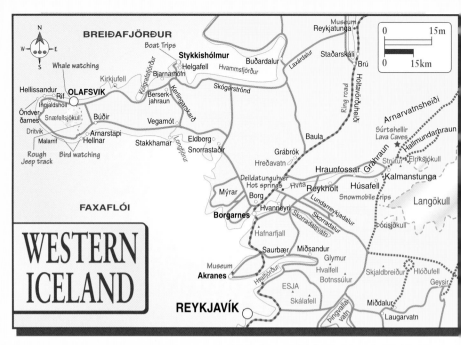

To approach the mountain, which can be climbed with care and, to be safe, the aid of ropes, ice axe and crampons, drive an indistinct track round the north side of **Strútur**. Then cross the lava to the foot of the mountain and begin the route up following the ridge south of the most prominent ravine on its western side. Seek advice at Húsafell before undertaking the climb. The summit of Strútur 3,076ft (938m) also gives a

## Súrtshellir Lava Cave

Just over 1 mile (2km) in length, **Súrtshellir** is an extensive lava tube or tunnel in the **Hallmundarhraun** lava field. The lava is named after a cave-dwelling mystical being from **Grettir's Saga** and flowed from the north-western edge of Langjökull. To get there, take the F578 jeep track from the farm **Kalmannstunga** at the head of the Hvítá Valley. It's a rough track, but may just be passable in an ordinary car, if you ask locally for advice. The caves, and those of nearby **Stefánshellir**, were formed when a lava channel, carrying lava from the vent of the volcano, emptied at the end of the eruption. There are several entrances to the caves, formed when the thin crust of the tunnel collapsed. To explore the caves, which are a protected site, a torch is essential. Good footwear and a walking stick are useful, because the floor is often icy. The caves are known to have been inhabited, most likely by outlaws, and tenth-century cattle bones have been found in one of them. Stalactite-like lava drips and icicles hang from the roof, which in most places is above head height.

fine view. The route starts from the saddle north of **Kalmannstunga,** and is easy, though long.

North of Eiríksjökull spreads a vast area of marsh and moorland dotted with many thousands of small lakes and rivers. **Arnarvatnsheiði** is a popular area for angling and attracts many breeding birds. Several jeep tracks, for high clearance four wheel drive vehicles only, criss-cross the area. The many huts among the lakes are privately owned and are used by anglers. Arinbjörn Jóhansson runs horseriding trips through the region that is an option for anyone wanting to explore further.

These two valleys are furthest south in the Borgarfjordur district. Route 52 is known as **Uxahryggur** and follows **Lundarreykjadalur** to the plateau at the foot of **Skjáldbreiður**. This 3,476ft (1,060m) shield volcano gives its name to all others of the type. From here ordinary vehicles can head south to Þingvellir. Strong winds, dust storms and drifting sand can make the route difficult.

**Skorradalur** has a pretty lake and its pockets of woodland make it popular with locals at the weekends. There is a campsite on the south shore of the lake, from where Route 50 leads over a low pass to Hvalfjörður. The abandoned farm **Draghálas** was home to the leader of the Ásatrú sect. The faith, which is an official religion in Iceland, is based around worship of the Norse deities.

Deildatunguhver, largest hot spring in Iceland

175

# From Borgarnes to Reykjavík

Leaving Borgarnes, Route 1 crosses the fjord by a bridge. Watch for the strong tidal currents as you cross. On the other side are the impressive screes of **Hafnarfjall**, which the road skirts to reach the shores of Hvalfjörður.

Out on the end of the peninsula sits the town of **Akranes**, which is among the largest fishing ports in Iceland, with a population of just over 5,000, and the locals will claim, the best soccer team in the country. The 'Book of Settlements' names Irish settlers as first to claim land here, a theory given credence by several Celtic place names. By the seventeenth century a small village had grown and now the town supports several small manufacturing industries, and the cement works.

For visitors, the **Folk and Maritime Museum** at Garðar, just outside Akranes, is worth a visit, if only to see the cutter Sigurfari and a range of other small fishing boats hauled up outside. The mineral museum **Steinaríki Íslands** has an impressive rock collection, as well as an exhibition on the construction of the tunnel under Hvalfjörður. Hotels, guesthouse accommodation, camping and restaurants complete the range of facilities for visitors. Akrafjall offers one of the best panoramas of the west of Iceland. The trail starts from the Akranes hot water utility car park and is signed to **Háihnúkur**, the 1,804ft (555m) southern summit of the mountain.

Since the tunnel under the fjord opened, the distance to the capital has been halved but visitors will miss out on the stunning scenery of **Hvalfjörður**, 'Whale Fjord', by tak-

ing the short cut. There is some debate as to whether the fjord gets its name from the whales hunted here, or the mythical man-whale Raudhöfði, who plagued the fjord. This larger than life monster was eventually tricked into swimming up the river at the head of the fjord, climbing up Iceland's highest waterfall and then expiring in the lake **Hvalvatn** at the top, where some years later, whale bones were found.

Route 47 follows the northern side of the fjord to **Saurbær**, where an impressive modern church was built in honour of Iceland's revered religious poet, Hallgrímur Pétursson, who was parish priest here from 1651-1669. He is best known for his Passion Hymns, which he is said to have composed while seated by the large rock east of the church. Behind the altar is a beautiful fresco, painted by the Finnish artist Lennart Segerstrale. The priest's life and work were cut short when he contracted leprosy. **Hallgrímskirkja** in Reykjavík was named after him.

When the British occupied Iceland in 1940, they established a military base and port in Hvalfjörður, the remains of which can still be seen. At the time, it was one of the most

## Highest waterfall

At the head of Hvalfjörður, a track takes off up the valley. From the end of the track it is an hour's walk to Iceland's highest waterfall, **Glýmur**. The falls drop 650ft (198m) from the marshy plateau and lake Hvalvatn into an abyss below. It is hard to get a good view of it.

important bases in the North Atlantic, and a safe haven for convoys of supply ships travelling between Europe and America. Close by is the former whaling station.

The peninsula that lies north of Reykjavík at the foot of Mount Esja, is called **Kjalarnes**. The first church to be built in Iceland was here, at the settlement farm of Esjuberg. In 1981, the site was excavated, but what had previously been assumed to be the remains of the church, turned out to be very much more recent.

## Mount Esja

An imposing massif, 3,011ft (918m) high **Esja** was most likely formed during the Ice Age and consists of layers of basalt and tuff. Its precipitous cliffs and screes form a moody backdrop to Reykjavík especially on a stormy day. Climbing Esja is a popular outing for city dwellers who snake up the ridge path from the car park at Mogilsár, by the woodland near the head of Kollafjörður. It's a fairly strenuous walk, especially the last leg, but well worth it for the views.

# THE SNÆFELLSNES PENINSULA

The **Snæfellsnes Peninsula** juts out from Iceland's west coast, like a long arm with a clenched fist at its tip, in many ways a microcosm of the whole island. Craters, lava flows, an ice cap, glaciated peaks, fjords, sandy beaches and high cliffs are its landscapes. A rugged mountain chain runs its length, capped by 4,743ft (1,46m) **Snæfellsjökull**, a mystical cone-shaped strato volcano.

The south side of the peninsula is farming country yet has conserved much of its extensive marshlands, which are an important habitat for birds. Fringed by golden sand beaches, the wild and windswept coast is pounded by surf as it faces the full onslaught of an unforgiving Atlantic. The north side of Snæfellsnes is more sheltered and there are fjords, which make good anchorage for fishing vessels. Most of the sights of the peninsula can be covered in two days, though longer would allow for whale watching, birdwatching on Breiðafjörður Bay, snowmobiling on the glacier or exploring some of the Saga sites.

## North coast of Snæfellsnes

With a treacherous maze of islands and channels at its mouth and a lack of good natural anchorages, **Hvammsfjörður** has never really developed much of a fishing industry. Its south shore was once wooded, hence the name **Skógarströnd**, 'Forest Coast'. It is natural then that **Stykkishólmur**, situated at the mouth of the fjord has developed as the main fishing port and shellfish processing base. It is good choice for a few days' stay at the Hotel Stykkishólmur or the smaller Guesthouse Eyjaferðir, the youth hostel or campsite. The town is linked by bus with the capital, while the **Baldur**

**ferry** runs twice daily in summer between the port and **Brjánslœkur** in the North West Fjords. The nineteenth century **Norwegian House**, a traditional timber building of character, houses the local folk museum, while Stykkishólmur's modern church is unusual both in its outside form, and its light and airy interior.

The many islands of **Breiðafjörður Bay** are a breeding ground for sea birds, with the great draw being the chance to see the rare white-tailed sea eagle which recently has nested there. With probably fewer than 100 pairs left in the country, this is one of Iceland's most endangered birds. The daily boat trips, which are run by Seatours, give an excellent chance of seeing this bird in early summer when it is still nesting, as well as the other species. The

Above: Rock arch near Arnarstapi
Below: Hraunfossar on River Hvíta

Above: Stykkishólmur
Below: Arnarstapi and Snæfellsjökull

bay and islands are quite sheltered so it is not too much of a
rough ride. The same company
also does the whale watching
trips from Ólafsvík.

# Helgafell

Just south of the town is the
farm and church of **Helgafell**.
Meaning 'Holy Mountain'
the 239ft (73m) high hill
commands a breathtaking
view. First settler in the region Þórólfur Mostrarskegg
named the mountain, and
stipulated that no one should
look at it without washing
first, nor should man or beast
be killed on it because it
was sacrosanct. Several
prominent early Icelanders
lived at Helgafell, including
the ambivalent Snorri the
Priest of Eyrbyggja Saga,
who swapped homes with

179

Guðrún Ósvífursdóttir, the tormented heroine of Laxdœla Saga. Legend has it that if you climb the hill for the first time, starting at her grave and neither looking back nor speaking, you may make three wishes. They must be well-intended, told to no one and you must be facing east when you make them.

Berserkjahraun is an area of impressive scoria lava originating from four craters and three different eruptions, all around 4,000 years old. For those interested in exploring the lava and craters, a track, which was once the old road, loops through the lava to rejoin the main Route 57. The next fjord, **Kolgrafafjörður**, has dramatic mountain scenery and a hiking route over **Tröllaháls** to **Hraunfjörður**, taking about 2 hours.

A new village which has sprung up in the last sixty years around the fishing industry, **Grundarfjörður** has a population of just over 800. There is a hotel down by the waterfront, and a local company Detours offers village walks and a visit to the fish factory. Across the bay is the prominent **Kirkjufell**, 'church fell', shaped

by Ice Age glaciers. Climbing the 1,500ft (463m) mountain is risky but there is a pleasant 4-mile (7km) walk around its base.

A cluster of three villages are grouped on the northern tip of the peninsula. **Ólafsvík** is a small town with two guesthouses and one of the best anchorages on the peninsula. Just by the cross roads for Route 54 over the pass, was the site of the notorious farm of **Fróðá**, which became the scene of several horrific deaths and mysterious hauntings in Eyrbyggja Saga. Until the year 1700, **Rif** was the busiest fishing station in the west of Iceland, then the river changed course and ruined its port. Christopher Columbus is said to have visited here in 1477 staying a winter at the nearby farm of **Ingjaldshóll**. It is believed that he might have been investigating the Norse voyages across the Atlantic. **Hellissandur**, a larger village, has a nice guesthouse which does guided walks, snowmobile trips on the ice cap and horse riding. The **maritime museum** is worth a visit.

## Whale watching

Nowadays, the village of **Ólafsvík** is better known as the jumping off point for Iceland's most exciting whale watching trips, on board the 100 ton catamaran *Brimrún*, which is stable and has ample deck space upstairs and a large lounge below. In summer blue and humpback whales gather to feed in an offshore trough, with the best time being July and August, when they usually come in closer to shore. Large groups of ten or more blue and humpback whales can be seen feeding in the area, along with occasionally other species of cetacean, such as short-finned pilot whales, orcas, white-beaked dolphins and sei whales. Try to pick a calm day but if you only have one chance, then go for it because the sight of the largest animal on earth is unforgettable. There are few other places in the world where blue whales can be seen with such a degree of certainty.

# The tip of Snæfellsnes

The uninhabited volcanic tip of the peninsula, with its almost desert-like landscapes, could not be more different from the rest of Snæfellsnes. Öndverðarnes, the westernmost point, can be reached by a track and there are marked walking trails in the area. Abundant sea birds nest on the cliffs along here and occasionally killer whales are spotted offshore. You can walk to some interesting volcanic features in the lava of **Neshraun,** among them **Vatnsborg,** a gaping crater-like hole, with lush ferns growing on its floor.

A couple of miles off Route 574, down a track towards the sea, is the sandy bay of **Djúpalónssandur.** From the car park and picnic table, a trail leads past a keyhole lava formation to the beach. Where the trail meets the beach there are several boulders lined up which were used to test a man's strength to see if he were fit to go out on the fishing boats. Only those who could lift all four were considered for the job. The beautiful pebble beach is said to be a good spot for hunting out 'magic stones'. No one can quite describe them, but perhaps the magic is in the special feel of their incredibly smooth surface.

Walk along the beach and follow the cliff top path northwards. It's about thirty minutes walk to **Dritvík,** once a bustling fishing station where from around 1550 to 1860 some 60 or 70 boats were launched from the bay in the height of the season, employing over 350 men.

Þúfubjarg is a cliff west of the old fishing settlement of **Malarrif,** which is just off the main road, and an hour's walk along the coast from Djúpalónssandur. On the cliffs are nesting guillemots, Brünnich's guillemots and razorbills. The rock pillar **Lóndrangar** is thought to be an ancient volcanic plug.

## Snæfellsjökull

At 4,743ft (1,446m) high, **Snæfellsjökull** is an active strato volcano, capped with ice and built up over the last 700,000 years. There have probably been in the region of twenty eruptions in the last 10,000 years, on and around the volcano, the largest and last of these around 1,750 years ago. It was first climbed in 1754 by the Icelandic adventurers Eggert Ólafsson and Bjarni Pálsson. An easy climb, there are several approaches to the summit, but the shortest route is from the jeep track that runs over **Jökulháls**, taking three to four hours to the summit, or six hours from **Stapafell**. The jeep track is only snow free late in summer, by which time most of the crevasses are exposed. It is nevertheless advisable to have rope, ice axe and crampons for the climb or use a local guide.

Snæfellsjökull is probably Iceland's second most famous volcano, after Hekla. Jules Verne used the mountain as the scene for his novel *Journey to the Centre of the Earth*, in which a German/Icelandic expedition descended through Snæfellsjökull's crater. It seems likely that Verne may have confused it with Hekla, the traditional entrance to

**Continued on page 184...**

## Borgarfjörður

### Borgarnes Information Bureau
☎ 437 2214
By Hyrnan Service Station by the bridge. Guided historical tours of the area.

### Agricultural Museum at Hvanneyri
☎ 437 0000
Located 9 miles (14km) from Borgarnes. Unusual knitwear and crafts on sale at the handicraft shop.
Open: 1-6pm, daily in summer.

## Reykhólt

### Snorrastofa
At Reykhólt ☎ 435 1490
snorrastofa@aknet.is
www.reykholt.is
Small museum dedicated to Snorri Sturluson and promoting literary research and local history. Open: 10am-6pm daily 1 June-25 August.

### Húsafell Travel Service
☎ 435 1550, Fax 435 1551,
husafell@husafell.is
www.husafell.is
Guesthouse, cabins, camping, swimming pool and activities in wooded surrounds. Popular with Icelanders. Located on Route 518, near the start of the Kaldidalur Track.

## Akranes

### Garðar Folk & Maritime Museum
☎ 431 1255
Located just outside Akranes. Open: 10.30-12am and 1.30-4.30pm, daily May-August and 1.30-4.30pm weekdays September-April.

### Icelandic Museum of Minerals
☎ 431 5566
Located on the outskirts of town just off Route 61. Open: 11am-6pm, daily May-August and September-April.

## NORTH SHORE OF SNÆFELLSNES

## Stykkishólmur

### Seatours Cruises
☎ 438 1450, Fax 438 1050,
saeferdir@saeferdir.is
www.saeferdir.is
3-hour trips among Breiðafjörður's islands, with fantastic rock formations and abundant sea birds in June and July. Also whale watching trips from Ólafsvík

Church at Buðir

**The Norwegian House**
Museum of local history
☎ 438 1640
By the port. Open: 11am-5pm, daily June-August.

**Baldur Car Ferry**
☎ 438 1450
saeferdir@saeferdir.is
www.saeferdir.is
Sails across Breiðafjörður between Stykkishólmur and Brjánslækur, stopping at the island of Flatey
en route. Departs Stykkishólmur at 9am and 4pm and Brjánslækur at 12.30 and 7.30pm. Daily in summer 1 June-31 August. No sailing on Seamen's Day. The ferry links in with buses to Reykjavík, Látrabjarg and Ísafjörður. Reservations advisable for vehicles.

**Shark Curing at Bjarnarhöfn**
☎ 438 1581
See how shark is cured in the traditional way, and taste it! Located on Route 577, 10 miles (16km) west of Stykkishólmur.

## Grunarfjörður

**Detours**
☎ 438 6939
www.detours-iceland.com
Village walks, fish factory tours and kayaking

## Ólafsvík

**Whale Watching**
Trips to see blue whales, humpback whales and other species run by seatours (see Stykkishólmur).

Troll-like rock formation

## Hellissandur

**Maritime Museum**
☎ 436 6961
Open: 1-6pm, daily in summer.

## SOUTH SHORE OF SNÆFELLSNES

## Hellnar

**Brekkubær**
☎ 435 6820
brekkubaer@hellnar.is
www.hellnar.is
Guesthouse accommodation, camping, alternative therapies, tarot readings in a magical setting of glacier views and a spectacular coastline.

## Arnarstapi

**Snjófell Travel Service**
☎ 435 6783, Fax 435 6795,
snjofell@snjofell.is
www.snjofell.is
Accommodation, camping, turf house restaurant, snowmobiling and glacier skiing, boat trips.

hell. Whatever the author intended, we may eventually discover the truth as the glacier is continuing to shrink and its 'bottomless' crater may yet be exposed.

Snæfellsjökull is believed by many to hold strange powers and to be one of the earth's 'power points'. It attracts a following of alternative thinkers, many of whom are based in the Arnastapi and Hellnar areas.

Two tiny fishing settlements on the south shore are nestled at the foot of the glacier. In **Hellnar**, the old salting house has been converted into a café, with a terrace looking out over the sea. It's an idyllic setting and if you are lucky you may see orcas just offshore. **Brekkubær** offers alternative healing therapies, Tarot and Viking card readings and has a guesthouse and campsite.

Just off the main road, west of the turn-off to Hellnar is a lake-filled crater known as **Bárðarlaug**. Nearby Laugarbrekka, was the home of Guðríður Þórbjarnadóttir. This remarkable lady accompanied her husband on a voyage to Vinland, where she gave birth to a son, Snorri, who is remembered as the first white man to be born in North America. She then embarked on a pilgrimage to Rome and became a nun, but returned to Iceland in later life. Today such travels are the norm, but not so in tenth-century Iceland.

From Hellnar, a beautiful coastal path follows along the cliff top east to **Arnarstapi**. The 2-mile (3.5km) route passes many interesting columnar basalt rock arches, sea stacks and blowholes, formed by wave erosion, while kittwakes nest on the cliffs here and arctic terns breed on the meadows behind. Arnarstapi has more of the feel of a village about it and still has a small fishing industry.

Snjófell run an attractive guesthouse and restaurant in a traditional-style, though new, turf building They also offer whale watching trips and a range of glacier based activities, including skiing and snowmobiling, the lazy option for those who want to get to the top of the volcano. If you get a clear night in early summer, it is well worth taking the midnight sun tour up the volcano for unforgettable views. For those happy to walk, follow the jeep track that starts by the mountain Stapafell.

# The south coast of Snæfellnes

Located at the end of a long arc of golden sand, **Búðir** on a calm sunny day is idyllic. Sadly, the weather is seldom calm so visitors may not have believed the framed newspaper cutting in the hotel, whose headline boasted: "Búðir hotter than Majorca!". In any case, the place is no beach resort and consists of a rustic campground, church, the turf ruins of an old trading post and fishing port and the recently rebuilt hotel.

Búðir sits at the edge of the **Búða-hraun lava**, whose many sinkholes and cracks support a rich and varied flora, including 11 of Iceland's 16 ferns. The buttercups are especially prolific and the English painter, W G Collingwood, on his visit during the nineteenth century, remarked on this as he painted them. A walking trail leads to the black timber church, which was reconsecrated in 1987, though originally built 140 years previously. The path, which was once the main bridle trail to Arnarstapi, continues to the crater which erupted Búðir's lava and there is a fine view from the top (2 hours round trip). Just west of the waterfall **Bjarnarfoss**, the acid laccolith **Mælifell** protrudes from the surrounding basalts, into which it erupted intrusively.

**Lýsuhóll**, just east of Búðir has a swimming pool and guesthouse and

## A grim tale

**A**xlarhyrna, the prominent mountain north of the crater at Búðir is connected with the gruesome legend of Axlar-Björn, who lived at the nearby farm of Öxl. Björn's pregnant mother had a craving for blood and feared greatly for the child she was carrying. As a youth Björn dreamed that a man offered him eighteen pieces of flesh, each tasting better than the last. The stranger then told him to climb Axlarhyrna and take whatever he found under a rock. This was an axe, and when Björn picked it up he was possessed with an urge to kill. After that, people began to disappear under mysterious circumstances. Björn and his wife were suspected, and when proof was found they confessed to eighteen murders and were sentenced to death. Björn had all his limbs crushed before he was beheaded, while Steinunn, pregnant at the time, was allowed to give birth first. The child turned out no better, and became the murderer Sveinn Skotti.

offers horseriding trips along the beach. Along this stretch of road are many ponds and marshes, which offer rewarding birdwatching. Further along the coast, **Löngufjörur** is a wonderful stretch of golden sand, accessed from the farm Stakkhamar, which has accommodation. The turn off is just west of the crossroads at **Vegamót**. At Vegamót, there is fuel, a café and shop, and from here Route 56 leads to the north coast of the peninsula.

Hotel Eldborg is a summer hotel just south of the main road before you reach the crater of the same name. The best example in Iceland of a spatter ring crater, **Eldborg** rises 200ft (60m) above the surrounding lava. Some geologists believe the crater formed five to eight thousand years ago, while others think there was a second eruption in historical times. From the farm at **Snorrastaðir**, which offers accommodation and horse riding, there is a trail to Eldborg, taking around two hours there and back. Formed from splashes of lava, which accumulated around the vent, the crater is steep-sided, though not a difficult climb.

North of the main road, are the columnar basalt formations of **Gerðuberg** and the cave-riddled lava and craters of **Gullborgarhraun**, which erupted 7,000-9,000 years ago. The mineral springs at **Rauða-melsölkelda** heated a natural bathing pool in the thirteenth century, traces of which remain on the site. From here to the town of **Borgarnes,** a broad expanse of marshland, cut through by some of the best fishing rivers in the country, forms the farming district of **Mýrar**.

Opposite: Látrabjarg bird cliffs

Cut-off from the rest of Iceland, the wild and sparsely populated West Fjords has a reputation for some of the worst weather and roads in the country, but those who visit claim this is a small price to pay for the outstanding scenery and warm welcome.

For centuries its resolute inhabitants eked out a living farming the narrow strip of land between mountains and sea. Then in the early twentieth century larger fishing vessels, equipped with motors, discovered great shoals of fish offshore. The sheltered fjords provided a perfect safe haven for the fleet and as people flocked to the region to process the catch, small villages sprung up almost overnight. Fishing is still the main source of livelihood but the quota system has spelled disaster for many communities. Fifty years ago it was the farms that were abandoned. Now it is the turn of the fishing villages.

Geologically the West Fjords region is the oldest part of Iceland, its rocks dating back 16 million years. The deeply indented coastline is scarred by intense erosion of the Ice Age glaciers, which almost severed it from the rest of the island. The narrow isthmus between **Kollafjörður** and **Gilsfjörður** is just 8 miles (13km) wide, and according to local legend, the work of two trolls, who decided to dig a channel here.

## Routes to the West Fjords

There are several routes to the peninsula. From Stykkishólmur on Snæfellsnes, the summer ferry Baldur crosses Breiðafjörður Bay twice a day to Brjánslækur. During the two and a half hour journey, the boat weaves among the bay's many islands and calls in at **Flatey**, one of only two still inhabited. The tiny island's village has many fine traditional timber houses, which have been restored. Visitors are attracted by the tranquil feel of the island, its old world atmosphere and prolific bird life. A café and guesthouse allow for an overnight stay.

Site of a twelfth century monastery, the island became something of a cultural centre and for centuries, the treasured medieval manuscript Flateyjarbók was preserved there. Later presented to the Danish king, the manuscript was finally returned to Iceland in 1971.

## The Dales

The ferry conveniently avoids the lengthy journey on Route 60 around the fjords and inlets of **Dalasýsla**, 'the Dales County'. But by taking it, visitors will miss out on a region steeped in history, based around the town of **Búðardalur** (population 300). **Eiríksstaðir** in **Haukadalur** is believed to be the birthplace of Leifur Eiríksson. Leifur became the first European to set foot in North America, which he named Vínland, around the year 1000.

Excavations at Eiríksstaðir have unearthed the remains of a Viking hall, which has been dated at 890-980. The reconstructed 10th century farmhouse is well worth a visit. **Hvammur** on the northern shore of Hvammsfjörður was the land claim of matriarch settler Auður the Deep-minded and later birthplace to

writer, historian and statesman Snorri Sturluson.

North of the 'Dales' is the region known as **Reykhólasveit**, based around the hotel at **Bjarkalundur** and village of **Reykhólar**, where sea-weed is harvested for fertiliser and dried using local geothermal sources. From the hotel, a walking trail leads to the impressive twin volcanic plugs of **Vaðalfjöll**. The summer Route 608 over Þórskafjarðarheiði takes off to the north, connecting with Route 61 to Ísafjörður.

## Laxdæla Saga

One of the most poignantly related and skilfully crafted of the great family Sagas, the stirring events of Laxdæla are based around the valley of **Laxárdalur,** in the 'Dales'. Route 59 follows the valley to Hrútafjörður, passing the farmstead of Hjarðarholt, which was home to Kjartan Ólafsson. Betrothed to Saga heroine Guðrún Ósvífurdóttir of nearby **Sælingsdalur**, Kjartan went to Norway to seek fame but when he failed to return in good time, Guðrún married his cousin Bolli. On Kjartan's return, love turned to bitterness and Guðrún incited the reluctant Bolli to kill him. Kjartan's brothers took revenge and Guðrún was left widowed. Later she remarried and ended her days in contemplation at Helgafell. The tragedy of her ill-starred relationships left many questions unanswered. When, on her deathbed, her son asked whom she had loved the most, her cryptic reply, "I was worst to the one I loved the best", only perpetuated the ambiguity.

# Strandir

Meaning 'Coasts', **Strandir** is the name given to the rugged eastern flank of the West Fjords region, which sees only a handful of visitors and a fair share of foul weather. **Hólmavík** is the only remaining town on the coast, its hotel, shops, bus links and intriguing **Sorcery and Witchcraft Museum** making it a use-ful stop off point for visitors. Fish-ing and a scattering of sheep farms employ most of the coast's inhabit-ants, who number less than a thou-sand. The traditional industry of shark curing continues alongside the collecting of driftwood, washed over from northern Scandinavia and Siberia. North of Hólmavík, the main Route 61 heads to Ísafjörður over the barren lake-studded moor of **Steingrímsfjarðarheiði**.

The coastal Route 643 continues north for a further 50 miles (80km). This is really a road to nowhere and therein lies its appeal. Once a bustling herring base, **Djúpavík** is virtually abandoned though the former factory workers' hostel is now a small hotel, with some good walking in the vicinity. At nearby **Gjögur**, once a legendary shark fishing station, is an improbably sited airfield, which is served by a twice weekly schedule to Reykjavík and is the only year round access to the area by public transport.

At end of the road are the tiny communities of **Trékyllisvík** and **Norðurfjörður**. There is camping here a shop, guesthouse and a beautifully situated swimming pool on the seashore, heated by natural hot springs. Beyond here, a hiking trail follows the uninhabited coast to **Hornstrandir**, some of the most inspiring, though tough, walking in Iceland but as all food and equipment have to be carried, it gets few takers. Boat transport can sometimes be arranged from Norðurfjörður. The easier route to Hornstrandir is by boat from Ísafjörður.

## Barðarströnd

The slow gravel Route 60 winds around the southern fjords, where the rare white-tailed sea eagle nests. There are no villages here and in fact the whole coast has fewer than 500 inhabitants, perhaps as a result of the seventeenth century hauntings by the ghost of Sveinn Skotti. A petty thief and son of a mass murderer, Sveinn was hanged on the cliffs above **Vatnsfjörður**.

This fjord, whose fertile hinterland is a nature reserve, was where Viking Hrafna-Flóki landed and attempted one of the first settlements in Iceland. The 'Book of Settlements' tells that the fishing was so good that Flóki neglected to make hay for his livestock, who perished over the bitter winter that followed. In spring he climbed a mountain and saw nothing by ice-filled fjords. It was this drift ice, and not the glaciers, that prompted the disillusioned pioneer to name the

land 'Iceland', on his departure.

Named after the hapless Flóki, is the **Hotel Flókalundur**, a convenient place to break the journey at the crossroads where Route 60 heads north to Ísafjörður. The hotel is also the base for sea kayaking expeditions in the area, run by Ultima Thule. Continuing along the coast, Route 62 turns to a welcome few miles of paved road either side of the ferry terminus at **Brjánslækur**. At low tide, the golden sand beaches west of here are especially inviting, and the bird watching good. **Rauðsdalur** is a guesthouse and base to explore the area.

## Látrabjarg and the Western Tip

Iceland's (and Europe's) westernmost point, sees few visitors in spite of the lure of the impressive 9-mile (14km) long bird cliff of **Látrabjarg**. Rising to 1,456ft (444m) at its highest point, the cliff is home to Iceland's greatest concentration of seabirds. A special draw are the thousands of puffins, which are happy to let visitors approach to within feet of their cliff-top perches A walking trail runs along the cliff top, which is riddled with puffin burrows, so especial care is needed to avoid tripping over. It is possible to walk the full 13 miles (20km) to the stunning golden beach of **Rauðisandur** to the east. Beyond here is the superbly located guesthouse at **Melanes**, reached by the rugged and steep Route 614 from Patreksfjörður fjord to the north.

Several times a week in summer a bus connects with the ferry arriving at Brjánslækur and continues via Látrabjarg to Ísafjörður, or vice-versa. To explore the bird cliff, most

# THE WEST FJORDS

visitors base themselves at **Breiðavík**, a hostel and guesthouse beside a beautiful arc of golden sand. Originally built as a remand home, behind its austere façade is a genuine welcome from the family who run it and a wealth of knowledge about the local area and its inhabitants.

The rough track to the cliff is open to all vehicles with care and passes the former fishing settlement of **Hvallátur**, where many of the cottages have been restored as holiday homes. The place has a timelessness about it that seems to echo the centuries of hardship and endurance, and the drama and tragedy of the many rescue attempts mounted from the village to save the crews of stranded ships.

Among the most remarkable rescues was the British trawler *Dhoon*, which ran aground below the cliffs in December 1947. With little thought for their own safety and in appalling weather, the local farmers and fishermen managed to save all but one of the crew. Lowering themselves down the cliff face by ropes, as if collecting eggs, they secured a line to the wreck and hauled the exhausted crew 656ft (200m) to safety.

Incredibly, some years after, while filming a re-enactment, another ves-

190

## Laugar in Sælingsdalur

### Dalamanna Folk Museum
☎ 434 1328
Open: 10-12am and 1-5pm, daily
1 June-31 August.

### Eiríksstaðir (near Búðardalur)
☎ 434 118  www.leif.is
1 June-31 August 10am-6pm.
Eirik the Red's farm and birthplace
of his son Leif the Lucky. Replica of
a 10th century longhouse where
'real' Vikings welcome visitors, tell
stories and show how people lived
at the time.

## Örlygshöfn, Látrabjarg

### Hnjótur Museum
☎ 456 1511
Fascinating local history, maritime
and aviation collection.
Open: 9am-6pm, daily, 1 June-
1 September.

## Arnarfjörður

### Jón Sigurðsson Museum
Hrafnseyri
☎ 456 8260
Museum and café dedication to
the independence hero. Open:
daily 17 June-1 September.

## Ísafjörður

### Maritime Museum
☎ 456 3293
A cluster of renovated timber
buildings with fascinating displays.
By the port. Open: 1pm-5pm,
daily, 15 May-30 June and 10am-
5pm July-mid September

### Vesturferðir
☎ 456 5111, Fax 456 5185,
vesturferðir@vesturferðir.is
www.vesturferðir.is
Jökulfirðir & Hornstrandir trips,
sightseeing cruises &
information. Website has tide
tables and GPS points.

### Sjoferðir Boat Trips
☎ 456 3879 Fax 456 4879
sjoferðir@sjoferðir.is
www.sjoferðir.is

### Hornstrandir Boat Trips
☎ 456 5690
hornstrandir@hornstrandir.is
www.hornstrandir.is
Boat trips to Jökulfirðir,
Hornstrandir and Isafjardardjup
islands. Drop off and pick up
service for hikers and backpackers.

## Strandir

### Sorcery and Witchcraft museum
Holmavik ☎ 451 3525
Open: 10am-6pm, daily June-
August

## Bolungarvík

### Ósvör
☎ 456 7172
Reconstruction of a traditional
fishing station.

Maritime
Museum,
Ísafjörður

sel ran aground on the spot and the rescue team went into action yet again. A collection of memorabilia and photographs of the events are displayed in what must be one of Iceland's most fascinating museums at nearby **Hnjótur**. Behind the museum is a sombre and poignant memorial to the rescuers, the rescued and all those lost at sea in the dozen or more known strandings on this coast alone, during the twentieth century.

# The Route to Ísafjörður

In clear weather, this drive can be among the most stunning in the country. The roller coaster route dips from fjord to fjord, crossing several high passes along the way, a challenge to the nerves of the driver and suspension of the car. Several short sections are paved, but those that are not can be rough and rutted. The southern fjord and village of **Patreksfjörður**, named after ninth-century Hebridean Bishop Patrick, is the largest. At the head of the fjord, lies the rusting hulk of one of Iceland's first trawlers, driven ashore on the spot some years ago. The smaller community of **Tálknafjörður** and shrimp fishing village **Bildudalur** compete for visitor attention. While Bildudalur has the airport, rival Tálknafjörður boasts a swimming pool.

North of here Route 63 joins Route 60 to head over **Dynjandisheiði**, with views down to Geirþjófsfjörður. Outlawed for a suspected vengeance killing, Saga hero Gísli Súrsson spent thirteen years on the run but was tracked down and slain at the head of this uninhabited fjord in 977. Below the road and marking the spot where he died, a poignant silhouette of the outlaw is carved on a rock.

**Dynjandi**, the West Fjords' best known waterfall, and arguably among the most spectacular in Iceland, is located at the head of the northern arm of **Arnarfjörður**. It tumbles over the edge of the mountain in a fan-shaped cascade, 328ft (100m) high. Several smaller falls downstream lead to one of Iceland's most scenic campgrounds.

Past a small hydroelectric scheme on the river Mjólká, is the farm of Hrafnseyri, birthplace to independence hero and statesman Jón Sigurðsson, who was born there on 17 June 1811. A coffee shop, small museum, restored turf farm and chapel are on the site. A side road continues along the fjord to the foot of the region's highest peak 3,273ft (998m) high **Kaldbakur**. The locals have built a substantial cairn on its summit so that the region can claim its only 3,280ft (1,000m) peak. An indistinct path up the mountain follows the valley of Fossdalur from the shore of Arnarfjörður.

Reached by a tortuous switchback route is the next fjord north, spectacular **Dýrafjörður**, which boasts some of the finest mountain scenery in the region. Þingeyri was the West Fjords' first trading post. Across the fjord from Þingeyri is **Mýrar**, the largest eider farm in Iceland, boasting over 5,000 pairs. The nearby farm of **Alviðra** has a guesthouse and claims to have first been settled by none other than a son of King Harald Finehair of Norway. An alternative for those keen on exploring the fjord is the summer hotel at **Núpur**. Some worthwhile walking trails over the peninsula may tempt the energetic.

**Önundarfjörður**, named after its first settler, is almost bisected by a stunning golden sand beach. On a rare sunny day, its shallow water heats up and locals bathe here boasting of their own version of the 'Costa del Sol' or 'Florida Keys'. The parsonage of **Holt** was birthplace to seventeenth century Bishop Brynjólfur Sveinsson, who made a gift of Iceland's priceless Flatey Manuscript to the Danish king. Holt's attractive timber church dates from 1869 and has several relics from the days of Bishop Brynjólfur. The nearby youth hostel and guesthouse at **Kirkjuból** has a dramatic setting amidst good walking country.

The fishing village of **Flateyri** was once a whaling station. It sits beneath the towering peak of Eyrarfjall, which dumped a massive avalanche on the village in 1995. In the wake of the tragedy, defensive barriers have been erected to stall any future falls, which are all too common in this region of steep-sided mountains.

A 4-mile (7km) long tunnel now links Önundarfjörður and Ísafjörður, cutting out the once hazardous Breiðdalsheiði Pass. A side branch of the tunnel leads down to the village of Suðureyri. Its main claim to fame is that it sees no sun for over three months each winter, longer than any other village in Iceland.

The focal point for the region and, with a population of just under 3,000, its largest town, **Ísafjörður** huddles at the foot of 2,375 ft (724m) high **Eyrarfjall**. The cluster of brightly painted houses are spread over **Eyri**, a spit of land that juts into the fjord and forms a safe port. The oldest houses in town, happily left standing as factories and warehouses sprang up around them, are four timber buildings dating from the mid-eighteenth century. The lovingly restored **Túrnhús** was once a salting plant, but now houses the **West Fjords Maritime Museum**, which is

## Sun Coffee

Life in the fjords has always been tough. Even with the vastly improved roads of today, there is still a sense of real hardship about winter in the remote fishing villages. Not least because of the mountains which, towering above the ice-sculpted fjords, block out the sun. From November to February many villages live in perpetual shade. On the day when the sun's rays return to bless their homes with life-giving light and warmth, the whole village celebrates with 'Sun Coffee' and that most delectable of Icelandic treats, pancakes.

worth a visit for its collection of nautical memorabilia. With a daily bus service and choice of flights, the town is well connected with the capital, and has two hotels, a guesthouse and camp site.

## Exploring from Ísafjörður

Routes 60 and 61 converge at Ísafjörður forming a circular route that can be driven over several days, though a week will allow time for a few worthwhile detours The broad fjord of **Ísafjarðardjúp** on which it sits, almost severs the region. Nowhere else in the country have the Ice Age glaciers been so active and the mountains of this broad fjord are among the most beautiful in the region. Heading towards the mouth of the fjord, the road ends beyond

**Continued on page 196...**

Above: Adalvik Bay in the uninhabited Hornstrandir reserve

Left: Abandoned village, Hesteyri

Opposite top: Hiking near Flædareyri, Jökulfirðir

Opposite bottom: 100-metre high Dynjandi Falls

Bolungarvík, the West Fjords' second largest town. Hugging the southern shore of the fjord, Route 61, which was only completed in 1975, leads to Suðavík. There are few visitor facilities, though ample spectacular scenery, between here and Djúpmannabúð, a guesthouse, fuel station and camp site near the head of the fjord.

The main road heads south over Steingrímsfjarðarheiði, while Route 635 continues along the northern shore of Ísafjarðardjúp to Kaldalón. Here, a small glacier tumbles off Drangajökull, the only ice cap in the north of Iceland, which has almost halved in size during the last 100 years. Beyond Kaldalón, the chilly-sounding Snæfjallaströnd takes over as the road comes to an end. Meaning 'Snowy Mountain Coast', the snow lies lower and longer here than in any other coastal area. Hiking trails lead from here to uninhabited Jökulfirðir and Hornstrandir.

## Boat trips

Several boat trips run in summer for those interested in exploring the islands of Ísafjarðardjúp or the uninhabited nature reserves to the north. Islands have traditionally been sought-after farm sites and two in the fjord are still inhabited: Vígur, an idyllic spot with Iceland's only wind-mill and colonies of eider and puffin; and Æðey, meaning 'Eider Island', which also has impressive bird populations.

Hornstrandir and Jökulfirðir, the remote peninsula and fjord country north and east of Ísafjarðardjúp is one of hauntingly beautiful landscapes. Though once farmed, by 1950 most of its inhabitants had abandoned their simple homesteads for a more comfortable existence in Ísafjörður or further afield. No longer grazed by sheep, the vegetation is undisturbed and wildflowers flourish on a scale unknown elsewhere.

Hundreds of thousands of birds breed on the precipitous and mist-shrouded cliffs of the peninsula's north coast, which is pounded by an unrelenting Arctic Ocean. In the sheltered fjords, eiders gather in great flocks and dainty red-necked phalaropes dart around tirelessly following the sea shore. This is also the only part of Iceland where arctic foxes can be reliably observed in their natural habitat. At sundown, their shrill bark is unforgettable, as is the swagger of a skilled hunter that lives dangerously, catching birds in flight from a cliff-top perch.

When the region's inhabitants departed, they left behind their homes, churches and with them, over a thousand years of history. Though some buildings have fallen to ruin, many have been meticulously maintained by their children and grandchildren, keen to preserve the memory of a way of life that had survived unchanged for centuries.

Most of the region is now a nature reserve and is accessible only on foot and by boat. From Ísafjörður, Sjóferðir run a boat service to Hesteyri and to other parts of Jökulfirðir and Hornstrandir on request. There is hostel accommodation at Grunnavík, run by a delightful couple who grew up in the village, which lies in a sheltered bay at the entrance to Jökulfirðir. They also offer transportation by boat to the start and end of hiking routes. There are several good day walks from Grunnavík, which is also the start of a challenging

*Continued on page 198...*

196

# WALKING IN HORNSTRANDIR

The region's walking trails are the old bridle paths used by local people until the area was abandoned. Some are clear, others indistinct. Some are marked by cairns, but often these have collapsed. If you have time, why not help to repair them so that these historical routes are not lost? There are also many rivers to wade, which in early summer or after heavy rainfall, can be tricky. Add to this the difficulty of rocky coastal sections, some passable only at low tide and it is not hard to see that the region is best suited to experienced hikers with navigation and map reading skills. As in any mountain area, the weather can be extreme and change suddenly. The inexperienced and those who are less confident should join a guided group trek.

## WALKING FROM HESTEYRI

For a taste of the wild, **Hesteyri** makes a great base from which to explore. The following walks are not especially challenging for fit walkers but some are long and require clear weather and basic map reading skills as the paths are not always obvious.

### 1 AÐALVÍK (7-9 HOUR CIRCULAR WALK)

From Hesteyri follow the main trail up the valley and over the 1,000ft (300m) pass to Aðalvík. Once down on the flat, don't cross the river, but follow the coast south along a gorgeous sandy beach, then cut back up another valley, over a second pass to return to Hesteyri.

### 2 THE WHALING STATION (2 HOURS THERE & BACK) & KJARANSVÍKURSKARÐ (7-9 HOURS CIRCULAR WALK)

Cross the river and head north-east along the shore of the fjord. The old blubber ovens and chimney stack are intact, though in danger of collapse. For a longer walk continue (at low tide only) along the shore to the head of the fjord, and beyond to the 1,400ft (426m) pass for a fantastic view of the north coast. Return to Hesteyri via the high path, marked by cairns, above the fjord.

### 3 HESTEYRAREYRI AND SLÉTTUNES (4 HOURS THERE AND BACK) & GRÆNAHLÍÐ & SÆBÓL (10-11 HOURS CIRCULAR WALK)

From Hesteyri walk south along the beach to the ponds at the point. Then join the path up the hill to the headland and beyond to a point overlooking the lighthouse. The view of Jökulfirðir and Ísafjardarðjúp is magnificent. For a full day walk continue along the cliff top to Grænahlíð and drop down to the bay at Sæból, stopping to view the church at Staður on the return to Hesteyri.

### 4 KAGRAFELL (5 HOURS UP AND DOWN)

The peak behind Hesteyri offers a fantastic view and is for the most part an easy climb. Take the main trail to Aðalvík and from the cairn on the pass head up the south-west flank of the 1,663ft (507m) mountain.

14-day trek through the region, ending at the village of Hesteyri. To walk to the ice cap **Drangajökull** from here is a four-day round trip with overnights at the old village hall at **Flæðareyri**, where there are toilets and a camp site.

The former doctor's house at **Hesteyri** is now a hostel and its setting, overlooking the fjord and surrounded by fields of wood cranesbill and buttercup, is quite idyllic. Along the fjord stand the remains of the former whaling station, later a herring factory. Many visitors come to Hesteyri on a day trip from Ísafjörður, but there are enough day walks to fill several days.

Choosing more remote Hornvík, on the north coast, as a base, gives access to the stupendous bird cliffs of **Hornbjarg** and **Hælavíkurbjarg** but there is no accommodation, though a basic campsite, in the bay. The scenery here is most dramatic and the feeling of isolation absolute. Accommodation and boat transport in the region, together with advice and other arrangements, can be booked through **Vesturferðir** in Ísafjörður.

# BACKPACKING ON HORNSTRANDIR

The following trip can be done in 12 days but it is better to allow a couple of extra days in case of bad weather. The route is for experienced hikers only, with route-finding skills. All food, a tent and other necessities must be carried. It may be possible to arrange for a food drop along the route, depending on what the boat schedules are:

**Day 1** Grunnavík to Flæðareyri

**Day 2** to Hrafnsfjarðareyri

**Day 3** to Furufjörður

**Day 4** day trip to Reykjafjörður

**Day 5** Furufjörður to Barðsvík

**Day 6** to Bjarnanes

**Day 7** to Hornbjarg and Hornvík

**Day 8** to Hlöðuvík

**Day 9** to Fljótavík

**Day 10** to Aðalvík

**Day 11** to Hesteyri

**Day 12** exploring from Hesteyri.

**Unloading gear at Hornvík Bay**

# 9 The Uninhabited Highlands

Landmannalaugar

*I*celand's interior consists of a broad plateau lying at an average height of 2,000-2,600ft (600-800m) above sea level. The highest landforms are capped by the ice fields of Vatnajökull, Langjökull, Hofsjökull and Mýrdalsjökull, the four largest on the island.

Ice aside, the materials most abundant in the interior are black ash and sand. The retreating Ice Age glaciers left behind huge mounds of them, dumped here and there as moraine. Bare ridges and mountainous outcrops of tuff project from the plateau while sheets of lava provide a change in texture, though not in colour. At first sight the over-whelming impression is one of utter desolation.

No wonder Iceland's early settlers saw little reason to venture into these areas. Only outlaws and fugitives from justice took refuge here. Many could not survive, but one who did, and in doing so achieved legendary status, was the eighteenth-century fugitive Eyvindur Jónsson, who spent

## Elves, trolls and ghosts

*I*celanders are by nature superstitious and many maintain a strong belief in the supernatural. This is not surprising in a country where extraordinary natural events and phenomena take place on a regular basis. People might disappear without trace, never to be seen again. Elves, trolls and ghosts were convenient scapegoats to cover up for all sorts of unexplained events, as well as unacceptable behaviour. Almost half of Icelanders claim to have had an encounter with a ghost. Formerly, these were malevolent beings capable of killing and haunting though nowadays most are in the form of harmless apparitions or sensory experiences.

Most Icelanders will not actively claim to believe in elves, but nor will they deny their existence. According to a popular folktale, the elves, known also in Iceland as the 'Huldufolk' or 'Hidden People' are descended from certain children of Adam and Eve, hidden from God on his visit, because Eve had not had time to wash them. Elves live in hills, rocks and fields around us and there are ample stories of roads diverted to avoid disturbing an elf community or farmers not cultivating hay on a particular piece of land.

At the bottom of the belief table are the trolls, huge, ugly and ungainly, living in the mountains and preying on unsuspecting wayfarers. Most are night trolls, who are unable to stay out during the day for fear of the sun's rays, which can turn them to stone. The number of petrified trolls which dot Iceland's landscape would seem to indicate that they are either unlucky or just stupid. Some of the best are to be found in Þórsmörk, Drekagil near Askja and on the road to Laki.

seventeen years on the run, hiding out in some of the interior's most inhospitable places.

Nevertheless, in the early days, trails through the highlands were blazed so that people could attend the annual Althing. Going through the interior was often easier than crossing the hazardous glacial rivers around the coast. Later, trails like the Kjölur track, became established trade routes.

By the eighteenth century, the traffic had almost ground to a halt. Raids on the convoys by fugitives were becoming commonplace. People were disappearing without trace and not only were outlaws to blame. Elves, trolls, ghosts and monsters from Iceland's folklore, ensured that for the next 150 years, the highlands were left alone.

The island's long hours of winter darkness and monstrous lava and rock formations are the perfect food for a fertile collective imagination. With precious little light from their oil lamps and huddled together in one room for warmth, telling stories was the obvious way to pass the hours. There are six huge volumes of folktales, the work of eighteenth century scholars Jón Árnason and Magnús Grímsson, who travelled the length and breadth of the island gathering and recording this priceless contribution to the country's literary heritage.

For those who travel today the immediate attractions are the vastness of the landscapes and the 360° views, plus the excitement of being simply miles away from the nearest habitation. Even at the busiest of the highland campgrounds, walk over the next hill and you will find utter solitude. Four wheel drive enthusiasts have the chance to subject their vehicle to the kind of conditions for which it was built. Lastly, the landscapes themselves are just devastatingly beautiful.

# THE KJÖLUR ROUTE F35

This links the north and south of Iceland travelling between the glaciers **Hofsjökull** and **Langjökull**. The distance from Gullfoss to the Blandá Power Station is 101 miles (161km), with camping and hut accommodation at Hvítárvatn, Kerlingarfjöll and Hveravellir. Driving time is around five hours. Fuel is only available along the way at Kerlingarfjöll, so fill up at Geysir or Blönduós before setting off.

**Kjölur** was once a trading route for convoys between the north and south of Iceland. In recent years, the road has been greatly improved, the rivers all bridged and the road can be driven (with care) in an ordinary car but check the terms of the insurance to see if you are covered.

The following description is of the route from north to south. Leaving the valley of the **Blandá** the road climbs above the river to the area that has been flooded to feed the power station. By the last of the lakes is a viewpoint with a picnic table. The road continues through highland pasture, much of which has been sown with grass seed and reclaimed in response to criticism over the land lost to flooding in the Blandá project. As the distant ice caps appear in view, the road crosses the **Seyðisá River** and the pasture turns to gravel flats. At the turn off to **Hveravellir**, steam can be seen rising in the distance.

*continued on page 204*

201

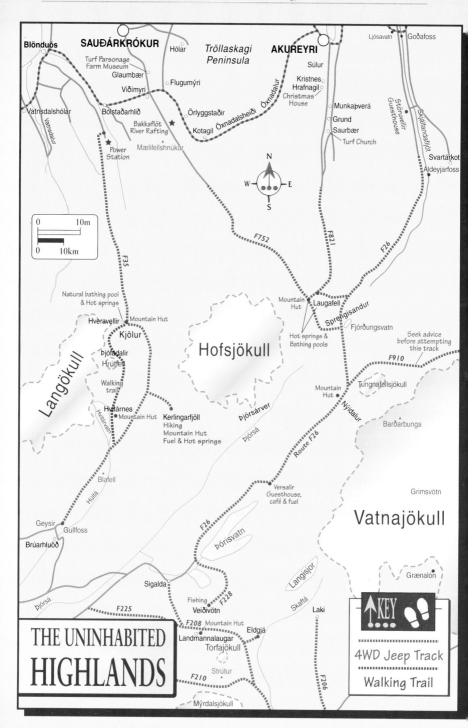

THE UNINHABITED HIGHLANDS

KEY

4WD Jeep Track

Walking Trail

Above: Viti crater and Lake Öskjuvatn, at 227m the deepest lake in Iceland

Below: Luminous green moss on the Northern Fjallabak Route

## Hveravellir

This is one of the prettiest of Iceland's geothermal areas and its naturally heated bathing pool is a wonderful place to relax. You can regulate the water temperature by removing either the hot or cold inflow pipe. Test the water before you get in, especially if no one else is in the pool. There are two huts, owned by the Touring Club of Iceland, which it is advisable to pre-book. The campsite is bumpy, prone to flooding, has flushing toilets and running cold water.

There are both steam vents and hot springs on the site, including milky blue pools that have built up wonderful silica ripples around them. The most active hot spring is called **Eyvindahver**, and is said to be where the outlaw Eyvindur boiled his sheep. Ruins of his shelter can be seen in the lava behind the spring. A trail continues into the lava and after about twenty minutes there is a sign to **Eyvindarhellir**, (Eyvindur's Cave). The cave entrance is so well concealed that it was a perfect hiding place for the outlaw. Continue for a further hour and a half to the crater **Strýtur**, a shield volcano. In clear weather, the view is far reaching.

The weather station at Hveravellir is manned all year round. In winter they get supplies brought in by snowmobile and the occasional jeep which may venture in here. The road continues beyond Hveravellir to a place nestled at the edge of Lang-

jökull, called **Þjófadalir** (Thieves' Valley). A gang of school boys are said to have killed an old woman and fled here, living for a time from sheep they had stolen. A walking trail leads south of here, following the old Kjölur route to Hvítárvatn.

Returning to the main road the next stretch is over old moraines and if the weather is clear there can be great views of the icecap **Langjökull**, at 367 sq miles (950 sq km) in area, Iceland's second largest. Impressive **Hrútfell** looks like a badly iced cake, its several glaciers spilling down from the domed summit. **Kerlingarfjöll**, a range of beautiful rhyolite mountains, have been developed as a summer recreational area. There are huts to stay in, many geothermal springs in the area, and some fine, alpine style walking. To reach the area take the F347. The track continues beyond Kerlingarfjöll and around the southern edge of **Hofsjökull**, but is very rough and only recommended for those with considerable experience of driving these sort of routes.

Back on the F35, there is a loop to the hut at **Hvítárnes** by the stunning glacial lake **Hvítárvatn**. Formed of glacial melt water there are occasionally small icebergs on the lake. The hut, is believed to be haunted by a young girl who lived in the area when it was farmed. It is said that males who sleep in a particular bed in the hut are affected. Cross the River **Hvítá**, by the bridge and climb to the pass at **Bláfellsháls** and a large mound of rocks. It is considered bad luck to drive past without adding to the cairn, a local superstition.

The final stretch of road goes through one of the worst eroded pasturelands in Iceland. The topsoil, now all but gone, was once 6ft

## Bláfell

The shapely peak of **Bláfell**, 3,949ft (1,204m) high, was home to a troll by the name of Bergþór, who lived there in a cave with his wife. Bergþór had Christian tendencies, highly unusual for a troll, but his wife could stand neither the sight nor stench of a believer and soon moved away. When Bergþór was dying he sent a message to the pastor at Haukadalur asking him to reserve a place in the graveyard for which he would be rewarded. The pastor was not too keen on this idea but one night there was a knock at the door and they discovered Bergþór's stick and took this to be a sign that he had died. A party went to the cave and found the body but no sign of the reward only an old kettle with some tea leaves. One lad took a handful of these and stuffed them in his trouser pocket. In anger, they buried the body just outside the church yard. The boy who had taken the tea leaves suddenly found his pockets grow heavy and discovered they had turned to gold. So everyone rushed back up the mountain, but the cave, kettle and tea leaves had all gone.

(1.8m) thick. Clumps of it remain like some type of bizarre geological formation.

Just before Gullfoss, Route F338 takes off around the southern edge of Langjökull, following the power line which feeds the ferrosilicon plant in Hvalfjörður. There is one tricky river crossing and the route is slow going, though quite dramatic and desolate. There is a small hut at the base of **Hlöðufell**, from which the F337 leads, via a spine-chilling descent, to Laugarvatn.

# THE SPRENGISANDUR ROUTE F26

The route links the north and south of Iceland travelling between Hofsjökull and Vatnajökull, a total distance from Goðafoss to the Sigalda Power Station of 152 miles (244km). There is camping and hut accommodation at Nýidalur, and guesthouse accommodation at Hrauneyjar and Stóruvellir. Driving time is around eight hours. Fuel is only available along the way at Versalir, so fill up at Goðafoss or Sigalda before setting off. There are several unbridged rivers, of which the one 3 miles (5km) north of Nýidalur, can be tricky at times.

The Sprengisandur route was long believed to be the abode of outlaws and elves though visitors nowadays need only fear bad weather. It is probably not worth doing it unless the weather is good, because without the views, it is frankly a long and tedious drive with not a lot to see along the way.

## From Sigalda to Nýidalur

The first part of the route from south to north crosses the area flooded by the hydroelectric schemes on the

Continued on page 208...

Opposite: Ófærufoss Falls at Eldgjá
Above: Frostastaðavatn, near Landmannalaugar
Below: Ódaðahraun lava, Central Highlands

# ICELAND'S SILENT ENEMY – SOIL EROSION

Someone has taken the time to calculate that one square yard of Iceland's surface has been robbed of its top soil for every day in the life of every Icelander that has lived. When the land was first settled birch woodlands may have covered up to one quarter of the country and willow and other dwarf shrubs dominated the vegetation above 1,000ft (305m), giving vital protection to the lush understorey plants and fragile soils. Sheep were only introduced in the ninth century so this vegetation had evolved in the absence of herbivores. Now 1,100 years on, over half the vegetation cover and soil have gone and woodland has been reduced to a pitiful one per cent.

Not only the sheep but also the nature of the soil itself and the delicate balance between mean annual temperature and the length of the growing season, can be blamed. In a harsh environment, even a tiny temperature change may make the difference between erosion and successful re-growth.

A major policy of soil conservation, erosion control and land reclamation is underway. Large tracts have been fenced off from sheep and re-sown, using grass seed. Raising public awareness has been important too and now visitors, as well as locals, think before driving off road. Scars from wheel tracks in the moss can last for centuries but even footprints are forever. At many of Iceland's more vulnerable sites, especially waterfalls, areas have been roped off to protect them from you, the visitor. So, think before you step over to get that special photograph.

Þjórsá River. Just north of here, a 17-mile (27km) track leads to **Veiðivötn**, a cluster of lake-filled craters, which are popular with Icelanders who come for the fishing. The moss-clad slopes of the craters and cobalt-blue of the water makes the place pretty idyllic in fine weather and there are numerous tracks to explore from the campsite.

A guesthouse in the middle of nowhere, **Hrauneyjar**, by the power station complex, has a café, basic provisions and fuel. **Þjórsárver** is an area of marsh-land south of the icecap Hofsjökull and a key breeding ground for many of the world's population of pink-footed geese. This has led to concerns over the continuing development of the rivers for hydroelectricity production.

**Nýidalur** is a lonely, windswept sort of place and the sight of the Touring Club of Iceland's two huts after mile after mile of desert, is more than welcoming. There is a campsite here if you are brave enough to camp at over 2,624ft (800m). The valley runs along the side of the small ice cap, 4,985ft (1,520m) high **Tungnafellsjökull**. A long full day hike leads to the head of the valley and back, with some hot springs as a reward. Another option for hikers are the lower ice-free slopes of Tungnafellsjökull, which give good views over the desert.

## Nýidalur to Goðafoss

Three miles (5km) north of the huts, just after the river, the F910, known as the **Gæsavatn Track** begins. This route to **Askja**, which skirts the northern edge of Vatnajökull, is tricky, with many, many river crossings and difficult sandy stretches. Anyone attempting it should do so in convoy and only after seeking advice locally.

The F26 continues to the chilly looking lake **Fjórðungsvatn** where those heading for **Skagafjörður** and Akureyri take the F752. The unbridged **Bergvatnskvísl** looks innocuous enough but can be difficult after prolonged rainfall. To avoid it take the F881 further north which links up. Both these routes lead to the hut at **Laugafell**, owned by the Touring Club of Akureyri, where there is a lovely natural bathing pool and hot springs. The routes divide here to descend steeply to Skagafjörður and Akureyri.

From Fjórðungsvatn, you now follow the course of **Skjálfandafljót River** the whole way to Goðafoss. It is well worthwhile stopping at **Aldeyjarfoss**, where the river tumbles into a gorge lined with basalt columns.

## ROUTES TO ASKJA AND KVERKFJÖLL

Some people visit **Askja** on a day trip from Lake Mývatn, but if you have time, the area really is worth two or more days, especially if you plan to include **Kverkfjöll** as well. Moreover, it is a long and bumpy drive and to have to do it twice on the same day, seems to make little sense.

There are two main approach roads, both taking off from Route 1, the F88 east of Mývatn, and the F905 west of Egilsstaðir. The first is 60 miles (96km) long, the second 50 miles (81km). Both take three to four hours, and meet 18 miles (28km) from Askja. There are mountain huts at **Herðubreiðarlindir** and **Dreki**, both owned by the Touring Club of Akureyri and at **Kverkfjöll**, owned by The Touring Club of Iceland. Camping, which is only allowed at designated sites in this region, is possible at all three places, but the only one with showers is Herðubreiðarlindir. There is no fuel or other visitor services available, though the wardens at the huts are generous with their information and help.

Historically, there are few accounts of travels in this region of Iceland. The glacial rivers and lack of grazing ground were formidable obstacles. It may well have been 1875, following the eruption of Askja, that the area was first thoroughly investigated, though the outlaw Eyvindur is known to have taken refuge in the region during his years on the run.

## To Askja west of the Jökulsá, via Herðubreið

The F88 follows the Jökulsá River's west bank and the route was first driven in 1939. As you pass, stop and observe how smooth much of the surrounding rock is. This has been caused by the same floods that formed the Jökulsá Canyon downstream. After about 13 miles (20km) the route crosses the edge of a lava flow. It is worth a stop here for a view of some of the finest examples of ropy lava in Iceland.

Further ahead, a freshwater river, the **Gráfarlandaá**, is forded. There is a small waterfall above the ford, and many wildflowers grow along the river banks. Beyond here, the track enters the huge lava flow from the shield volcano **Kollóttadyngja**, which extends to the foot of **Herðubreið**. This imposing 5,516ft (1,682m) mountain is one of Iceland's most memorable. It was formed by a sub-glacial eruption during the Ice Age. First climbed in 1908, the mountain rises 3,600ft (1,100m) above the surrounding land which gives an idea of just how thick the Ice Age glaciers were.

Herðubreiðarlindir is the name given to the springs which emerge from under the lava to form a lush oasis in the central highland desert. High altitude rarities such as the dwarf buttercup and drooping saxifrage are found here, as well as the common and striking arctic river beauty *Epilobium latifolium*, which stains the gravel flats with bright splashes of purple. Around thirty species of bird are found in the area and on the small lakes south of the huts.

The outlaw Eyvindur spent the winter of 1774-75 at Herðubreiðarlindir living on angelica roots and raw horse flesh. He is said to have remarked that this was the worst of his many years on the run. Remains of his shelter can be seen on the trail a stone's throw north-west of the mountain hut, which dates from 1958. The warden lives in the second hut. To protect the vegetation, camping is only allowed in certain areas.

## Dreki and Askja

The route to Askja goes straight over the lava in a tortuous series of twists and bends. This section must be taken slowly. Once the lava is over, you are into the sand, which can be problematic if the weather has been dry and windy, which it usually is around here.

Bathing pool in the Hveravellir geothermal area, Kjölur mountain track

# WALKS FROM HERÐUBREIÐARLINDIR

## ↑1 THE LAKES (1.5 HOURS)

Follow the stream south of the hut until you reach the first of the lakes. The path continues around the further of the lakes and then loops back towards the hut. An excellent walk for birds and flowers.

## ↑2 TO HERÐUBREIÐ (3-4 HOURS)

The marked trail starts from the hut and continues over the ropy lava to the foot of the mountain. Three miles (5km) each way. To climb the mountain, continue a further 5 miles (8km) around the base of the mountain anti-clockwise until you meet the path up on its west face. The climb is not especially difficult except for the last part, when you need to watch for falling rocks. This would be a very long and strenuous 10-12 hour day.

## ↑3 TO ASKJA (2 DAYS)

A two-day walk following the same route around the base of Herðubreið but instead of climbing the mountain, continue the marked trail to the south of the shield volcano Kollóttadyngja. Stay overnight at the hut at Bræðrafell, owned by the Touring Club of Akureyri (5-7 hours) 11-12 miles (17-19km). Next day follow the marked trail due south to Dreki hut (6-7 hours) 12-13 miles (18-20km).

Torfajökull Rhyolite Mountains near Strútslaug

The **Dreki** hut sits on a sea of white pumice at the foot of the **Dyngjufjöll** massif. While the hut and toilets are weighed down with rocks, the campsite does not inspire confidence. To be sure of your tent staying upright weigh the guy ropes and pegs down with rocks, which previous campers will have conveniently left. Winds can be fierce here and it snows even in mid summer. Guarding the hut and campsite are the dragons after which the ravine, **Drekagil**, gets its name.

With care you can walk up the ravine, watching out for falling rocks, to a small waterfall at its head, taking about twenty minutes each way. Here in the walls of the gorge, are impressive pillow lavas, squeezed out under pressure of water, a bit like toothpaste. Another short walk, memorable at sunset or sunrise, is up the slope to the right of the gorge. From Dreki,

the **Gæsavatn track** F910 leads to **Nýidalur** on the Sprengisandur route. This very challenging route should only be attempted in convoy after seeking advice locally from the warden at Dreki hut.

**Askja** lies a further 5 miles (8km) on. The road is slow and it takes about thirty minutes to reach the end of the track, from where it is about a forty-minute walk to the crater **Víti**, meaning 'Hell'. The sulphurous fumes may be off-putting, but there is no denying that a swim in hell is a memorable experience. The water temperature ranges from lukewarm to tepid. In others words, not warm enough to be comfortable, especially if it happens to be snowing, which is likely. The climb down into the crater can be very slippery, and care is needed around the crater rim as well. It is thought that Víti, which was formed in 1875, erupted the

## THE ÖSKJUVEGURINN TRAIL

This is a 3-4 day wilderness backpacking route from Dreki, via Askja to **Svartárkot** in Bárðardalur, using huts owned by the Touring Club of Akureyri for the overnight stays. It traverses the heart of the **Ódáðahraun lava desert** and it would be hard to imagine a more desolate, yet strangely alluring place. The route is marked the whole way. Hikers can use the scheduled bus tour to Askja to get to the start of the trail, but transport the other end is a problem. It is a 14-mile (23km) walk on Route 843 from the trail head to the bridge over Skjálfandafljót River, where it joins the Sprengisandur route. Here there is a chance to hitch a lift, or take the scheduled bus. The first day of walking goes from Dreki, via Askja to the hut at Dyngjufell 12 miles (19km) and 8-10 hours. Day 2 follows a jeep track to start with, then heads through the eastern edge of the Frambruni lava flow to the hut at Botni, 13 miles (21km) and 6-8 hours. The final day follows an old jeep track along the Suðurá River to Svartárkot.

The walk can be extended to make a 5-day trek by combining it with the 2-day walk from Herðubreiðarlindir to Dreki. Note that apart from the huts, there are no other facilities for visitors and you must take all your food and cooking utensils. Booking in advance is advisable as the weather is merciless in this corner of Iceland. The route is for experienced and fit backpackers only.

huge volume of pumice which spread over much of north east Iceland, covering one tenth of the island. Following the sudden emptying of the magma chamber, its thin roof collapsed, forming the circular caldera of Askja (the word Askja means caldera). Later the depression filled with water, forming Iceland's deepest lake, 745ft (227m) deep.

It was winter when Askja blew in 1875 and a thick layer of pumice fell on more than 3ft (1m) of snow. Pumice is a good insulator and in places this 125 year old ice has still not melted away. A walk up the ridge behind Víti gives a great perspective of the entire area, which if you can spare it, is worth a full day to explore further.

# To Askja, east of the Jökulsá

The track F905 starts from just east of Möðrudalur, on the old Route 1. It then becomes F910 and there are a couple of freshwater rivers to ford before you reach the first of the lava flows. The lava is post-Ice Age but has been smoothed over by flooding and then swamped with pumice from Askja. It is a moody and atmospheric place. There is a new bridge (1986) over the **Kreppá** and 10 rather slow miles (16km) to the junction where F903 takes off to **Hvannalindir**. Turn right here and follow the track round to the next junction that leads to **Kverkfjöll**. Cross over the Jökulsá Bridge and keep going until you meet the junction with the F88.

# Routes to Kverkfjöll

There are two routes, the first the F903 via the springs at Hvannalindir, a smaller version of the oasis at Herðubreiðarlindir. The second route is the F902 and the distance is roughly the same.

A huge central volcano at Vatnajökull's northern edge, **Kverkfjöll** has been built up in repeated eruptions during and after the Ice Age. There is thought to have been a major eruption in the fifteenth century and possibly others since then, though it is only since 1970, that the area has been studied. A fault runs through the mountain, forming the cleft and a massive geothermal field, which is one of the largest in Iceland. There is a hut at the foot of the mountain run by the Touring Club of Iceland, where camping is also possible. From the end of the road, you can walk to the ice caves formed by a warm river running through the glacier. They may not be safe to enter so seek advice from the hut warden. It is possible, with care, to walk across the glacier to **Hveradalur** and back in a day. Hveradalur is where the bulk of the hot springs are located, but again, seek advice before going on your own. In summer, the wardens do guided walks on the glacier.

## Sunrise and sunset

|            | North   | South   |
|------------|---------|---------|
| **Jan 1st**     | 11.32am | 11.19am |
|            | 3.00pm  | 3.44pm  |
| **April 1st**   | 6.28am  | 6.46am  |
|            | 8.07pm  | 8.19pm  |
| **July 1st**    | 1.57am  | 3.05am  |
|            | 0.32am  | 11.57pm |
| **October 1st** | 7.22am  | 7.36am  |
|            | 6.41pm  | 6.58pm  |

# THE FJALLABAK ROUTES

The Fjallabak wilderness lies north of the ice cap Mýrdalsjökull. Most visitors agree that its scenery is among the most dramatic in Iceland, and for four-wheel-drive enthusiasts, its tracks are the most fun to drive.

Central to the region is the **Torfajökull** volcanic system, which threw up the surrounding many-hued rhyolite mountains during repeated eruptions under ice. The area has thousands of hot springs, steam vents, craters, lava flows, lakes and even a waterfall or two, and is a veritable paradise for hikers and mountain bikers. Access to the region is through the scheduled bus services to either Þórsmörk (hikers only) or **Landmannalaugar** and **Eldgjá**, via Route F208 or F225. The Southern Fjallabak route has no scheduled bus services.

Landmannalaugar Mountain hut and Campsite

## Northern Fjallabak route

From the west there are two tracks to Landmannalaugar off Route 26. The F208 is shorter and faster but is less scenic because it follows the power line. F225, the longer route, skirts the base of Hekla, Iceland's most notorious volcano that last blew in February 2000. Its ash can be seen to either side of the track. There are a couple of small rivers to ford, set among grassy plains and a backdrop of moss-clad fells.

214

## 1 BLÁHNÚKUR AND BRENNISTEINSALDA LOOP (3-4 HOUR CIRCULAR WALK)

From the campsite follows the track up the valley to the first stream. If there is no plank across, you will need to ford it. Then head up the ridge of the mountain **Bláhnúkur**. The greenish deposits at its base are a crude form of perlite. The path is steep and unrelenting and follows the ridge to the summit 3,050ft (930m) taking about an hour. From the summit there are views of Iceland's three largest ice caps. The way down the other side is mostly not as steep, but it can be gravelly underfoot. About half way down the path splits right down a side ridge. At the bottom, wade the river, and follow the track through the bizarre and twisted lava formations to where the steam rises at the foot of Brenninsteinsalda. Here there are steam vents and sulphur pits. Follow the marked path left of the mountain if you want to climb it, otherwise take the same path in the opposite direction back to the campsite.

## 2 SUÐURNÁMUR (3 HOUR CIRCULAR WALK)

The path up the ridge of this multi-hued mountain takes off the other side of the river that you ford to reach the campsite at Landmannalaugar. The ridge walk offers superb views, but the descent into Vöndugil can be tricky. Seek advice from the wardens.

## 3 BRANDSGIL (1 HOUR THERE AND BACK)

Continue on the track up the valley from the campsite and skirt the base of Bláhnúkur to reach the wonderful gorge of Brandsgil.

## 4 THE LAUGAVEGUR TRAIL (4 DAYS)

Probably the most famous trek in Iceland, this route was the first long-distance path to be waymarked. The four day trek between Landmannalaugar and Þórsmörk traverses the heart of a remote region, with rhyolite mountains, abundant hot springs, ice caves and glaciers its highlights. The Touring Club of Iceland owns the huts along the way, which it is essential to pre-book, unless you plan to take a tent. Basic food supplies can be bought from the mobile shop at Landmannalaugar and at Þórsmörk. The first day from Landmannalaugar starts with a steady climb to **Hrafntinnusker** (3-4 hours). Those with the energy can walk to the ice caves from here, about a two-hour round trip. The second day, goes past many beautiful thermal springs, through the heart of the rhyolite, with a steep descent to **Álftavatn** (4-5 hours). A newer and better hut and campsite at Hvanngil, 4 miles (6km) further, is an alternative to Álftavatn. Climb the mountain behind Hvanngil for an incredible view of its surrounds. The third day is over black sands to the hut at **Botnar**, where you should take a detour down to the gorge of the **Markafljót** (3-4 hours). The final day gives wonderful views of the glaciers as you approach **Þórsmörk** (4-5) hours. Some people do the trek in just two days, but this allows little time to enjoy the scenery along the way, and explore around the huts. The walk can be extended for a further two days by continuing from Þórsmörk over a 3,280ft (1,000m) pass to Skógar (see under Þórsmörk).

At the cross roads by **Lake Frostastaðavatn**, it is worth taking a short detour to the lake-filled explosion crater **Ljótipollur**, which was formed in the fifteenth century. Its green-blue water is 46ft (14m) deep and contrasts exquisitely with the rust red of the crater walls. The road climbs to a saddle above Frostastaðavatn where there is a great view of the first of the rhyolite ridges. A tongue of lava, from 1480, dips into the lake on its far side. On the other side of the road, a small moss-clad crater is worth the climb up, but stick to the marked path so as not to damage the fragile moss.

Set amidst mountains that look like they have been created by an artist run amok with a palette, **Landmannalaugar** is one of Iceland's most scenic spots. It is also very popular, which means that its camp-site, spread out over the gravel flats of a river bed, resembles a sprawling tented city. The only other accommodation is the Touring Club of Iceland's mountain hut, which usually needs booking.

Landmannalaugar sits at the edge of **Laugahraun**, a huge wall of viscous, slow flowing, acid lava which, in 1480, oozed from a fissure on the side of **Brennisteinsalda**, the pink and beige cone-shaped mountain behind. Hot water emerges from under the lava to form a wonderful natural bathing pool. The surrounds of the pool are marshlands, which support a surprising variety of plants and birds, given the height of the place above sea level 1,935ft (590m). Particularly entertaining are the red-necked phalaropes, which spin in circles to stir up their food. The vegetation is very fragile and it is extremely important not to disturb it in any way. In summer a mobile shop brings supplies to Landmannalaugar, which is helpful to hungry hikers arriving from a trek.

Route F208 now roughly follows the power line, which takes the northern route around Mýrdalsjökull, in case Katla erupts. There are several rivers to ford, though none especially deep, except after heavy rainfall. This is a wonderfully scenic roller coaster ride of a route, which hauls up and down steep slopes and in and out of river beds. Superb black gorges and electric-green moss banks provide unusual subjects for photography, and even if the weather is foggy, which it often is, the place has an atmosphere all of its own.

**Eldgjá** is a 5-mile (8km) long fissure, blasted out by an explosive eruption in the tenth century, which is probably linked with the Katla volcano. Drive up the fissure for ten minutes from the turn-off, and ford the river to reach the car park. From here it is a thirty to forty minute walk up the fissure to the waterfall **Ófærufoss**, which tumbles in three stages over the edge of the gorge. Camping is not allowed in the fissure but there is a campsite and hut, about 6 miles (10km) south of there. Beyond Eldgjá, the road follows the course of the **Skaftá River** over broad expanses of open pasture, with views of the glaciers to join Route 1.

# The Southern Fjallabak route

There are two approaches to **Hvanngil**, by Route F210 from **Keldur**, or F261 from **Hvolsvöllur**. The second is scenically superior and there is much of interest along the way. Several farms in the Fljótshlíð valley offer accommodation, and the wonderful views of the glaciers make this a tempting prospect. The last farm, **Fljótsdalur**, is a youth hostel with basic facilities and rustic charm. It is run by Englishman Dick Phillips, who pioneered walking trips into the region north west of here.

The route follows the base of the **Tindafjöll** massif and glacier, the remains of a major volcanic system which blew its top off. The route follows the **Markafljót River** and it is worth a 90 minute detour on foot to walk the trail along the river's impressive gorge. There are a couple of glacial rivers to ford before Hvanngil, where there is a new hut and campsite. If you have time, it is worth spending a night or so here, because there are plenty of good walks, though as yet few marked trails. The hill behind the hut, a one hour walk there and back, gives a panoramic view of the surroundings.

The route continues over **Mælifellssandur**, the black sand outwash plain on the northern edge of the icecap. At the foot of the hill **Mælifell**, a track takes off to the left. Follow this for several miles fording the oddly named **Brennivínskvísl** (Brennivín is the national spirit of Iceland) until you can drive no further. From here follow the path up the river and over a low saddle, skirting the northern flank of the mountain **Strútur**. Descend to and cross another river and climb again until you see a flat grassy plain with braided river channels. Walk around it to reach **Strútslaug**, a natural bathing pool in a warm river at the foot of **Torfajökull**. ($1^1/_2$-2 hours walk each way).

Back on the main road, ford the **Holmsá,** which can be tricky after heavy rainfall, and keep on the F210 (the best of the several options) until you descend to the valley and join Route 208.

## Exploring the Highlands by bus

Scheduled bus services cover the Kjölur, Sprengisandur, North Fjallabak and Askja routes, running daily in summer.

Icelandic family gathers for saga reading

217

# DRIVING IN

All of Iceland's highland tracks are unsurfaced. Many are graded once or twice during the summer, a few not at all. **Each highland route has an official opening time and it is forbidden to drive the route until then**. This is because in spring the top layer thaws out first but does not drain because the land is still frozen below. If the roads have not dried out properly, you are likely to get badly bogged down and do a lot of damage. The routes are all best driven in a high clearance four-wheel-drive vehicle, except for the Kjölur route which can be covered in an ordinary car. Do check the conditions of the road and your insurance, especially if you are hiring a vehicle,

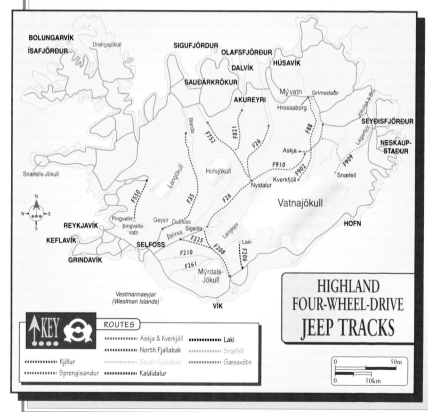

HIGHLAND FOUR-WHEEL-DRIVE JEEP TRACKS

KEY

ROUTES

- Askja & Kverkjöll
- North Fjallabak
- South Fjallabak
- Kaldidalur
- Kjölur
- Sprengisandur
- Laki
- Snæfell
- Gæsavötn

# THE HIGHLANDS

Above: Mt Herðubreið, Central Highlands
Below: Near Landmannalaugar, reducing wheel pressure to drive on snow

219

# • DRIVING IN THE HIGHLANDS •

These are the average opening times of the major routes:

| Route | Average opening |
|---|---|
| Laki | 12 July |
| **North Fjallabak F208** | |
| Sigalda-Landmannalaugar | 17 June |
| Landmannalaugar-Eldgjá | 28 June |
| Eldgjá-south to Route 1 | 8 June |
| **South Fjallabak F210** | |
| Keldur-Hvanngil | 5 July |
| Fljótshlíð-Hvanngil | 5 July |
| Hvanngil-Mælifellssandur | 5 July |
| Landmannaleið F225 | 19 June |
| Kjölur F35 | 15 June |
| Sprengisandur F26 | 1 July |
| Skagfjarðaleið F752 | 3 July |
| Eyjafjarðarleið F821 | 9 July |
| Askja (Dreki hut) F88 | 20 June |
| Askja (crater) | 20 June |
| Kverkfjöll F902 | 20 June |

information on opening times ia given out regularly during the summer by the Public Roads Administration. www.vegagerdin.is

## Travelling with care

The isolation of the highlands and the possibility of extreme weather, even in high summer, mean that if things go wrong, then they can go badly wrong. **If you are bringing your own vehicle, make sure you have all the necessary spare parts and that you know the basics of its mechanics. If hiring a vehicle, make sure that the insurance covers you to drive in the highlands. Remember that your insurance is invalid for any damage or breakdown that occurs off the official tracks and when crossing rivers**. The costs of recovering a vehicle from a remote area can be very high. **Always carry a tow rope and a shovel.** Before you start your journey, ring Vegagerðin, the Icelandic Highways Department, for information on your intended route.

## Crossing rivers

There are many unbridged rivers in the highlands and special care is needed to cross them.Locate the proper fording place. There may be more than one, so choose the one that has been used most recently.

The flow of glacial rivers varies. It is highest during and after heavy rainfall, or at the end of a hot sunny day. Flow is usually at its lowest early in the morning. All rivers have a higher flow in spring from the melting winter snow. Glacial rivers are fast flowing and muddy, making it difficult to see large rocks on the river bed.

If in doubt, wait for another vehicle and cross in convoy. It helps to watch another more experienced driver cross first. Seek local advice from the wardens at the mountain huts, from other car or coach drivers. **Engage low gear, low ratio and four-wheel-drive. Do not change gear once you have entered the river and do not stop. Do not take risks.** Some people have died crossing Iceland's rivers. If in doubt, wait. It may be boring, but it's not fatal.

## Driving in sand

High winds can cause drifting sand in the highlands. Where this builds up on the roads it can be problematic, especially in dry weather. Take a run at a sandy stretch, engaging second or third gear, low ratio and four-wheel-drive. Keep a constant speed and do not change gear. If you get stuck, do not spin the wheels, you will only dig in deeper. Planks or sand mats can be helpful under the wheels.

## Driving off-road

**All driving outside official roads and tracks is prohibited by law in Iceland.** This is to protect the fragile environment. It may look fun to make tracks in the sand but you will leave a scar that may take hundreds of years to heal. Vegetation is very sensitive and the ground often waterlogged. Driving on such ground you will sink in and leave deep tracks, which the wind will undercut, starting a new cycle of soil erosion. Over half of Iceland's soil cover has already been lost to erosion.

## Facilities in the Highlands

Apart from mountain huts (see Fact File Accommodation) there are practically no facilities in the highlands. Travellers need to be self sufficient in terms of fuel and food, and take a tent unless huts have been pre-booked. At Landmannalaugar there is a mobile shop selling basic provisions during July and August. At Kerlingarfjöll on the Kjölur route (☎ 852 4223 www.kerlinarfjoll.is email: info@kerlingarfjoll.is) there is fuel as well as hut accommodation and basic provisions, while on the Sprengisandur route at Hrauneyjar (☎ 487 7782 www.hrauneyjar.is email: hrauneyjar@hrauneyjar.is) there is a guesthouse, fuel, café and basic provisions.

# By air

Icelandair has flights every day of the week from London and Glasgow to Keflavík Airport, located 31 miles (50km) from Reykjavík. Other European destinations served by the airline include Amsterdam, Barcelona, Hamburg, Frankfurt, Munich, Copenhagen, Oslo, Stockholm, Zurich, Paris and Milan.

**Icelandair**
London W1T 7LY
☎ (0207) 874 1000,
Fax (0207) 387 5711
london@icelandair.is
www.icelandair.co.uk
There are regular services from the USA cities of Baltimore, Washington, Boston, Minneapolis, New York and Orlando.

**Icelandair**
Columbia, Maryland 21044,
☎ 1 800 223 5500,
america@icelandair.is
www.icelandair.com

**Air Iceland**
(See Fact File Around Iceland) fly from the Faroe Islands and Link Reykjavík with Constable point and Kulusuk in East Greenland.

**Iceland Express**
☎ 0870 850 0737
www.icelandexpress.com
fly daily from Stanstead in the UK and Copenhagen in Denmark to Keklavík.

# By sea

Between mid-May and early September, a car and passenger ferry links Aberdeen in Scotland and Seyðisfjörður in the East of Iceland, via the Shetland and Faroe Islands.

**P&O Scottish Ferries**
Aberdeen AB9 8DL
☎ (01224) 572615
Fax (01224) 574411,
www.smyril-line.fo
www.poscottishferries.com

Eimskip operate a cargo service between Immingham in the UK and Reykjavík. The service carries vehicles as cargo, and has limited passenger accommodation. Between the USA and Iceland there is a cargo service only.

**Eimskip UK**
Immingham, DN40 1AH, England,
☎ (01469) 550200
Fax (01469) 550298,
www.eimskip.com

**Eimskip USA Inc**
1 columbus Center, Suite 500,
Virginia Beach VA23462 USA
☎ (757) 627 4444
Fax (757) 627 9367,
gyl@eimskip.com

222

# THE ICELAND EXPERIENCE

A visit to Iceland is no mere holiday, it is an experience of a lifetime. Nowhere else on earth can one observe so much natural beauty in so small an area.

Planning your Iceland Experience is like putting together a rather complex jigsaw puzzle. Just leave out a few pieces and the final picture is incomplete. There are so many travel options, from simple 'go-as-you-please' arrangements, right through to fully inclusive guided tours of the island. Suffice to say, in order to get the best out of your holiday, you may need the assistance of those who have travelled the same path before, and have up-to-date information on the many choices available.

At Arctic Experience we pride ourselves in being able to tailor a holiday, or expedition, to the exact requirements of the individual.

Our brochure includes a diverse selection of holidays and travel ideas, which may well give you food for thought. The advice we give is of course free, and the prices for services we arrange are very competitive. We also carry an extensive range of maps on Iceland and Greenland.

Contact us for further information.

**ARCTIC EXPERIENCE**
...where holidays come naturally
24 hour brochure line:
## 01737 214214
www.arcrtic-experience.co.uk

29 Nork Way, Banstead,
Surrey SM7 1PB

## Arriving at or departing from Keflavík Airport

A **'Fly Bus'** service operates between Keflavík Airport and the air terminal at Hotel Loftleiðir in Reykjavík. Buses depart from Hotel Loftleiðir 2 hours prior to the flight departure time and the journey to the airport takes about 45 minutes. Buses meet all arriving flights. The fare is approximately £9 ($16) each way, payable inside the airport terminal and at Hotel Loftleiðir.

## Passport & Visa

A valid passport is needed to visit Iceland, except for citizens of Denmark, Norway, Finland and Sweden. No visa is required for citizens of the United Kingdom, Irish Republic and other European countries, United States of America, Canada, Australia, New Zealand, for visits of up to three months. Citizens of Austria, Belgium, France, Germany, Greece, Italy, Liechtenstein, Luxembourg, the Netherlands, Portugal, Spain and Switzerland may travel to Iceland using their national identity card. For visa information contact the Immigration Service, www.utl.is

**Embassy of Iceland**
2a Hans St, London,
SW1X OJE, England
☎ (0207) 259 3999
Fax (0207) 7245 9649

**Embassy of Iceland**
1156 15th Street N W, Suite 1200,
Washington DC, 20005-1704
☎ (202) 265 6653
Fax (202) 265 6656

## Vaccinations

There are no mandatory vaccinations required for Iceland.

## Tour Operators

### In the UK

**Discover the World**
Banstead, SM7 1PB,
☎ (01737) 214214,
Fax (01737) 362341,
sales@arctic-experience.co.uk
www.arctic-experience.co.uk

**Dick Phillips**
Whitehall House, Alston,
CA9 3PS, ☎ (01434) 381440,
icelandick@nent.enta.net
www.icelandictravel.com

**High Places**
Sheffield, S6 3AE,
☎ 0114 275 7500,
Fax 0114 275 3870,
www.highplaces.co.uk

**Regent Holidays (UK) Ltd**
Bristol BS1 2HR,
☎ (01179) 211711,
regent@regent-holidays.co.uk
www.regent-holidays.co.uk

**Scantours Ltd**
London, WC2H 7DH,
☎ (0207) 839 2927,
Fax (0207) 839 5891,
info@scantours.co.uk
www.scantoursuk.com

**Travelscene**
Harrow, HA1 1LQ,
☎ 0870 777 9987
reservations@travelscene.co.uk
treks@highplaces.co.uk
www.travelscene.co.uk

## In the USA

**Icelandair Holidays**
☎ (1800) 779 2899
holiday@icelandair.is
www.icelandtotal.com

**Nordic saga Tours**
☎ (1800) 848 6449
NSTours@nordicsaga.com
www.nordicsaga.com

**Nordique Tours**
☎ (1800) 995 7997
info@nordiquetours.com
www.nordiquetours.com

**Scanam World Tours**
☎ (1800) 545 2204
info@scanamtours.com
www.scandinaviantravel.com

**Scantours**
☎ (1800) 223 7226
info@scantours.com
www.scantours.com

## In Canada

**Great Canadian
Travel Company**
☎ (1800) 661 3830
iceland@gctc-mst.com
www.greatcanadiantravel.com

## In Iceland

**Destination Iceland**
Vatnsmýrarvegur 10, Reykjavík,
☎ 591 1020
booking@dice.is    www.dice.is

**Discover the World**
Sætún 8, 105 Reykjavík
☎ 561 3200
bara@dtw.is    www.dtw.is

# ACCOMMODATION

If you are travelling in June and August it is almost always essential to pre-book your overnight stops, unless you plan to camp or use dormitory style sleeping bag accommodation. New Year (in the capital) is also a busy time.

In this book we give suggestions for places to stay in Reykjavík and a selection of the more unusual and characterful establishments around the island. We do NOT include full accommodation listings. This is because almost all the information you need in order to book can be obtained on the internet or by telephone. On the following pages we give all the necessary contacts for you to get the information and make a booking. Alternatively, use the services of a tour operator offering tailor-made independent travel (see under 'Tour Operators'). As they can get better prices than the public prices, it does not necessarily work out more expensive.

Outside of the capital and larger towns many establishments are only open in the summer months between 1 June and 1 September. A few stay open until mid-September. For visitors using public transport, it is worth noting that many farms, guesthouses and hostels offer a pick up service from the airport, main road or nearest town. It is always worth asking when you book.

Hótel Borg, Reykjavík

**Áning** is a free publication listing accommodation throughout the island. It can be downloaded from the internet from www.heimur.is/world or obtained once you arrive in Iceland at hotels and information centres

## Accommodation Costs

Approximate prices, per person per night in summer, in a twin-bedded room including breakfast. Prices may be 25%-35% lower at other times of year. Check special rates for children. Mountain huts and cheapest sleeping bag accommodation prices are dormitory style.

### Reykjavík
'Top of the Range' £95-£135 (US$170-$240)
'Mid to Top range' £70-£85 (US$120-$155)
'Mid Range' £50-£60 (US$85-$110)
'Guesthouse' £28-£40 (US$45-$70)

### Around Iceland
**Edda Hotels** £33 (US$58) without bathroom £50 (US$90) with bathroom
**Icelandair Hotels** around £60 (US$110) with bathroom
**Fosshotels** £55-£72 (US$94-$130) with bathroom
**Farm Guesthouses** £36-£55 (US$60-$90) without and with bathroom
**Youth Hostel** £16 (US$28) no breakfast
**Sleeping bag accommodation** £13-£18 (US$23-$32) no breakfast
**Mountain hut** £12-£16 (US$21-$28) no breakfast

## Accommodation In Reykjavík

### Top of the Range
**Hótel Borg**
Pósthússtræti 11,
☎ 551 1440, Fax 551 1420
hotel.borg@hotelborg.is
www.hotelborg.is
Central location, beautiful
nineteen thirties décor.

**101 Hótel**
Hverfisgata 10
☎ 580 0101
101hotel@101hotel.is
www.101hotel.is
Stylish new 'Design Hotel' in the
city centre. Monochrome and
minimalist theme.

### Mid to Top Range
**Radisson SAS Hótel Saga**
Hagatorg,
☎ 525 9900, Fax 525 9909,
sales.reykjavik@radisson_SAS.com
www.hotelsaga.is
International style large hotel, 10
minutes walk from heart of city.
Parking

**Hótel Klöpp**
Klapparstígur 26
☎ 511 6062, Fax 511 6071
klopp@centerhotels.is
www.centerhotels.is
Stylish new small hotel with
central location.

### Hótel Skjáldbreið
Laugavegur 16
☎ 511 6060, Fax 511 6070
skjaldbreid@centerhotels.is
www.centerhotels.is
New central hotel in an historic building

### Hótel Óðinsvë
Oðinstorg
☎ 511 6200
odinsve@hotelodinsve.is
www.hotelodinsve.is
Quiet, central location. Light and airy, Scandinavian style small hotel. Good restaurants.

## Mid Range
### Hótel Leifur Eiríksson
Skólavörðustígur 45
☎ 562 0800, Fax 562 0804
hotel-leifur@islandia.is
www.hotel.is
Nice central location and pleasant rooms.

### Hótel Reykjavík
Rauðarárstíg 37
☎ 514 7000
grandhotel@grandhotel.is
www.grand.is
Modern hotel in a near central location.

### Hótel Plaza
Aðalstræti
☎ 511 2700
icelandichotels@icelandichotels.is
www.icelandichotels.is
New hotel in central location. Well-equipped rooms.

### Hótel Nordica
Suðurlandsbraut 2
☎ 444 5000
icehotel@icehotel.is
www.icehotel.is
Renovated in 2003, with new deluxe rooms. 30 minutes walk to central reykjavík.

### Hótel Loftleiðir
(By the domestic airport)
☎ 505 0900, Fax 505 0905,
icehotel@icehotel.is
www.icehotel.is
Plenty of facilities but not much character, 20 minutes walk from heart of city.

## Guesthouses
Small establishments, generally not offering rooms with private bathroom.

### Centrum Guesthouse
Njálsgata 74
☎ 511 5602
mail@guesthouse-centrum.com
www.guesthouse-centrum.com
Reasonable prices and near central location.

### Ísafold Guesthouse
Bárugata 11
☎ 561 2294
isafold@itn.is
attractive historic family home in quiet, central location.

### Dómus Guesthouse
Hverfisgata 45
☎ 561 1200
domus@simnet.is
www.domusguesthouse.is
Historic house in central location. Also offers sleeping bag accommodation.

### Dúna Guesthouse
Suðurhlið 35d
☎ 588 2100
ghduna@simnet.is
www.islandia.is/duna
Not central but well priced. Also offers sleeping bag accommodation.

# Accommodation around Iceland

## Edda Hotels

☎ 444 4000
edda@hoteledda.is
www.hoteledda.is
A chain of 15 summer hotels
offering rooms with basin and
sleeping bag accommodation,
some rooms with shower/WC.
They usually have their own
restaurant but not self-catering
facilities.

## Foss Hotels

☎ 562 4000
bokun@fosshotel.is
www.fosshotel.is
A group of 13 hotels around
Iceland with a central
booking system. Most rooms
are with private bathroom
and the majority of hotels
have their own restaurant.

## Youth Hostels

Booking office:
☎ 553 8110
info@hostel.is, website
www.hostel.is. Some hostels
are open all year, others
from May/June to
September. 27 hostels
around the island.

## Icelandair Hotels

☎ 444 4000
icehotel@icehotel.is
www.icehotel.is
A group of hotels with central
booking system. All have a
restaurant and rooms with private
bathroom.

## Keats Hotel

☎ 460 2000
keahotels@keahotels.is
www.keahotels.is
Hotels in Akureyri, Reykjavík and
Mývatn

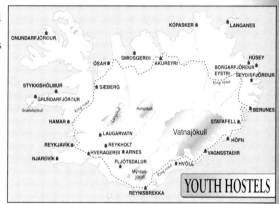

## Farm Guesthouses

There are over 120 of these located around Iceland. Many are part of
the Icelandic Farm Holidays network, which produces a list of farms
and takes bookings. Some farms are like youth hostels, others may
offer holiday cabins or are more like country hotels with a range of
facilities. Many offer the choice of made up beds or sleeping bag
accommodation but it is important to specify what you wish to book
when inquiring. Some, but not all, offer self-catering facilities.

Staying on farms is a great way of getting contact with the local
people. On some, the standard of accommodation and meals is as good
as that of the hotels. Many farms also offer horse riding, jeep trips,
angling, boat trips and other activities. Cabin accommodation is self-
catering and linen can usually be supplied, though at additional cost.

### Icelandic Farm Holidays
☎ 570 2700
Ifh@farmholidays.is
www.farmholidays.is

# Fact File

## Mountain Huts

These are located mostly in uninhabited areas. Orange painted huts are for emergency use only and are located on mountain roads and along uninhabited coasts. They are not for general visitor use. Huts in recreational areas of the highlands are owned and maintained by the following hiking clubs and are open to members and non-members for a fee. It is usually essential to book in advance.

**Touring Club of Iceland**
(Ferðafélag Íslands),
Mörkinni 6, 108 Reykjavík
☎ 568 2533
fi@fi.is   www.fi.is

**Touring Club of Akureyri**
(Ferðafélag Akureyrar),
Strandgata 23, 602 Akureyri,
☎ 462 2720
ffa@li.is   www.ffa.is

**Útivist**,
Laugavegur 178, 105 Reykjavík
☎ 562 1000
utivist@utivist.is   www.utivist.is

## Camping In Iceland

It used to be possible to camp almost anywhere in Iceland and while it is still the case in some out of the way places, camping is restricted to official sites within National Parks and Conservation Areas. Where the land is obviously private, as in farming country, permission should always be sought first. There are now campsites in almost all towns and villages, in most protected areas and on some farms, which also offer guesthouse facilities. For a list of campsites contact www.camping.is Fees for camping are fairly standard, in the region of £3-£4 (US$5-$6) per person but the facilities offered can differ hugely. The best sites may have hot showers, drying facilities, a laundry and indoor cooking and eating space. At the other end of the scale, there may just be an earth closet! **Reykjavík Campsite**, Laugardalur (by the main swimming pool), ☎ 568 6944.

## Accommodation of Special Character

This section gives details of unusual hotels, guesthouses and a unique self catering lodge, chosen for their spectacular location, historic interest or just because they are different from the rest.

### West

**Hotel Glymur**
Hvalfjörður
☎ 430 3100
info@hotelglymur.is
www.hotelglymur.is
Views, hot tub and fabulous art work

**Guesthouse Ensku Húsin**
near Borgarnes
☎ 437 1826
litlabrekka@aknet.is
www.aknet.is/enkuhusin
Historic building, beautiful riverside location

**Hotel Búðir**
Búðir, Snæfellsnes
☎ 435 6700
budir@budir.is
www.budir.is
Stunning coastal location, views, good food.

**Brekkubær Eco Guesthouse**
Hellnar, Snæfellsnes
☎ 435 6820
brekkubaer@hellnar.is
www.hellnar.is
Coastal location, alternative therapies.

## North

**Hotel Tindastóll**
Sauðarkrókur
☎ 435 5002
sml@simnet.is
www.hoteltindastoll.is
Historic building, hot tub.

**Árgerði Country Guesthouse**
Dalvík
☎ 555 4212
argerdi@argerdi.com
www.argerdi.com
Beautiful rural location, historic building.

## East

**Hotel Aldan**
Seyðisfjörður
☎ 472 1277
booking@hotelaldan.com
www.hotelaldan.com
New hotel in historic building in a beautiful fjord and village.

**Hotel Framtið Djúpivogur**
Djúpivogur
framtid@isholf.is.
www.isholf.is/framtid
Historic building, beautiful fjord and village location.

**Hotel Djúpavík**
Standir, West Fjords
☎ 451 4037
djupavik@snerpa.is
Guesthouse in former herring workers' hostel, stunning fjord location.

**Gauksmýri**
near Hvammstangi
☎ 451 2927
gauksmyri@gauksmyri.is
www.gauksmyri.is
Farm guesthouse, horse riding and horse breeding, bird watching.

**Lava House**
near Mývatn/Húsavík area
☎ 561 3200
(or in UK 01737 214214)
sales@arctic-experience.co.uk
www.arctic-experience.co.uk/tour4j
Luxury self-catering riverside country lodge, sleeping 10-12. Hot tub.

**Húsey Hostel**
Egilsstadir region
☎ 471 3010
www.husey.de
Hostel style farm accommodation. Great for seals and bird watching.

**Guesthouse Egilsstðir**
Egilsstadir region
☎ 471 1114
egilsstadir@isholf.is
www.isholf.is/egilsstadir
Historic building, antique furnishing, lakeside location.

## South

### Hotel Skaftafell
Skaftafell
☎ 478 1945
hotelskf@centrum.is
www.hotelskaftafell.is
Breathtaking location 15 minutes walk from a glacier at the foot of Iceland's highest peak.

### Hotel Anna
near Skógar
☎ 487 8950
eyjathe@isholf.is
www.simnet.is/moldnupur
Delightful traditional farm guesthouse in spectacular location.

### Hotel Eldhestar
Hveragerði
☎ 480 4800
info@eldhestar.is
www.eldhestar.is
'Eco' farm guesthouse and riding centre, with hot tub.

### Hotel Rangá
Hella
☎ 487 5700
hotelranga@hotelranga.is
www.hotelranga.is
Luxury lodge-style hotel in the country.

### Frost & Fire Guesthouse
Hveragerði
☎ 483 4959
info@frostandfire.is
www.frostandfire.is
Guesthouse with hot pool, sauna and hot springs on the doorstep.

## ACTIVITIES & SPORTS

## Angling

The main season for salmon fishing is late June to mid-September and for trout fishing from late April to late September. For salmon fishing permits must be arranged months, even years, in advance, while for trout, permits can often be arranged on the spot. Sea angling can be arranged locally from most towns and villages around the island.

### National Angling Association
☎ 553 1510
angling@angling.is
www.angling.is

### Icelandic Farm Holidays
(see Accommodation for details)

## Climbing

### Icelandic Alpine Club
☎ 581 1700
info@isalp.is    www.isalp.is

useful website: www.fjallamennska.is

# Cycling
## Bringing your own bike
Both touring and mountain bikes are suitable, but wide and robust tyres are important and your bike must withstand constant jarring and dust once you leave the surfaced roads. Make sure you are a competent bike mechanic and bring a sensible range of spares.

useful website: Icelandic Mountain Bike Club www.fjallamennska.is

## Hiring a bike
Hire available by the day or by the week. Advisable to book in advance. A number of youth hostels and guesthouses also have bikes for hire for day use.

### In Reykjavík
Borgarhjól Hverfisgata 50 ☎ 551 5653, Fax 551 5657

### Lake Mývatn
From the camp site ☎ 464 4103.

### Akureyri
Skipagata 4 ☎ 461 2248.

## Where to cycle
**The Ring Road** – Mostly tarmac, some sections busy and along most of the south coast there are no alternative routes available. Bikes can be taken on buses only if space permits and at additional cost. No pre-booking.

**Across the highlands** – the north to south routes may look appealing but there is little variety of scenery and the cycling is monotonous. High winds and dust can make it miserable.

**Fjallabak Routes** – fantastic scenery, rugged terrain and tracks and some unbridged rivers.

**Snæfellsnes Peninsula** – plenty of interest, fairly flat and mostly surfaced roads with little traffic.

**North-West Fjords** – light traffic, mostly gravel roads, a lot of up and down but some great scenery.

**Around Lake Mývatn** – not a big choice of route but plenty of interest. The circular route around Tjörnes incorporating the Jökulsá Canyon is an option.

# Hiking
To enjoy Iceland's wonderful scenery to the full you need to be prepared to walk. Many tour operators offer hiking and backpacking holidays in Iceland for those who do not want to do it on their own (see under 'Tour Operators'). Another option is to join trips arranged by one of the local hiking clubs, The Touring Club of Iceland, Útivist or The Touring Club of Akureyri (see under 'Mountain Huts'). Useful website: www.fjallamennska.is

Opposite: Hiking at Laki

Above: Midnight Sun, near Dalvik, Eyjafjörður

Below: Hofðabrekka Farm Guesthouse, South Iceland

235

## Tips for walkers

Check the weather forecast. Ask advice from local people and don't set out if the forecast is not good. Always carry proper clothing including rainproof jacket and trousers, warm fibre-pile jacket, trousers, hat and gloves and wear walking boots and not sports shoes or trainers. Bright clothing makes you easier to find if you get lost or injured. Take extra food for emergencies and a compass, and know how to use it. Don't walk alone. Take great care when wading through rivers. Wear boots, sandals or shoes. Use a stick for support and to test the water depth and link arms with others. Spend time looking for the best place to cross. The narrowest place usually has the deepest water and the swiftest water flows on the outside of a bend. The best place may be at the widest point, or between bends where the flow is more even. Any river, particularly a glacial river that comes above knee level, is potentially hazardous. If in doubt, don't cross. By waiting a few hours, the flow may subside.

Always seek advice from local people and wardens and let them know of your intended route. For wilderness hikes and backpacking trails a compass and GPS are essential items. Iceland's nature is fragile. Don't leave any litter, even fruit peel and don't leave cigarette butts. Don't damage the vegetation, especially the moss and stick to marked trails when possible.

### Hiking maps and routes

Some of the most useful are the leaflets obtained from wardens in the National Parks and Conservation Areas but always seek advice about your intended route as well. The general map series 1: 100 000 gives a surprising amount of detail, though does not mark walking trails. Some special area maps with walking trails of Hornstrandir, Landmannalaugar-Þórsmörk, Snæfell, Lónsöræfi, East Fjords and Skagafjörður are available in Iceland.

Suggested walking routes are included throughout the text. They are not graded as grading of routes is a very subjective thing and the weather can turn an easy walk into a test of endurance and survival.

## Horse Riding

Many farms throughout Iceland offer short horse riding excursions of one to three hours. Usually it is enough to ring the day before to arrange a trip. Icelandic Farm Holidays (see Accommodation for details) have a list of horse riding establishments.

All year round trips run from just outside Reykjavík at:

**Laxnes Horse Farm**
☎ 566 6179
info@laxnes.is   www.laxnes.is

**Ishestar**
☎ 555 7000
info@ishestar.is   www.ishestar.is

**Eldhestar**
☎ 480 4800
info@eldhestar.is   www.eldhestar.is

Longer trips of up to a week or more are a popular way of experiencing the country, details fromTour Operators.

## Kayaking

**Ultima Thule Expeditions,**
☎ 567 8978
Sea Kayaking in Iceland's West
Fjords Region
ute@ute.is    www.ute.is

**Kajakaferðir**
☎ 896 5716
kajak@kajak.is    www.kajak.is
2 hour kayaking trips around
Stokkseyri.

## Rafting

Rafting takes place on swift-flowing and icy glacial rivers though
insulated survival suits are provided. Most trips are on grade 2-3
rapids, though more challenging trips may be available to experienced
rafters.

### *Hvítá River (near Geysir)*
**Arctic Rafting**
☎ 580 9900
activity@activity.is
www.activity.is

### *Þjórsá and Markafljót Rivers (South Iceland)*
**Arctic Rafting**
☎ 568 3030
bookings@arcticrafting.is
www.arcticrafting.is

### *Jökulsá Austari & Jökulsa Vestari (Skagafjöður – North Iceland)*
**Bakkaflöt**
☎ 453 8245
bakkaflot@islandia.is
www.bakkaflot.com

## Skiing

Both cross-country and downhill skiing are popular among Icelanders
but facilities are less developed than in Europe and North America.
Most villages and towns have a drag lift for downhill skiing but the best
facilities are at Akureyri ☎ 462 2930 and just outside Reykjavík at
Bláfjöll ☎ 561 8400 and Skálafell ☎ 566 7095. The season is usually
from January to April, depending on snow conditions. Facilities are
open in the evenings (for floodlit skiing) and at weekends. Summer
skiing is possible at Kerlingarfjöll (on the Kjölur mountain track)
☎ 552 2300. Equipment hire available on site or through Sportleigan
☎ 551 9800 at the BSI bus terminal in Reykjavík.

## Snowmobiling, Dog Sledding and ATV

**Activity group**
☎ 580 9900
activity@activity.is
www.activity.is
offer a range of activities all year
from the capital

**Snowmobile Tours**
☎ 487 1500
snow@snow.is
www.activity.is
Tours on Mýrdalsjökull

**Vatnajökull Glacier Tours**
☎ 478 1000
vatnajokull@vatnajokull.com
www.vatnjokull.com

# Whale & Dolphin Watching

### Keflavík on Reykjanes Peninsula
**Moby Dick**
☎ 421 7777
mobydick@dolphin.is,
website www.dolphin.is

### In Reykjavík
**Marine Marvels**
☎ 533 2660
hafsulan@hafsulan.is
www.marine-marvels.com

**Elding Whale Watching**
☎ 555 3565
elding@elding.is
www.elding.is

### Ólafsvík on Snæfellsnes
**Seatours**
☎ 438 1450, Fax 438 1050
saeferðir@saeferðir.is
www.saeferðir.is

### Eyjafjörður
**North Sailing**
☎ 867 0000
nieis@nieis.is
www.nieis.is

### Húsavík
**North Sailing**,
☎ 464 2350
info@nordursigling.is
www.nordursigling.is

## BUSINESS HOURS & SHOPPING

Shops are open Monday to Friday 9am-6pm. In the summer many shops are closed on Saturdays but some knitwear and souvenir stores are open in the morning. The Kringlan Shopping Mall in Reykjavík is open Monday to Friday 10am-7pm and Saturday 10am-2pm. Corner shops, selling basic foodstuffs, hot dogs, snacks and confectionery, are open all day and evening until 10 or 11pm. A supermarket (open 10am-11pm) and bookshop (open 9am-9pm) in Austurstræti in central Reykjavík are open seven days a week. Normal office hours are 9am-5pm.

## What to buy

Silver Jewelry, Knitwear, including hand-knitted sweaters, gloves & hats as well as machine knitted items. Icelandic foods – dried fish, pickled herring and chocolate are just some of the typical foodstuffs that could make an unusual gift. The duty free store at Keflavík Airport has an excellent stock.

### Art & Ceramics

Icelanders love collecting works of art and there are many galleries in the capital and around the country, where visitors can view and purchase contemporary local art and ceramics.

## Tax Free Shopping

More than 550 shops in Iceland offer tax free shopping for visitors. Around 15 per cent of the purchase price of certain goods is re-fundable to foreign visitors on departure at Keflavík Airport. The value of items on each till receipt must be at least ISK 4,000, and the goods must be packaged and sealed by the store. Ask for the appropriate form and refund voucher when you pay for the goods. The purchases must be presented unopened to customs officials on departure and the refund voucher will be stamped. Note that bulky knitwear and wool items need not be shown and may be packed in checked in baggage.

## CHURCH SERVICES

The established church in Iceland is Lutheran. Church services are held on most Sundays at 11am or 2pm. There are Catholic churches in Reykjavík and Akureyri. Mass in English is held in Reykjavík on Sundays at 6pm.

## CUSTOMS & DUTY FREE ALLOWANCE

There is a duty free shop for both arriving and departing passengers at Keflavík Airport. Credit cards are accepted. Alcoholic drinks are very expensive in Iceland. You may take in free of duty one litre of spirits and one litre of still or fortified wine or 2.25 litres of wine if no spirits or beer are taken. The minimum age for alcohol is 20 and 18 for tobacco. Six litres of beer may be taken in place of either spirits or wine. 200 cigarettes are allowed free of duty.

Up to 3kg of food, to the value of ISK 13,000 can be taken in free of duty, but import of eggs and uncooked or partly cooked meat and meat products is prohibited. There are special rules concerning the import of used riding and angling equipment and clothing. Such items must be disinfected and accompanied by a vet's certificate.

## DISABLED VISITORS

Some car rental companies have vehicles suitable for disabled visitors and some hotels have special rooms available. Most coach excursions involve steps on and off the coach and are not suitable. The City of Reykjavík publishes a leaflet in English titled 'Accessible Reykjavík' detailing facilities in the city for disabled visitors. Available from the Tourist Information Centre.

## EATING OUT IN REYKJAVÍK

In Reykjavík there is a huge choice of restaurant including many different ethnic restaurants, cafés and fast food outlets. The following serve traditional Icelandic food and contemporary cuisine. Bookings are recommended.

**Skólabrú**
Skólabrú 1
☎ 62 44 55

**Lækjarbrekka**
Bankastræti 2
☎ 551 4430

**Við Tjörnina**
Templarasund 3
☎ 551 8666

**Perlan**
Revolving restaurant on top of the hot water towers.
☎ 562 0200

**Apótek**
Austurstræi 16
☎ 575 7900

**Tveir Fiskar**
Geirgata 9
☎ 511 3474

**The Lobsterhouse
(Humarhúsið)**
Amt Mannsstígur 1
☎ 561 3303

**Sjávarkjallar Inn**
Aðalstræti 2
☎ 511 1212

## Vegetarian Restaurants

**First Vegetarian**
Laugavegur 20b
☎ 552 8410

**Grænn Kostur**
Skólavörðustígur 8
☎ 552 2028

## ELECTRIC CURRENT

220 volts, 50 hertz alternating current. Round two-pin prongs are usual.

## FURTHER READING

Many of the Icelandic Sagas have been translated into English. *Egil's Saga*, *Laxdale Saga* and *Njal's Saga* are particularly readable. Nobel Prize winning author Halldór Laxness' works have also been translated. *Independent People*, *Salka Valka* and *Atom Station* are recommended.

Books on Iceland may be purchased in the UK from the Tour Operators and Dick Phillips; in Iceland from Iceland Review, Nóatún 17, Reykjavík, ☎ 511 5700, Fax 511 5701, www.icelandreview.is publisher of many excellent books on Iceland in English.

## LOCAL TIMES

Iceland is on Greenwich Mean Time (GMT) throughout the year. When it is 12 noon in Reykjavík during the summer, it is 1pm in London and 8am in New York City.

## LOST AND FOUND

Contact the police station, Borgartún 33, Reykjavík, ☎ 569 9018. Open: Mon-Fri 10am-12pm and 2pm-4pm.

## LUGGAGE STORAGE

At the BSI Coach Terminal, Vatnsmýrarvegur 10, ☎ 591 1000. Open: daily 1 June-20 August 7.30am-10pm and 21 August-31 May 7.30am-7pm.

# MAPS OF ICELAND

Touring Map 1:500 000

General Section Regional Maps (3 sections) 1:250 000

Atlas Maps (87 sections) 1:100 000

Topographical Maps (102 out of 199 published) 1:50 000

Geological Maps (7 out of 9 published) 1:250 000

Special Maps of popular areas: South-West Iceland 1:100 000; Þingvellir 1: 25 000; Hekla 1: 50 000; Vestmannaeyjar 1: 50 000 and 1: 10 000; Skaftafell 1:100 000 and 1:25 000; Mývatn 1:50 000; Húsavík/Mývatn 1:100 000; Þórsmörk/ Landmannalaugar 1:100 000; Hornstrandir 1:100 000

These may be obtained from Landmælingar Íslands (National Land Survey of Iceland), Stillholt 16-18, 300 Akranes, Iceland, ☎ 430 9000, e-mail lmi@lmi.is, website www.lmi.is and in the UK the Tour Operators Discover the World and Dick Phillips.

# MEDICAL & DENTAL EMERGENCIES

**Ambulance** ☎112
**Police** ☎112
**Doctor (evenings and weekends)** ☎1770

The casualty department of Reykjavík's City Hospital is open 24 hours a day, ☎ 525 1700. Other hospitals around the country also have facilities to admit casualty patients.

At weekends in Reykjavík an emergency dental service is available by phoning ☎ 575 0505. Note that dental charges in Iceland may be very much higher than in the UK. For all medical treatment, including ambulance services, a charge is made. EU visitors should bring form E111, which entitles them to payment of the same charges as Icelandic citizens. Cash or credit cards are accepted.

# MONEY MATTERS

The Icelandic monetary unit is the króna (plural krónur). Coins are 1, 5, 10, 50 and 100 krónur. Notes are 500, 1,000, 2,000 and 5,000 krónur. Non residents may bring with them an unlimited amount of domestic or foreign currency. The same applies when leaving Iceland.

Money can be exchanged at banks throughout the country. Open: 9.15am-4pm, Monday to Friday. Outside of normal banking hours money can be changed at:

**Keflavík Airport**, exchange facilities open for all arriving and departing passengers. Better rate in the transit hall than after clearing customs.

**The Change Group** (Western Union Money Transfer) at the Tourist Information Centre, Aðalstræti 2, Reykjavík. Open daily June-August 8.30-6pm and 9am-5pm weekdays and 10am-2pm Saturdays September-May. Commission rates can be high, ask before you change.

241

Above: Skólabrú Restaurant in Reykjavík
Below: Off-road in the winter
Opposite: Ófærufoss Falls in Eldgjá

# • FESTIVALS •

Icelanders love to dress up, go out and celebrate. Once the proverbial ice is broken, they can be very welcoming to visitors and it is worth asking at the tourist information bureaux if there are any local events planned during your stay.

## New Year's Eve

After dinner at home, families visit a community bonfire and then everyone goes home to watch the New Year's Eve gala TV revue. Ending at 11.30pm, the streets liven up again as people head out to let off their fireworks. By 11.45pm the symphony of light and sound begins as the whole community lets off fireworks in unison. New Year in Reykjavík is possibly the most celebrated, yet totally unrehearsed, firework show in the world with all proceeds from the sale going to charity.

## Þorrablót (February)

With its roots in a long forgotten pagan ritual, Þorrablót is a festival of food and drink celebrated in February. Icelandic delicacies, including the dreaded rotten shark and singed sheep heads are washed down with brennivín schnapps and plenty of song and dance.

## Bolludagur, Sprengidagur and Öskudagur

Everyone bakes 'Bollur', a kind of cream filled choux pastry, on the Monday before Shrove Tuesday. The Tuesday is known as 'Sprengidagur' or 'Explosion Day' when a hearty meal of salted lamb and split peas is served. 'Öskudagur', Ash Wednesday is for children. They go from house to house on a kind of 'Trick or Treat' frenzy.

## The First Day of Summer

In a country where winter can drag on forever, it seems a little optimistic to celebrate the first day of summer in April (usually on the third Thursday). Even so, this is a public holiday with plenty of festivities, particularly in the capital.

## Seamen's Day (Sjómannadagur)

The first Sunday in June is celebrated, particularly in the fishing villages. There are rowing and swimming races, tests of strength and simulated sea rescues, and an atmosphere that is fun-filled and light-hearted.

### Independence Day (17 June)

Commemorating 17 June 1944, when the Republic of Iceland was established, and marking the birth date of independence hero Jón Sigurðsson, this is a day of parades, street theatre, music, side shows and dancing.

### Verslunarmannahelgi (first weekend in August)

The Monday is a public holiday, allowing shopkeepers, for whom the holiday was intended, to have a long weekend. Everything is closed and Icelanders by their thousands leave for the countryside to camp or to attend one of a number of special events. Visitors may want to avoid popular destinations like Þórsmörk at this time. To join in one of the events head for Galtalækur (alcohol-free), Akureyri or for the biggest buzz or all, the Westman Islands.

### Réttadagur (mid-September)

A celebration to mark the end of the sheep round-up, this major event in the farming calendar is celebrated with singing, dancing and usually a lot of merry-making.

### Christmas

Long before Christianity, the lengthening of the days after the passing of the winter solstice was celebrated. Today, Christmas in Iceland is a festival of light in both the spiritual sense and in the lavish Christmas lights that festoon the trees, hedges, balconies and window surrounds of almost every home and garden, wasteful perhaps, but to Icelanders one of the benefits of cheap and renewable hydro-electric power. Preparations begin weeks ahead. During the build-up to Christmas, the thirteen mischievous Christmas Lads come down from the mountains. With names like Hurðaskellir (Door Slammer) and Bjúgnakrækir (Sausage Thief), they are unlikely Santa Claus figures. However, children who leave a shoe on the window ledge at night, with luck receive a small gift for each of the thirteen nights before the festival.

Tins of biscuits are baked and traditionally new clothes sewn for every member of the household. Anyone left out might fall prey to a vicious beast called the Christmas Cat. Nowadays, the clothes are bought, as are gifts, exchanged after the traditional dinner of smoked lamb, pork or ptarmigan, on Christmas Eve. Christmas Day is altogether quieter, a time for families to be together. The whole of Reykjavík sleeps and everything is at a standstill.

Hotels can also change money and travellers' cheques but the rates may be lower. ATM (cashpoint machines), are located in most towns around the country and can be used to obtain cash with cards displaying the VISA, Eurocard/MasterCard, Electron, Maestro, EDC, Cirrus & Eurocheque signs.

Changing back all unused Icelandic currency before departure from Iceland is recommended. This can be done at the bank in the departure lounge at Keflavik Airport. You may need to produce receipts of previous exchange transactions.

Credit cards are very widely used in Iceland and are accepted at a large number of establishments. You can often pay for a taxi or even for drinks at a bar with your credit card. VISA and MasterCard are the most widely used but American Express, JCB and Diners Club are also accepted.

## MOTORING IN ICELAND

### Bringing your own vehicle

Special rules apply to motorists bringing their own vehicles, in particular diesel vehicles. Contact the Icelandic Embassy for up to date details on these and insurance matters or www.tollur.is

### Car Rental

Car rental is expensive compared to most other parts of Europe and North America. This is because all vehicles have to be imported and the rough roads give most cars a short life expectancy. Car rental can be arranged locally on a daily basis but may include only 100km of mileage with high charges for extra mileage. Unlimited mileage may only be offered with longer rentals. It is often better value to get a 'Fly Drive' package through a tour operator abroad. Special rates may be offered outside of the main summer season. Rental companies will usually deliver to your accommodation.

#### *In Reykjavík*

**ALP Car Rental**
☎ 562 6060
alp@alp.is
www.alp.is

**Avis**
☎ 591 4000
www.avis.is

**Budget Car Rental**
☎ 567 8300
info@budget.is,
www.budget.is

### General Driving Tips

- Vehicles are left hand drive and driving is on the right hand side of the road.
- Safety Belts are mandatory for both front and rear passengers.
- Headlights must be used day and night all year round.

- Filling stations are open daily from 7.30am to 8pm or 11.30pm. A few in the capital are open 24 hours but opening hours in country areas may be shorter. Esso and Shell fuel stations are marked on maps available free to visitors. Except for the Sprengisandur and Kjölur mountain tracks, fuel is not available in the highlands.
- Driving on gravel roads – slow down when you meet another vehicle to avoid throwing up loose stones. The shoulder of a gravel road is often loose. Tarmac can turn to gravel abruptly. Slow down on the approach to gravel.
- The road sign 'Blindhæð' indicates a blind summit. Slow down and keep to the right.
- Bridge – slow down for single track bridges.
- Animals have priority on unfenced roads. Slow down for them. If you hit an animal you are liable to pay compensation to the owner.
- Children often play in the streets in urban areas.
- Speed limits are 56mph (90kph) on tarmac roads; 50mph (80kph) on gravel roads and 31mph (50kph) in populated areas.

## Breakdown assistance round Iceland

Garages offering vehicle repairs (Verkstæði) and fuel stations are located in almost all towns and villages, and in some country areas. There are virtually no services for motorists in the uninhabited highlands but if you have rented a vehicle, the rental company is responsible for rescue, unless you have broken down while driving through rivers or off marked tracks.

## Road Conditions

Information on road conditions and opening of mountain tracks from Vegagerðin (Public Roads Administration) ☎ 1777 (354 522 1000 from abroad) or on their website www.vegagerdin.is

## PHOTOGRAPHY TIPS

Film is very expensive in Iceland so bring more than you expect to use. Lenses – a wide angle is useful for waterfall shots and for introducing a dramatic foreground to your landscape pictures. Light conditions can be tricky, especially on cloudy days. With slide film it is important to over-expose to compensate for this. Dust can be a problem, so make sure your gear is protected. Batteries – bring a spare set as they can be hard to find outside the capital. Video Camera – bring a spare battery pack and charger with two-pin adaptor.

## POSTAL SERVICES

Post offices are open Monday-Friday 8.30am-4.30pm. Postage stamps are also often obtainable from hotel reception desks and at souvenir shops selling postcards.

## PUBLIC HOLIDAYS

New Year's Day
Maundy Thursday
Good Friday
Easter Sunday
Easter Monday
First Day of Summer
  (usually third Friday in April)
Labour Day May 1
Ascension Day
Whit Sunday
Whit Monday
National Day June 17
August Bank Holiday
  (first Monday in August)
Christmas Eve (noon onwards)
Christmas Day
Boxing Day
New Year's Eve (noon onwards)

## SAFETY WHILE VISITING

Iceland is thankfully a safe and crime free country to travel in but in
Reykjavík at night, watch your valuables, particularly in bars and night
clubs. At swimming pools do not leave valuables in the changing rooms
unless they are safely locked away. Valuables can usually be left with
reception.

You will probably at some stage during your stay in Iceland become
aware of the smell from the hot water in hotels. It is perfectly harmless
and clean but an unavoidable side-effect of hot water that comes
directly from geothermal areas. It is often very hot, so take care when
having a shower.

Many of Iceland's most interesting sights are potentially hazardous.
Take particular care in the vicinity of geothermal areas, glacial rivers,
glaciers, waterfalls and other natural wonders. In some places, rope
barriers have been erected for your safety and to protect sensitive
areas. Entering these roped off sections may cause damage to sensitive
natural features and may be dangerous to you. Remember that off the
beaten track, many hazardous areas are not marked and you should
use extra caution there.

## TELEPHONE

There are no area codes in Iceland and all telephone numbers are
seven digits. To call Iceland from abroad, dial the country code (354)
followed by the seven digit number. To call abroad from Iceland, dial
00 44 for the UK and 00 1 for USA followed by the area code without
the initial zero. Public telephones are card or coin operated, using 10,

Fact File

50 or 100 krónur coins. It is also possible to telephone and send faxes from post offices around the country. Hotels phone charges may be high.

## Mobile Phones

Check with your service provider if you can use your phone in Iceland. Three companies, Iceland Telecom, Islandssimi and TAL cover most of the inhabited areas of Iceland, including all villages with over 200 people. If your phone is not blocked you can buy an Icelandic mobile phone number from the offices of these companies, to be used with pre-paid GSM cards, which can be bought at petrol stations. Phones can be rented from Iceland Telecom, Ármúli 27, Reykjavík. In the uninhabited areas, some coverage is available on the NMT network – NMT phones can be hired from Iceland Telecom.

## TIPPING

Tipping is never expected in Iceland but if you would like to show appreciation for especially good service it may be appreciated in restaurants, hotels and by your driver and guide on an escorted tour.

## TOURIST INFORMATION

### In the USA
**Icelandic Tourist Board,**
655 Third Avenue, New York,
N.Y. 10017, USA,
☎ (212) 885 9700,
Fax (212) 885 9710,
usa@icetourist.is
www.goiceland.org

### In the UK
**Discover the World,**
(see Tour Operators)

**Icelandair,**
(see Getting to Iceland)

### In Iceland
**Tourist Information Centre,**
Aðalstræti 2,
101 Reykjavík, Iceland,
☎ 590 1500
www.tourist.reykjavík.is
Open: 1 June-15 September, daily
8.30am-7pm; 16 Sept-31May
weekdays 9am-6pm, weekends
10.00am-2.00pm

There are information bureaus in towns, villages and areas of special interest throughout Iceland. Accommodation establishments and many campsites also stock information leaflets and can give advice on local attractions. Many leaflets and maps are published in English and available free to visitors on arrival in Iceland. The following, which are updated each year, are especially useful: Reykjavik City Map, What's On in Reykjavík, Around Iceland & Áning (hotels, guesthouses and campsites).

249

# Fact File

## TRAVELLING AROUND ICELAND

## By Air

**Air Iceland**, Reyjavík Airport, 101 Reykjavík, ☎ 570 3000, Fax 570 3001, website www.airiceland.is

Air Iceland fly the following routes from Reykjavík several times daily: Vestmannaeyjar, Isafjörður, Akureyri, Sauðárkrókur, Egilsstadir, Hornfjörður (Höfn). Flights also operate less frequently to Gjögur and Bildudalur in the West Fjords and from Akureyri to Grímsey Island and þórshöfn.

Air Iceland Passes cover four (around £180 or US$288) to six (around £234 or US$374) sectors and can only be bought through Icelandair offices abroad. Also on offer is a Fly As You Please pass that offers 12 days unlimited travel for around £365 or US$660.

## By scheduled bus

**BSÍ Destination Iceland (DICE)**, Vatnsmýrarvegur 10, 101 Reykjavík, Iceland, ☎ 591 1020 Fax 591 1050 , e-mail travel@dice, booking@dice.is website Buses: www.bsi.is www.dice.is

BSÍ run all scheduled bus services in Iceland. Routes and timetables are detailed in a brochure published each year in English. The brochure, which is indispensable for anyone planning to use public buses to tour the island, can be obtained from BSÍ or from tour operators abroad. Around the Ring Road, services run daily in summer as follows:

| | |
|---|---|
| **Reykjavík-Höfn,** | 7 hours, £56 or US$101 |
| **Höfn-Egilsstaðir,** | 4 hours, £38 or US$68 |
| **Egilsstaðir-Mývatn-Akureyri,** | 4 hours, £40 or US$74 |
| **Akureyri-Reykjavík,** | 6 hours, £44 or $82 |

Several bus passes can be purchased locally at the BSÍ office:
**Full Circle Pass** (no time limit) valid for the circular route
around the Ring Road          £190 or US$342
**Full Circle Pass + West Fjords**   £281 or US$505
**Omnibus Pass** (time limit) unlimited travel on scheduled
routes (not highland routes): 1 week £209 or US$376; 2 weeks £303
or US$545; 3 weeks £371 or US$668; 4 weeks £411 or US$740
**Off Season 1 Week Omnibus Pass** £123 US$221
**West Iceland and West Fjords Pass** £127 US$229

## Mountain Bus Routes

In the summer months special bus services, some with a guide, operate in the uninhabited highlands. Bus pass holders get discounted fares on some of the routes, or a special Highland Pass can be purchased.

Fact File

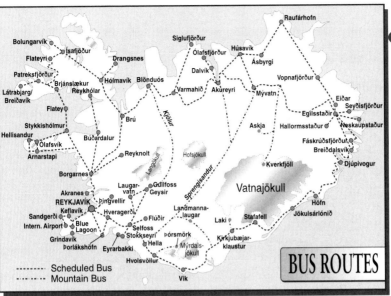

BUS ROUTES

- - - - - Scheduled Bus
- · - · - Mountain Bus

## USEFUL WEBSITES

Iceland general: www.icetourist.is
Reykjavík: www.visitreykjavik.is
Reykjanes Peninsula: www.reykjanes.is
West Iceland: www.west.is
West Fjords: www.akademia.is/vestfirdir/
North Iceland: www.eyjafordur.is
East Iceland: www.east.is
South Iceland: www.sudurland.net/info

## WEATHER

For weather information telephone 902 0600 extension 44;
office@vedur.is   www.vedur.is

## WHAT TO TAKE WITH YOU

### General Items

- Lip balm, sun-screen & skin lotion to protect your skin from sun and high winds.
- Any medicines you may need during your holiday – these may be difficult to obtain outside of the main towns.
- Travel insurance (plus EU citizens only – E111 form in case of needing medical treatment in Iceland).
- Camera, film and binoculars.

- Contact lens users should also bring glasses because dry air and dust can make wearing them very uncomfortable.
- Sunglasses, particularly if you are planning to drive around Iceland or take an excursion on one of the glaciers.
- A pocket knife, thermos flask and cup to make your own packed lunches.
- A small rucksack for day walks.
- Eye shades to help you sleep through the light summer nights.

## Clothing

A good wind and rainproof jacket (with hood) and trousers, preferably of a breathable material, are essential at any time of year.

In summer take a thick sweater and a lighter one and/or a fibre-pile jacket. A scarf, hat, gloves and warm socks are all essential. Thermal underwear may be needed if you are camping or planning a whale watching trip. Loose fitting trousers are comfortable to wear and allow room for thermal leggings underneath. Avoid denim jeans for walking because they restrict movement, are cold and clammy when wet and take a long time to dry out. In winter take all the above items plus a warm coat or jacket with a hood.

For special activities such as rafting, snowmobiling, whale watching and horse riding trips, special clothing may be supplied. Ask when you book.

Bring swimwear and a bathing towel for the many naturally heated swimming and bathing pools. At most swimming pools you may hire a swimsuit and towel.

## Laundry

Try to take enough clothing to last you during your holiday. Though some Reykjavík hotels offer a laundry service, most establishments outside of the capital do not. A few campsites and youth hostels around Iceland offer laundry facilities.

## Footwear

Terrain in Iceland is often wet under foot and very rough. Many of the sights you will visit involve some walking so proper walking shoes or boots are essential. Boots give good ankle support and the tread on the sole will help you feel confident on uneven and gravelly surfaces. Your boots should be water repellent, have plenty of tread on the sole and be well worn in. Bring a pair of trainers or comfortable shoes for travelling in and for around town. Shoes with heels are really only for evening wear.

Landmark Publishing Ltd

Ashbourne Hall, Cokayne Ave, Ashbourne, Derbyshire DE6 1EJ England
Tel: (01335) 347349  Fax: (01335) 347303  e-mail: landmark@clara.net
Website www.landmarkpublishing.co.uk

Published in the USA by
**Hunter Publishing Inc,**
130 Campus Drive, Edison NJ 08818
Tel: (732) 225 1900, (800) 255 0343  Fax: (732) 417 0482
Website www.hunterpublishing.com

3rd edition
ISBN 1 84306 134 1

**Print:** Gutenberg Press Ltd, Malta
**Editor:** Kay Coulson
**Cartography:** James Allsopp
**Design:** Samantha Witham & James Allsopp

**Front cover:** Hiking at Laki
**Back cover top:** Svartifoss Falls; basalt columns, Skaftafell National Park
**Bottom:** Reykjavík

**Picture Credits**
All photography supplied by the author except:
**Geoffrey Harlow:** 34TR, 102